S0-BBD-958

# Actionable Strategies
# Through Integrated Performance, Process, Project, and Risk Management

For a recent listing of books in the *Artech House Technology Management and Professional Development* Series, please turn to the back of this book.

# Actionable Strategies
# Through Integrated Performance, Process, Project, and Risk Management

Stephen S. Bonham

ARTECH
HOUSE

BOSTON | LONDON
artechhouse.com

Library of Congress Cataloging-in-Publication Data
A catalog record for this book is available from the U. S. Library of Congress.

British Library Cataloguing in Publication Data
A catalogue record for this book is available from the British Library.

ISBN-13: 978-1-59693-119-0
ISBN-10: 1-59693-119-1

Cover design by Igor Valdman

© 2008 Artech House. All rights reserved.

Printed and bound in the United States of America. No part of this book may be reproduced or utilized in any form or by any means, electronic or mechanical, including photocopying, recording, or by any information storage and retrieval system, without permission in writing from the publisher.

All terms mentioned in this book that are known to be trademarks or service marks have been appropriately capitalized. Artech House cannot attest to the accuracy of this information. Use of a term in this book should not be regarded as affecting the validity of any trademark or service mark.

10 9 8 7 6 5 4 3 2 1

*To Pamela, Henry, and Shelby*

# Contents

## CHAPTER 6

### Project Portfolio Management

## CHAPTER 7

### Risk Management

# Preface

To help organizations gain better control over their complex webs of internal activities, four basic approaches (performance, process, project portfolio, and risk management) have gone from being textbook references and divisional implementations to full-on industries of software products, journals, conferences, trade groups, consultants, books, standards, and laws. Operational risk management has become such a concern to societies around the world that governments have been implementing laws (e.g. Basel II, Sarbanes Oxley, Loi de la Sécurité Financière, etc.) to force companies to implement it. Strategic performance management has become so popular that a swath of frameworks (e.g. Balanced Scorecard, Performance Prism, ENAPS, etc.) and software products have flooded the market. Project portfolio management is now so pervasive that I have yet to find a mature company that hasn't implemented it to some degree. And the continual drive from the enterprise-level to improve processes using such frameworks as Six Sigma, ITIL, Kaizen, and SCOR is standard fare in today's product and service delivery industries. As will be shown, sufficient overlap exists in each of these disciplines to warrant some consolidation of effort. The result will be to reduce such collateral inefficiencies as redundant workloads, wasted executive involvement, and cultural frustration. While strategic performance management, enterprise level process management, project portfolio management, and enterprise level operational risk management each strive to fine-tune the capabilities of an organization, they each, independently, can introduce new layers of inefficiency.

These inefficiencies became more apparent as I bounced between the two fields of project management and strategic design. In the project management field, our project teams, program managers, and portfolio offices constantly engaged in performance tracking, process analysis, and risk management. To meet performance metric goals, ensure proper understanding of processes, and completely mitigate the risks, we would address all of these issues early and often. Then when I left the world of projects and became involved with designing strategies, I found that such integration didn't occur as it did on the successful projects, programs, and portfolios I was familiar with. Risk managers didn't look past core processes or the top three projects, performance experts looked at processes only, process experts were just starting to apply their skills to the project pipeline, and project portfolio directors had no clue of such enterprise-level activities as regulatory compliance, the Balanced Scorecard, or Six Sigma. Why is this a problem? Because so much time and resources tend to be put into the distinct success of each of these four efforts that it can be difficult for the leaders of these efforts to remove the horse blinders, speak the same language, understand mutual needs, and deliver strategies that aren't just a least common denominator shell or a set of disconnected substrategies. But, even more so, it is important because a lack of communication early and often between these silos can hobble strategic execution and fog enterprise visibility. Investing in risk mitigation at the expense of performance improvement, or building a project-oriented organization at the expense of process improvement can lead to short-term wins at the expense of long-term, strategic gain.

In the IT project management world, there is an acronym used to refer to a type of software implemented called COTS (or Commercial Off The Shelf). In the strategic design world, there is an acronym used to refer to a type of strategy not executed called SOTS (or Strategy On The Shelf). Integrated activity management helps set the different forces of the organization in a direction that makes strategies actionable. Strategic goals can be tracked for execution using key performance indicators, and strategic risks can be tracked for mitigation using key risk indicators. Goals and risks can, in turn, each be managed to resolution using such project portfolio frameworks as OPM3 and P3M3 and such process improvement frameworks as Kaizen and ITIL. But, the true benefit of integration is realized when these strategic tracking, controlling, and supportive disciplines work together to create actionable strategies, rather than in isolation to create misdirected shelfware.

The closest reference to an integrated management of an organization's activities may be Kaplan and Cooper's evolution of the classic activity-based costing (or ABC). In their 1998 Harvard Business School Press article, they built on ABC by explaining how to manage activities so as to reduce their associated costs [1, 2]. Such an approach attempts to draw direct links between measurable activities and cost accounting. However, since then, others have questioned the linearity of such linkages [3, 4]. With a lack of completeness in how activities can be quantitatively tracked, subjective management techniques sprout up. This book doesn't look at how to selectively track costs associated with such activities as processes or projects. Rather, it reviews the overlap between four basic methods of managing activities so that synergy, cost reduction, and efficient execution of the strategy can result. When running a company, government, or nonprofit organization, it is understood that there are some basics to success that should not be ignored: the organizational structure, the culture, the leadership styles, the management acumen, the financial diligence, the marketing approaches, the customer satisfaction, the employee growth and the product quality, for example. But, here we will focus on the dynamics of the organization as embodied in processes and projects, and as viewed through performance metrics and risks. Specifically, we will look at an efficient way that activities can be managed at the strategic level in today's rapidly changing markets.

Strategic-level activity management traditionally only looks at financial performance metrics that identify costs, revenues, and various financial ratios. In the nineties, performance measurement frameworks (e.g. Balanced Scorecard) showed how companies could expand on such metrics. Now, organizations are realizing that performance dashboards can cause a company to miss the status of other critical activity indicators such as risks and project investments. Strategic activity management now embodies the complete execution and viewing space provided by all four of what we will refer to as activity management "silos." Managers in any industry, government or nonprofit organization need to understand the links and overlaps between all the silos of activity management. We will go through many frameworks, models, and organizational structures offered by each of the strategic activity management industries that have grown recently. We will find that these "industry standard" or "best practices" models make constant references to overlap between one or two of the other activity management silos. The summation of all these overlaps will, in turn, lead us to our integrated model presented throughout the book. Ultimately, our new model will show how board members, executives and middle managers in any type of organization, small or large, will learn how to avoid wasteful allocation of resources when managing strategic activities.

As we progress through the integrated model proposed in this book, we will be riding on a foundation of four themes: strategic operations, organizational maturity, supportive vs. controlled execution, and dynamic execution.

- *Strategic Operations:* Operational metrics, day-to-day tasks, short-term issues, and simple projects are the responsibility of staff and line managers. Summarized key performance indicators, strategic quality improvement initiatives, project portfolio architectures, and enterprise-wide management of operational risks are the responsibility of all stakeholders. How staff and line managers (who are also stakeholders) support operational activity management will be referenced briefly. But, the core of the book will be to focus on the bigger, enterprise-level picture. This can get confusing when using the term "operational" with risks versus using the same term with performance metrics. When used with risk, it is meant to differentiate risks from those that deal with external market or credit threats (i.e. nonoperational risks). When used with performance metrics it is meant to differentiate metrics from those that deal with internal, line operations vs. those that support executive decision making (i.e. strategic performance management). As we integrate the four silos (or disciplines) of activity management, we will address such semantic conflicts clearly.

- *Organizational Maturity:* Unfortunately, when a book introduces such words as strategy, global or enterprise, many feel that it is only addressing issues found in larger companies. By clearly showing how an integrated model supports all maturity levels of an organization we will strive to eliminate such a perception.

- *Execution Support:* Performance and risk management aren't just reporting processes, they are also improvement and mitigation activities. Metrics should be periodically reviewed and updated, and projects should be launched to wipe out the threats of risk realization. Project portfolio and process management aren't just auditing and standardization exercises, they are also opportunities to consolidate training, standardize methodologies, manage vendors, implement knowledge management, and support asset purchases. Most companies approach our four activity management silos from a perspective of applying more control over the chaos of their internal dynamics. But, if mechanisms are put in place to help with the success of each of the activity management disciplines, then chaos can diminish along with the need for controls. That is, we will show that controlling structures should not be rolled out without equal consideration for support structures.

- *Dynamic Execution:* Each decade we hear that markets are moving faster, employee needs are becoming more complex, international competition is increasing, regulations are becoming more constrictive, and competitive advantage is ever-more fleeting. Nonetheless, with the information revolution, many feel that external and internal changes are accelerating even faster than in decades past. To address this, experts on strategy continue to update their understanding of why companies succeed or fail. For example, recent thoughts on strategic execution have focused on how failed companies make decisions that can be as logical as the decisions made by companies that succeed. Evidence is starting to show that the edge goes to those companies that prepare for multiple options and that can execute quickly to any of those options. In other words, they need to be astute to external turmoil and they need to be able to act as a single force that executes dynamically. As we will see, this final theme is a key reason for the need to integrate components of the four disciplines of activity management.

Strategic operations introduces the "what," organizational maturity proposes the "who," support versus control explains the "how," and dynamic execution includes the "when," "where," and "how." In designing the flow of content, I wanted to clearly lay out these four themes in the first chapters before diving into the specifics of each activity management silo. This allowed for a clearer evolution of the integrated model and a better fit into current-day strategic management theory. The final chapter expands on organizational structures and rounds out the concept of integrated activity management maturity.

## References

[1]  Cooper, R. and Kaplan, R. S., *The Design of Cost Management Systems: Text, Cases and Readings*, Prentice Hall, 2 Ed., 1998.

[2]  Kaplan, R. S. and Cooper, R., *Cost and Effect*, Harvard Business School Press, 1998.

[3]  Noreen, E. and Soderstrom, N. "The Accuracy of Proportional Cost Models: Evidence From Hospital Service Departments," Review of Accounting Studies, 1997, Vol. 2, pp. 89–114.

[4]  Anderson, M.C., Banker, R. D. and Janakiraman, S. N., "Are Selling, General And Administrative Costs 'Sticky'?" The Journal of Accounting Research, Vol. 41, pp. 47–63, 2003.

# Acknowledgments

I had the pleasure of meeting with several senior executives from various industries while compiling the book's primary research. My sincere appreciation goes to Steve Norgaard, Dr. Diane McCallister, Dave Keanini, Tom Myers, Jeff Tetrick, Kevin McHugh, and Shachar Feldman. Each of them were able to show me in much detail how they have integrated all of the four components of strategic activity management into their organizations. I am also indebted to the crack editorial staff at Artech House. Their professionalism and excitement helped keep the book on course. Finally, and most importantly, I am deeply thankful to my wife, Olivia, for her patience and extended support in completing this project.

## CHAPTER 1

# Strategic Activity Management

## Fast Industries

One of the key skills of a manager is the ability to multitask. As requests, issues, complaints, and risks pile up, they need to be quickly prioritized against all other urgent needs, then either responded to immediately or tabled. One doesn't need to dig deep to realize that this process is becoming gradually more complex for all; one just needs to look at his or her e-mail list, phone message light, or cell phone. As e-mail, voicemail, and text messages increase the volume of activity barreling toward a manager, quick and thorough responses can be difficult. Administrative assistants, e-mail filters, unlisted phone numbers, and delegated tasks are all examples of ways that some have tried to control the informational dam break. These upgraded habits of new-millennium managers are hints as to how the velocity of business has changed. A macroview of the effects of new business speed limits can be seen at the corporate and market levels through evermore complex information technology (IT) projects, rapidly evolving global threats, and increasingly costly government regulations. In fact, empirical studies are showing that there is strong evidence "that markets are shifting more frequently and more severely." The problem, however, is that "organizations have not become more adaptable to meet the increasing pace and magnitude of change" [1]. Nonetheless, as industries get faster, managers continue to search for better ways to multitask, and companies continue to search for better ways to execute.

In *The Strategy Paradox*, Michael Raynor surmises that one of the reasons companies are not as adaptable as they once were is that environments now change far too rapidly. There is no shortage of companies that have developed strategies that hope to address as many unforeseeable events or risks as possible; companies are keenly aware of the need to be more flexible these days. Nonetheless, adaptive strategies only work well if you have a well-trained runner on the starting line when the gun is fired. When jet fuel prices skyrocketed in 2001, most airlines hedged on fuel, but only Southwest and Continental airlines hedged 100%. While United, Delta, National, and Legend airlines all blamed part of their ultimate bankruptcies on fuel prices, other airline companies attributed part or their successes to a good gamble on fuel prices' going up [2, 3]. The bankrupt airlines were being flexible with partial hedges on fuel prices, but it wasn't enough to allow them to adapt quickly to the changes. Only the two airlines that were prepositioned to take advantage of the change won out. Were they lucky, or were they actively reviewing risks and committing to mitigation strategies (i.e., poised for the starting gun)?

The partial, or balanced, execution used by the bankrupt airlines are seen by some as safe approaches to tumultuous environments and by others as a way to sit on the sidelines, thereby missing out on the glory of a win (or the humiliation of a defeat). To boldly jump into the game as an industry shaper, a company should have a high level of self-confidence; it should be able to clearly understand its capabilities, its customers, its competition, and its environment. Besides having 20/20 visibility, a company must also be able to walk the walk better than its competitors. It should be able to do things more quickly and efficiently than the competition, and it must be able to invest in new projects that have a higher probability of success than the competition's projects. Developing and then producing products, creating and monitoring new advertising campaigns, improving and supporting efficient financial systems, and building and running new business units all require some initiating project and some ongoing processes. Those that can act quickly ("be first to market"), uniquely ("own the market"), efficiently ("achieve great margins"), and consistently ("bury the competition") have competitive advantages. However, the ability to uniquely, efficiently, and consistently execute on a dime is half the equation; being prepared to execute through proactive positioning and clear visibility is the other half. But how can a company execute if the target is always moving? How can an organization anticipate a moving target if sitting on a shifting set of capabilities? In essence, can a company execute a game of precision and strategy (think of a game of billiards) while traveling at high speed over rough waters?

In such a turbulent environment, basic requirements need to be established to reduce the randomness of a ball's being sunk. First of all, you need to be able to see the table, the cue, and the balls; then you need to be a very good player. Risk management and performance management are two old-school concepts that are seeing new light through improvements in technology, case studies, new frameworks, trade organizations, and literature. At the same time, while process improvement and project portfolio management have been around since the 1960s, they too have been gaining steam. All four of these methods were created to increase the visibility into the workings of the company or improve how the company executes on its strategy; they provide a way to better manage corporate activities. But it is in the integration of these activity management methods that organizations can achieve additional value and reduced waste. Is the company including risks and the status of project investments in its performance reports? Or do board members, executives, and senior managers receive enterprise risk, process performance, and project status information separately? Is each level of the organization acting on accurate and timely performance metrics? Or is the company at risk of bringing forth (or percolating up) unneeded or erroneous data? Is there a structured way (i.e., a process) to improve project success as well as control project approval? Or are projects left on their own to be successful? Are processes in place to report and resolve risks? Or is the culture so eroded that employees allow problems to fester and snowball? These are just a few of the questions that can be resolved through an integrated activity management approach.

A company, like a living creature, is defined by its structure and its actions. Many variables influence how each is developed, as well as their effects on each other. For activity management to add value, it should sit on a dependable foundation of frameworks and accountabilities. Staff needs to know what it is, how it works, and whom to go to for help. Unfortunately, even such organizational models can be as malleable as the dynamics of a company. Marius Leibold, Gilbert Probst, and Michael Gibbert, authors of *Strategic Management in the Knowledge Economy*, believe that in the "knowledge economy," change and adaptation have become so much more commonplace than in earlier business climates that corporate structure, as well as corporate activity, has become "a variable rather than a given or stable element." The business environments of the new millennium are not for someone who wants to find a niche and then go to the beach. These are environments where achieving a niche is the first step, and holding on tight during the wild roller coaster ride that follows is the long-term reality. Complete understanding of the environment, intense critical thinking, and perfect timing are all key ingredients to both surviving and performing well at such extreme levels. In other words, precision execution in dynamic environments has become the new competitive advantage. We will show that integrating the management of performance, process, project portfolio, and risk in the new-millennium cyclone will help a company slice through the market waves.

## In High Seas

The Asian market collapse of 1997 (the so-called Asian Contagion) had a dire effect on companies with large footprints in the affected countries. With the collapse occurring in a span of about 12 hours, companies like General Electric (GE) and Allied Signal had to react quickly. Both of these companies were able to implement contingency plans in less than six weeks because they had not only learned to identify such problems (risk management) but practiced the processes needed to realize their plans [4]. When companies find themselves in a situation in which they need to react quickly to new market developments, they need to execute adaptively (e.g., like a slalom skier), and they need to execute systemically (e.g., like a school of fish). The combination of the two allows for rapid, accurate execution of a group. But when such execution is occurring in an unpredictable environment (e.g., as on a boat in high seas or in a current-day market), we refer to it as dynamic execution, or successfully executing as intended in a dynamic environment.

### Adaptive Execution

A company is made up of several components, such as facilities, systems, equipment, knowledge, and reputation. A company is also defined by how it gets these components to interact. In a chaotic environment, such interactions occur as independent activities with no clear deliverables and no clear direction. In a controlled environment, these interactions are connected head to tail in such ways as to deliver predictable deliverables; the activities become dependent on each other. This serial interlinking of corporate activities to deliver predefined outputs can take two forms: processes or projects. How processes and projects are identified, managed, improved, and eliminated has been the subject of much research. But as companies reel from the new economic culture of rapid and constant change, they are realizing that if uncontrolled, process and project change can occur at dangerous speeds.

New-millennium companies that are adapting more quickly to market change have been doing so at the expense of order. The basic approach to staying ahead of market changes is to improve processes or launch new initiatives. Overtime, however, what once appeared to be a method to improve the competitive advantage of the company in fact drives the company into a state where visible control can disappear. To be flexible in the face of such change, a company must be able to constantly adapt processes and complete projects dependably. Corporate inefficiencies need to be hunted down and eliminated, project failure rates need to be dramatically reduced, organizational change hurdles need to be smoothed out, regulatory compliance efforts need to be weighed against enterprise risk management needs, and crystal clear visibility into the actual performance of the company needs to be available. The efficiencies of the company need to be visibly improved at ever-faster rates.

However "running harder and harder" is not the route for enduring, resilient organizational survival in the knowledge economy; "running differently is" [5]. That is, a company shouldn't spin its wheels while being constrained by what Yoshio Maruta, chairman of Kao Corporation, refers to as "past wisdom"; it should be willing to adapt its formula to changes in the competitor landscape [6, 7]. Does this mean that a company must constantly shift its strategy or management approach in the face of uncertainty to survive? No, a company should have an ability to adapt between techniques as an important first step to building a successful company [7]. Even famous industry shapers experimented with various risky techniques (i.e., adapted) early in their successes: manufacturing outsourcer pioneer Nike pushed the limits of low-wage workers before having to adjust to global pressures regarding worker's rights [8], shipping shaper Federal Express got caught up in its growth fever before it had to retreat and reassess strategies with its Zipmail and initial European expansion problems [9, 10], and online garage sale innovator eBay took a hands-off approach before it realized it had to adapt to market and regulatory pressures by gradually increasing its list of banned items (e.g., alcohol, firearms, and lottery tickets). In other words, stick to a vision, mission, or market, but be willing to adjust your path in reaching success with any of these strategic elements. Establishing formal activity management approaches helps ensure that those paths are stable and easy to follow.

## Systemic Execution

In a perfect world, business components (units, divisions, departments, and project teams) all work toward delivering results that help drive a business in the exact direction desired by executives. Such complete alignment is easier to achieve as executives are closer to the activities of line staff, such as in an early start-up. Over time, however, a company may find that while it executes, it does so like a room full of two-year-olds on chocolate rather than like the highly trained crew of a World Cup sail boat. While racing, the passion and expertise of such a crew are on overdrive, their peripheral awareness of what their teammates are about to do is acute, and their ability to prepare proactively and respond in a microsecond are razor sharp. In short, they move as if they were a part of the boat, a part of a single system.

If we referred to such a scenario as executing *systematically*, we'd be saying that it was executing as if it were a stepwise, methodical process. But we wouldn't be getting to the heart of what is really happening on the sailboat. Besides just following a list of steps for each independent task (in serial), crew members are also adapting to and amplifying each others' steps (in parallel). The synergy they achieve allows their interactions to improve the value of their team's overall output. Integrated execution is so embedded in each part of the sailboat team that they execute as one. In other words, the crew is executing *systemically*. Another famous analogy is Andrew Groves' likening systemic, or synergistic, execution to emergency room teams. In the wild, we see this with wolf packs, beehives, and ant colonies.

In companies, systemic execution is more than just about how to align strategies, substrategies, and IT operations; it is about how to integrate the moving parts of the company so that they build on each other to support a common direction simultaneously. Researchers C. A. Bartlett and S. Ghoshal found that this was just the culture Intel, 3M, Kao, and Asea, Brown, Boveri, Ltd. (ABB) were all striving to develop [6]. Yoshito Maruta, chairman of Kao Corporation, put it clearly when he said that his objective was to create a company that had "'biological self-control'—an organization that responds to crises just as the body does. 'If anything goes wrong in one department, those in other parts of the organization would sense the problem and provide help without being asked'" [6].

## Dynamic Execution

Getting a company to adapt systemically on a dime is akin to getting an ocean liner to move like a speedboat. If the larger boat were careening down a narrow river, then its chances of survival might be better if it were split into several smaller boats. This is a popular approach taken by companies that get too large to react: they restructure themselves around an *M* form, with strategic business units acting as the more maneuverable boats. Michael Raynor, however, believes that since the turns in the river are coming so quickly in present-day markets, the only way any of the boats will make the turn is if they are already pointed in the right direction. So, a risk-management-aware fleet commander will have different boats pointed in different directions before the turns arrive. While Raynor refers to the collection of such options as strategic flexibility, we will refer to activity-specific options as dynamic execution. Risk and performance management will help the company prepare for different dynamic scenarios, and project portfolio and process management will help the company execute as requested. Figure 1.1 shows how we split out these two groups of activity management and then refer to the set of four as the PePPR model. Performance management and risk management are the two elements of PePPR that start at the board level through governance mechanisms, then get

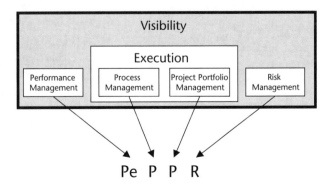

**Figure 1.1**   The PePPR model.

repeated throughout the various management layers. These will be referred to as the monitoring, or visibility, elements of PePPR. Process management and project management are the two elements of PePPR that start at the executive level and then also get repeated throughout the various management layers. These latter two elements will be referred to as the activity, or execution, elements of PePPR.

This book is about how to execute and integrate the activity management methods that have evolved since the information age began. References to leadership, organizational change, and knowledge management will be made, but this isn't the central theme. We will focus on how contemporary approaches to business strategy can be implemented given the recently renewed interest in activity management. An ever-tightening global competition has led to the ground swell of performance management implementations, mass business process reengineering (BPR)-based layoffs led to the stampede of enterprise process management systems, an incessant stream of failed IT projects over the last 25 years led to the explosion in project portfolio management, and corporate demise led to the flood of regulatory requirements for operational risk management. While the soft components of success (e.g., leadership, organizational change, and quick knowledge) in this exciting new environment are critical, our focus will be on developing the frameworks, models, and tools that will allow your company to support and control dynamic execution (see Figure 1.2(c) "Strategic Activity Management").

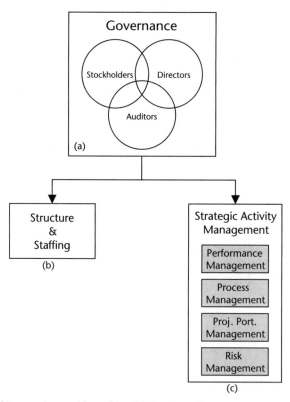

**Figure 1.2**  Vertical integration and board-level balancing of PePPR management.

### Visibility Management

As companies mature, governing boards of directors will alter their priorities and responsibilities to best ensure growth. When a company is small, "the board's emphasis is on performance, getting the venture up to speed as quickly as possible, and normally, taking the company public as soon as practical" [11]. But once a company goes public, the focus of the board shifts to managing risk. "The SEC, the stock exchange rules and most recently the Sarbanes-Oxley act come into play." Companies go from what Tom Perkins refers to as a guidance board to a compliance board. Is this the proper way to rebalance an organization as it grows? Perkins cited Jack Welch as one board member who feels that company boards are becoming too preoccupied with compliance and risk management. Instead, the board should ensure that it has its finger on the complete pulse of the direction of the company. To achieve such clarity, the board should look evenly at both the risks and the performance (Figure 1.2(a)).

How does PePPR management help support such a balance from the board level through to the executive ranks? Besides supporting a balance between such monitoring approaches as risk and performance management, PePPR management also supports a balance between monitoring and execution. Risk and performance management track what should and shouldn't be happening. Process and project portfolio management track what is happening and what will happen. The first two monitor and measure, and the last two execute and deliver. For example, how does an executive improve a performance metric or mitigate a risk? He or she initiates a process improvement review, launches a new initiative, or implements a process replacement project. Figure 1.3 illustrates how risk and performance tracking are managed from a set of dashboards. These dashboards (or scorecards) can be implemented as spreadsheets, desktop databases, or enterprise systems. Either way, such dashboards receive status information from running processes and ongoing projects. In this way, executives and board members are able to maintain their visibility of the organizational activities.

### Risk

While some industries have long understood the need to manage risks (e.g., financial, biotech, medical equipment), others have slowly incorporated such concepts into their normal operations with the ever-growing tide of information technology risk. Everyone now knows how risky it can be to invest in an IT-based project. Disaster recovery, information security management, and business continuity are other recent additions to what has become the enterprise risk management landscape. But no risk initiative has shocked corporations into adopting operational risk management procedures more thoroughly than the recent passage of such government regulations as Sarbanes-Oxley (SarbOx or SOX), Basel II, the Health Insurance Portability and Accountability Act, and Gramm-Leach-Bliley. Old-school risk management has now become an enterprise-level core competency of businesses that want to keep their heads above the market waters. However, companies that see risk management as more than just a compliance thorn understand it as a way to critically assess possible future outcomes and then to hedge bets and prepare for alternative scenarios. In fact, thorough risk analysis allows a company to react

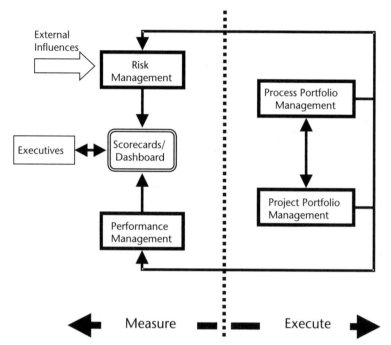

External
Influences

Risk
Management

Executives

Scorecards/
Dashboard

Performance
Management

Process Portfolio
Management

Project Portfolio
Management

Measure ▬ ▬ Execute

**Figure 1.3**   Integrating scorecards and dashboards.

quickly to solve new issues and to "proact" responsibly to prevent oncoming problems. This crystal ball ability to prepare will be elaborated in Chapter 7 and is what we'll refer to as *proactive* visibility.

## Performance

As enterprise risk management has gained steam across the business globe, so has performance management. Performance management is a new name for the old concept of executive information systems (EISs), where executives were able to monitor the performance of their companies via real-time updates of certain strategic metrics. Today, with the aid of new enterprise performance management (EPM) systems, companies are implementing all kinds of custom and standard performance measurement frameworks (e.g., Balanced Scorecard, Performance Pyramid, and European Network for Advanced Performance Studies [ENAPS]). Moreover, such systems are now supported by more thoroughly integrated back-end systems to allow for timely and more accurate metric updates. As a result, EPM system implementations are becoming quite popular and, according to research firm Zoominfo, even more popular than the risk management systems popularized by Sarbanes-Oxley and Basel II needs. At the time of this writing, Zoominfo, an online business-information search engine that combs over 3.8 million companies, found that there are about 150 companies that produce and sell operational risk management software and about 255 companies that produce and sell operational performance management software [12].

While risk and performance monitoring are the primary tools used by boards to guide chief executive officers and to comply with regulations, they are also the primary operational monitoring activities of upper management. Business continuity, investment risk, and regulatory compliance feed the need for an enterprisewide risk management framework. Process efficiencies, financial metrics, staff productivity, and project statusing feed the need for an enterprisewide performance management framework. These two primary activities don't end at the executive level; they continue on through all levels of management. A culture of risk and performance visibility can propagate if the company encourages and rewards those who identify and escalate possible risks and opportunities to improve metric data. The way to start is through open-book management and employee inclusion. That is, including employees in the performance enhancement and the risk mitigation steps after they've identified problems creates a sense of ownership and excitement that promotes openness and accuracy; performance reports are not "garbage out" because the information entered by enthused employees is not "garbage in." This statusing of completed activities is what we will refer to as *reactive* visibility and will detail in Chapter 4.

## Execution Management

In parallel to the growth in demand for technical solutions that improve corporate visibility, there is the growth in demand for solutions to improve corporate execution. Combining the research of professional analyst companies [13–16] with the output of an online business search utility [12] and my own personal references, I was able to find about 164 companies that provide enterprise project portfolio management software. Then, using a similar nonempirical approach, I found about 156 companies that provide business process management (BPM) software. Such a supply of technical solutions wouldn't be possible without an equally impressive need. The simple fact that new forms of automation exists to better track and control these activities is only half the story. The other reason for such a surge in interest with process and project portfolio management is the realization that the actions of a company are becoming more of a competitive differentiator than the structure of a company. In other words, in the highly dynamic nature of new-millennium industries, the stabilizing element of an organization is no longer found in its structure but in its evoked processes; "the traditional strategy-structure continuum becomes a meaningless relation" [17]. The new central relation that should now guide companies, according to Peter M. Senge and Goran Carstedt, authors of *Innovating Our Way to the Next Industrial Revolution*, is the strategy-activity continuum [18]. Such a continuum is realized through process and project management and their ever-shifting alignment with the dynamic strategies of our time.

### Process

Between projects and processes, processes tend to be the easiest to monitor and improve upon. They are fixed entities that can be identified by their input, their interconnected activities, and their output. They are repeatable sets of actions that companies depend upon for ongoing operations. The portfolio of all processes in a company defines how one would describe components of corporate execution. When describing the consistent activity outputs of a company (e.g., personnel reviews, invoices, products, environmental waste), their dependability is due to the existence of the company's supporting process portfolio. To maintain such output reliability, companies monitor and control their processes. To reduce costs, safety hazards, and inefficiencies, companies also strive to improve their processes. This monitoring, controlling, and improving of processes is known as process management. Where processes execute, process management ensures such execution isn't adversely interrupted.

From a gauge on the first steam engine to real-time, global inventory reports at Wal-Mart [19], technology has always played a large role in how processes are monitored. In businesses, process monitoring becomes process management when managers are also able to control and improve upon the performance of a process. When technology is used to help automate this, a newer industry term is used: business process management, or BPM. This automation of process management becomes even more critical as industries and markets force companies to constantly reconsider their approaches (i.e., change or improve their processes). Since process improvement efforts can vary in effectiveness across the enterprise, executives may establish framework standards so that these efforts can be supported and audited consistently between departments, divisions, and business units. Examples of such frameworks include Kaizen, Total Quality Management (TQM), Six Sigma, Critical Chain, Lean, and Just-in-Time. Another approach would be to require adherence to a maturity model such as ISO9000 or the Information Technology Infrastructure Library (ITIL). Chapter 5 will first go into much more detail on how enterprise process management can guide the execution of the company and then how it can be integrated with the other activity management fields.

## Project Portfolio

Projects, as opposed to processes, have both a definable beginning and a definable end. Rather than being made up of a series of repeatable steps, projects implement a set of steps that change as the project progresses (e.g., design, implementation, rollout). As companies grow in size, the capital outlays and resource allocations that go to projects increase to the point that it can become difficult for upper management to have a clear view of the status of its project (or capital expenditure) portfolio. Combined with a history of failed projects, such a lack of visibility can lead to a constant sense of gloom every time the subject of project status comes up. Project portfolio management is a control technique that provides (1) improved visibility of project portfolio progress, and (2) improved individual project success rates. That is, not only does structured process and project portfolio management support efficient corporate execution, but it also contributes to the increase in visibility that was provided by risk and performance management. Such improved visibility and odds of success are critical when a project consumes double-digit percentages of the capital budget; just one failure can cause a company to sink. Thus, project portfolio management is being adopted very quickly across corporations to better control portfolio alignment, improve capital expenditure visibility, and reduce the risks of project failure. Chapter 6 will elaborate further on the critical need for project portfolio management (PPM).

## Activity Management Silos

Over the last four decades, each of our four activity management areas has become strongly independent. We can picture them as a different dimension of silos that cross the boundaries of business unit and functional silos (see Figure 1.4). Software markets, literature, consulting services, conferences, professional organizations, and trade journals have all supported the siloing of these areas into specialty fields. As some of these contributors have specialized the fields even further (e.g., business continuity, business activity management, and product portfolio management), other contributors have started to merge the four fields. For example, software companies are now offering combined project and process performance management systems that include risk management. But what's wrong with adopting best-of-breed approaches to different needs? If I look at my human resources, procurement, accounting, and customer support systems, I am more efficient in each than a competitor who opted for an integrated system with fewer bells and whistles. The same goes for all my activity management systems. Why should I integrate my project portfolio management system with my performance and risk management systems? I like how they act as checks and balances on each other.

As independent management activities, PePPR components can cause staff to perceive shifting approaches to strategic execution. Take risk management for example. While the risk management director will require strict adherence to risk review processes, regulatory compliance, and business continuity plans, the project portfolio director, on the other hand, will push for investment audits to prove alignment, balance, and risk mitigation. Is enterprise-wide risk management centralized

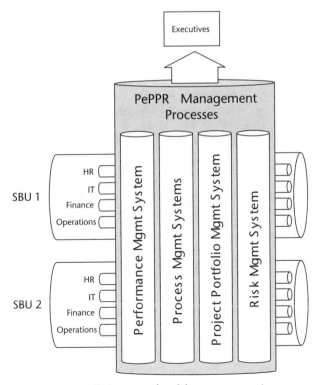

**Figure 1.4**  Vertically and horizontally integrated activity management.

with the project portfolio director who oversees risk mitigation projects, or is it centralized with the risk management director who identifies and investigates risks? Similar delivery contradictions can occur between process improvement champions and performance management directors. So, does a company really want its checks and balances stepping all over each other when advising executives or developing strategy plans? Or does a consolidated message on risk and performance sufficiently balance the status reporting of functional managers while keeping the message delivery simple? Feet-stepping can be a problem, but so can narrow thinking. For example, if a company primarily focuses on process improvement at the expense of the other three PePPR components, it can become trapped into not seeing "that the rules of the game are changing faster than the company, or that the game has changed altogether" [5]. The point to be made here is that we don't necessarily want to integrate software packages or to restructure functional departments; rather, we want to create a framework for integrating processes associated with activity management. While each of these four elements has its own particular focus, they also have more in common than being enterprisewide necessities of mature businesses; they rely on each other to be successful. Risk and performance management may make the horizon clearer, but process and project portfolio management allow a company to react and proact as a dependable unit.

## An Integrated Model

The previous section hinted at a couple ways activity management fields integrate. This section will show that there are other integration points besides the integration of risk and project management and the inclusion of risk mitigation and process improvement projects in the project portfolio. As illustrated in Figure 1.5, risk analysis can also occur on operational processes (1) and can feed performance management systems (6); performance management can track metrics associated with projects (5), as well as with processes(4); the project portfolio can include projects that are mitigating risks (8), improving processes (7), and updating the performance metrics of the company (9). Figure 1.5 also shows that there are inputs to each of the fields that don't involve their integration. But it is in the integration of activity management fields that synergistic value-adds can be realized. As the integrated PePPR management model is introduced in this chapter, the nonintegrated feeds shown as the four large arrows in Figure 1.5 will be addressed first, followed by an explanation of each of the fields' three feeds; the chapter concludes with a short explanation of the value-add of integration.

### Risk

In the industrial age, the philosophy was that if a company moved too quickly, it risked losing control. In the information age of business, however, companies feel that if they move too slowly, they risk falling behind in the race to succeed [18]. All the major risk types (e.g., credit, market, operational, reputational) affect the ultimate risk of failure. We'll lump credit, market, and reputational risks into a category called "nonactivity" risks. This allows us to then look just at operational, or activ-

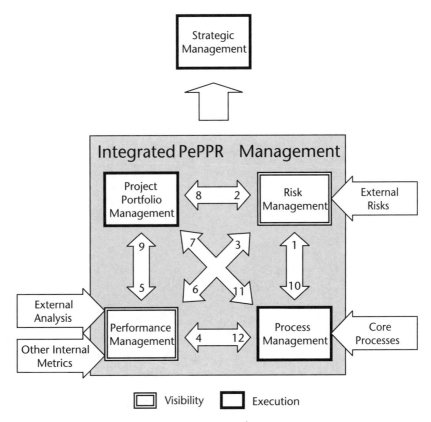

**Figure 1.5**   Integrating management support approaches.

ity-based, risks. In Figure 1.6, you can see how feeds 1 and 2 provide the information necessary to track risks associated with both processes and projects. The
metrics chosen to monitor process and project performance (dotted line arrows) are
also scrutinized to minimize the risk that they will be faulty (feed 3).

1. *Risk with process portfolio:* Equipment has a lifetime, methods get
   outdated, experts move on, and budgets are cut. These are all risks that can
   affect the smooth flow of processes in a company and the most common
   types of operational risk that would percolate up through a performance
   management system. They are also the types of risks a typical operational
   risk manager will monitor. Recently, with the passage of various regulatory
   acts, this process-centric focus by operational risk analysts has been a
   priority. For example, swarms of SarbOx/SOX consultants have invaded
   companies to identify and then mitigate such operational risks as uninsured
   front-loader operators, faulty inventory control software, and poor
   performance review templates.

2. *Risk with project portfolio:* Projects manage their risks according to the
   methodology chosen, the staff allocated, the timeline given, the budget
   authorized, and the functionality expected. These risks then filter up to the
   program and then the portfolio levels. The result is a prioritized list of

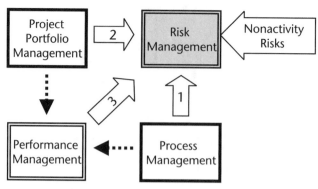

**Figure 1.6** Risk management integration types.

projects based upon their risk of failure. This allows risk managers to clearly see how capital outlays are balanced with the nondiscretionary financing of operational processes to determine the overall risk to a company's operations. Medium-sized projects, such as upgrading an IT server farm, repairing a road, or auditing a small company, may not seem worth the effort to a risk manager, but if such projects are tracked as a portfolio, the aggregate view of risk can prove valuable.

3. *Risk of poor or invalid performance visibility:* One of the problems with old executive information systems was their inability to rapidly alter the metrics available to executives. Such limitations in the technology's ability to adapt led to a reversion to the consolidation of status reports. If current performance dashboards aren't presenting the metrics required to support complete critical thinking, or if the data presented is inaccurate, strategic decisions could lead a company in disastrous directions. The more executives depend on performance measures, the greater the impact of such risks. It is quite common, given the squeeze by Wall Street analysts during quarterly reports, for financial statements to reflect expected results, only to have such results restated several years later. Is this the activity of fraudulent, desperate executives? Or is it the result of an over-reliance on faulty performance management metrics? While nonactivity metrics (e.g., financial) are the more popular, recent regulatory requirements are putting new focus on the accuracy of activity-based metrics (dotted arrows).

Operational risks are usually identified with the company's process portfolio and not with the project portfolio or with the validity of performance metrics. With integrated PePPR management, not only are risk managers now including the risk output from project portfolio directors, but they are also evaluating the risks of inaccurate performance indicators. With such forward thinking, companies can anticipate, and thus proact to, problems not just with their processes but also with their capital expenditures and the way they view their internal and external environments. As a result, executive visibility broadens and becomes more reliable.

## Performance

Where risk management helps companies look at the future to predict problems before they occur, performance management helps companies look at the past and present to react to successes and problems as they occur. Besides the traditional financial (or non-activity-based) metrics that feed performance dashboards, other sources of information help influence the success of performance management. For example, competitive and market analysis efforts result in critical information that allows executives to set goals. These goals are then translated into targets for sales, customer satisfaction surveys, employee training, process improvements, and project success rates. Also, activity metrics provide information on corporate dynamics. Feeds 4 and 5 in Figure 1.7 show the origins of data that feed activity metrics, and feed 6 shows how data from risk management (another monitoring activity) can compliment performance metrics. The dotted arrows illustrate how project and process risks can indirectly feed the performance management system.

1. *Metrics fed by processes:* When it is desirable to track an activity, accurate quantitative analysis is easier to establish for those activities that are fairly consistent, such as business processes. These processes are even easier to track if they include some IT component. With the aid of a growing software market, many tools are now available to help organizations automate the tracking of these metrics. Tools that will be reviewed in greater depth in Chapter 4 on performance management include data warehouses, analytics engines, and performance dashboards. Examples of such process metrics can include product quality statistics, customer feedback scores, sales forecasts, and safety program implementation rates.

2. *Metrics fed by projects:* Tracking the performance of projects can produce less quantitative results than when tracking the performance of processes. As a result, the performance ratings, or health of a project, tend to be fairly subjective. This leads to the need for more robust auditing teams and methodologies that help normalize statusing across projects. For example, a set of project managers may rate their projects as being on time, on budget, and on scope. But if the expectations of project sponsors shift in the middle

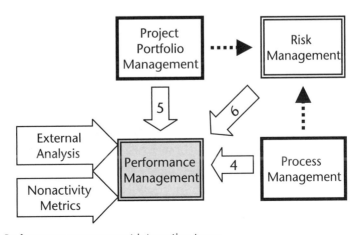

**Figure 1.7**   Performance management integration types.

of a project, such positive health ratings could be inaccurate. Project portfolio management offices can ensure that metrics representing the health of the entire portfolio become less subjective and more precise.

3. *Metrics fed by risks:* When executives view their performance dashboards, they see a swath of red, yellow, and green indicators. Their tendency then is to focus on the reds and to read any comments on why a process metric or project metric has gone south. Another aid to executives would be to see a proactive list of risks before problems arise for any particular metric. More advanced implementations of performance management dashboards provide this ability for managers to request, and then for executives to provide, support and guidance using risk analysis guidelines. A concrete company may report that cement prices are still low, but there is a risk of higher prices due to an increase in global demand; a workers' compensation insurance company may report a low claim rate but there is a risk of increased claims due to new Occupational Safety and Health Administration (OSHA) standards in the United States; and an upstream oil and gas company may report good reserve volumes but there is a risk that a competitor has been cross-drilling into its supplies for the last ten years. As will be shown, for such an integration feed to work, a company must have a culture of risk in place where employees are recognized, not punished, for identifying risks.

Performance management systems were originally designed to track metrics associated with operational processes. Now, with the aid of the project portfolio management office, consolidated project health metrics can complement the process metrics. While this expands a company's ability to react to threshold violations, it is through the integration of risk management that executives can proact to threshold violations. Where integrated risk management provided for a landscape view of the future, integrated performance management provides for such a view of the past, present, and future.

## Project Portfolio

A wide range of project types exists. A project can initiate to find something such as a supplier, an advertiser, a market, or a new drug. A project can initiate to create something such as a new product, a new bridge, or a new business. A project can also be created to improve something such as an athlete, a building design, or a business process. All of these can be categorized as growth oriented, productivity oriented, or both. Ultimately, their aim is to improve such performance metrics as revenue, customer satisfaction, and quality levels; to reduce such risks as regulatory requirements, acquisition threats, and patent expirations; or to improve such processes as product fulfillment, invoice collection, and software requests for proposals. While many process improvement efforts are labeled as such (feed 7), some can be labeled as risk mitigation or performance improvement initiatives. The dotted arrows in Figure 1.8 just reinforce the concept that the majority of risks and performance metrics tend to be based upon operational processes.

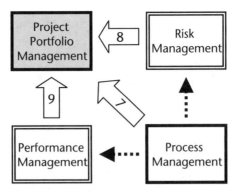

**Figure 1.8**   Project portfolio management integration types.

1. *Projects to improve processes:* Kaizen, Lean, Critical Chain, and Six Sigma are all methods used by companies to identify and then improve processes. Process improvement can involve initiation of a project to automate part or all of the process, to replace a process, or to eliminate a process. For example, the entire suite of human resources processes can be outsourced, and the finance department's spreadsheets can be replaced by an enterprise resource planning (ERP) system. Such projects should be reviewed, prioritized, and audited like any other project in the project portfolio.

2. *Projects to mitigate risks:* As risks are identified, they should also be prioritized by their impact on the company and the likelihood of their occurrence. With a given set of resources, the company can then select those higher-priority risks they would like to mitigate and then assign resources in the form of a project. If a glass furnace is reaching the end of its lifetime, a project can start to replace it before it fails; if competitors are providing superior customer communications, a project can start to improve and integrate Web sites, call centers, and advertisements; if a branch auditing office is inappropriately shredding customer documents after audits, a project can start to educate other branch offices of the repercussions of such actions. Again, such projects should be lined right up alongside process improvement projects in the project portfolio, then prioritized for risk, alignment, and return.

3. *Projects to improve performance metrics:* When the target levels for a set of performance metrics are found to be subpar as compared to an industry, further competitive and market analysis may need to be done. But when it is found that incorrect metrics are being observed or that the metrics being observed reflect incorrect information, projects are initiated to resolve these problems. Many times, such projects can grow into an immense undertaking of process reengineering, systems installation, and, just as scary, systems integration. Although the initial impetus was to provide greater and more accurate visibility through metric refinement, collateral benefits of such projects can include process improvement and risk reduction. For example, at a large, international medical instruments company, it was found that the sales force forecasted its sales inconsistently.

While different variables can affect sales across countries, the entire sales force could at least upload forecasts and actuals to a central system. After implementing a sales force automation (SFA) system, sales managers were able to normalize their forecasting metrics, which led to more accurate sales metrics.

Projects tend to get funded when they support the two basic strategic goals of a company: improving productivity or improving growth. With project portfolio management processes in place, the organization can better select and prioritize those projects that mitigate risks and those that improve processes. But a third type of project that should be included is the one that improves the way the company grades itself for performance. The value-add of looking at PPM from a point of view that integrates risk, process, and performance management is that it embeds operational risk management into the approval process, enforces process improvement strategies, and ensures continued refinement of how the company measures itself. Integrating PPM with the other three activity management concepts helps focus PPM activities beyond just strategic alignment, risk balancing, and financial return. Without a focus on such projects, risks will be realized, processes will never improve, and performance measures will be pointed in the wrong direction.

## Process

Process monitoring serves as the bedrock for risk management and performance management activities. Process improvement is also the prime source of projects for the portfolio of projects. However, it is far less common for organizations to integrate processes that support project portfolio, performance, or risk management into their portfolio. The process portfolio is primarily made up of those activities that support the ongoing operations of the company. A more mature company will also integrate such processes as initiative reviews and audits (Figure 1.9, feed 11), risk submission and tracking (feed 10), and metric improvement and implementation (feed 12). The dotted arrows show how some risk management and performance management processes can be indirectly derived from a need to support the project portfolio.

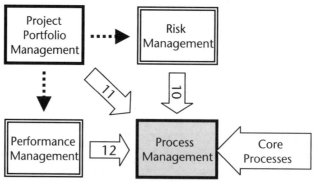

**Figure 1.9**   Process management integration types.

1. *Risk culture:* While major risk mitigation activities require funded projects, smaller risks tend to be handled with minor adjustments. If a department realizes it is understaffed for a given budget, it ramps up its hiring processes; if new regulations require companies to archive e-mails for at least three years, they increase their data-backup processes; if a new fuel in a manufacturing plant leads to hotter machines, the floor mechanics turn up the coolant valves. Such risk mitigation adjustments are numerous in any company with a healthy culture of risk awareness. Company cultures that have been devastated with layoffs, eaten away by micromanagers, and beat on by an endless stream of organizational change initiatives can lack pride, commitment, and a willingness to adjust for risk. With integrated PePPR management, processes are clearly defined for executives to be notified by managers about staffing shortfalls, by IT about server needs, and by operations about asset lifetime effects. Processes are also clearly defined as to how such notifications are rewarded and tracked for implementation. So, to avoid cultures where money is thrown at a risk to be diverted elsewhere by department heads with false budgetary pretenses, it is important to establish open-book risk management cultures supported by respected and enforced risk management frameworks.

2. *Project portfolio processes:* How do I submit an idea for a project? Does my idea align with the corporate strategy, the IT architecture, the culture of the organization, and the resources available to ensure approval and ultimate success? Also, is there a central source of knowledge from previous projects that I can use? Is there a set of methodologies the company prefers? Is anyone trained as a project manager, and is there an auditing process? These are all examples of project portfolio processes that, if integrated into the corporate process portfolio, will help ensure that good ideas turn into successful projects. Such control can minimize the funding of politically motivated, bad ideas, yet maximize the odds of realizing forecasted return on investment (ROI).

3. *Automated process management:* The dream scenario for executives would be not only to have a clear view into the performance of the company but also to be able to instantly influence that performance. A turbine mechanic can instantly adjust a valve, a train engineer can hit the accelerator, and an electrician can redirect current with a switch. But what can an executive do besides hope that his or her order is followed all the way through the layers of the company? Those processes that have strong automation and systems integration components have a higher likelihood of providing executives with dials, accelerators, and switches. Automation provides the controls, while integration links them and summarizes them like the many gears and dials of a mechanical watch. At one home improvement company, the vice president of marketing wanted his call center agents to read a script that up-sold roofs in Florida after a hurricane swept through. With secure access to the company's customer relationship management (CRM) system, he was able to make the change on the fly and thus improve sales according to weather patterns. In short, such automated process systems help integrate performance management into the process portfolio of the company.

The process portfolio is typically made up of operational processes that keep the company producing its products and services. But through the integration of the other three PePPR components, value can be added with the addition of risk identification/escalation processes, performance metric/data improvement processes, and project portfolio processes (e.g., approvals, audits, and support). Extending the process portfolio to include activity management processes helps institutionalize the flexibility and control that PePPR management provides.

## Strategic Value-adds

While executive-initiated strategic reviews are triggered by unforeseen market events, executive whims, or annual board requirements, business-unit-initiated strategic reviews are triggered more by real-time market forces. For example, according to Wayne W. Eckerson, author of "See It Coming," most executives never validate assumptions they have about what drives the business and, as a result, make poor "plans that leave the business vulnerable to 'unseen' market forces" [20]. It is in business-unit strategic reviews, however, that all four of our concepts merge—usually with the emphasis being on one of the concepts. In some companies, project portfolio management office directors pull more weight and drive strategic reviews with the need to promote better project support and control. In other non-project-centric companies, risk flags or performance goals drive the documentation of a strategy. Finally, some corporate strategies are guided by business processes that either have evolved from a culture or were created for an IT-based initiative. In short, while corporate strategies will always evolve from the executive view, it is also good to allow strategies to be influenced by the operational view of the marketplace. Fortunately, with recent applications in performance management to automate data analytics and metrics, some feel that this could "lead to more of a bottom-up questioning of corporate strategy" [21].

Integrating the components of PePPR management supports the strategic efforts of the company by reducing the redundant efforts spent on each individually. Sure, each PePPR component can be conducted independently of the other to promote checks and balances. But they should then be integrated to avoid experiencing the gaps that occur when they are siloed. The value-adds listed in this section show that by covering these gaps, potential problems can be avoided. Also, when implementing PePPR components, there is an opportunity for cross-training around common elements of the various methodologies and frameworks.

Integrating PePPR management components allows strategic planners to consider the balance of factors that affect how a company functions. The needs to improve the visibility of capabilities and to improve the execution of goals are the two tenets of this approach that should be core objectives of any organization. Besides just providing a framework to focus on corporate activities, PePPR management also provides a framework that consolidates the redundant activities of risk managers, project portfolio managers, process managers, and performance managers. That is, sufficiently common tasks exist that a team can easily cross-train and support each other in the enterprisewide control and support of PePPR components (introduced in Chapter 2 on maturity). Then, when strategic planning time arrives, infighting between activity management champions is replaced with concise and agreed-upon recommendations. Figure 1.10 and Table 1.1 show the integrated PePPR model in table form. Here, metrics, processes, projects, and risks are fed into the mix from above, integrated, and then fed out to the four PePPR management components. It is in the integrated matrix that the heart of this book beats.

As was presented in the previous section, the value-adds of integrated PePPR management can also be seen in each of the integrated components of the PePPR model. While each integration point provides value, some tend to be more common than others, thus providing less incremental value. One of the intentions of Chapter 2 is to show which are more basic and which are more advanced. It will be shown that, in general, process feeds to performance metrics, projects, and risks are a common activity in businesses. Also, risk identification and escalation procedures, as well as risk mitigation projects, are fairly basic elements of a business. But once we start looking at how the project portfolio and the performance management architecture feed PePPR management, we will see that this is less common but can be just as valuable as the basic integration points. As we progress through the book, a central focus will be on the elaboration of these value-adds.

## Systems versus Culture

In the 1990s, companies experienced a wave of operational support systems, such as enterprise resource planning (ERP), customer relationship management (CRM), sales force automation (SFA), and supply chain management (SCM), that promised better in-house control of such family jewels as accounting, customers, sales, and suppliers. Where small towns feel that they've breached the big time when they get their first McDonalds or Wal-Mart, start-ups feel the same when they've implemented a three-letter acronym (TLA) operational support system. Over the last

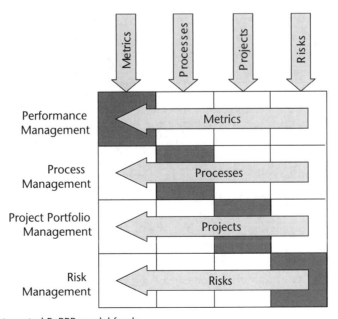

**Figure 1.10**   Integrated PePPR model feeds.

**Table 1.1** Detailed View of Integrated PePPR Model Feeds

| Feeds To | | Feeds From | | | |
|---|---|---|---|---|---|
| | | *Performance* | *Process* | *Project Portfolio* | *Risk* |
| | *Performance* | External analysis Internal metrics | (4) Operational *process metrics* | (5) *Project* portfolio status *metrics* | (6) Operational *risk metrics* |
| | *Process* | (12) Engrained *metric* improvement *processes* (performance culture) | Core processes | (11) *Project* portfolio management *processes* (project culture) | (10) Engrained *risk* identification/escalation *processes* (risk culture) |
| | *Project Portfolio* | (9) Performance *metric* improvement *projects* | (7) *Process* improvement *projects* | | (8) *Risk* mitigation *projects* |
| | *Risk* | (3) Are you tracking the correct *metrics* (metric *risks*)? | (1) Identifying and reporting on *process risks* | (2) Are *project risks* fed to the operational risk management dashboard? | External risks |

decade or two, such systems have been refined, battle-weary survivors have told their stories, and cultures (like continental shelves) have shifted in favor of business efficiency. Then, at the turn of the millennium, we saw the growth of software companies that promised to integrate all of these nonstandard systems with such tools as enterprise application integration (EAI), business intelligence (BI), data warehouse (DW), and business activity management (BAM). As companies dealt with the pains of systems integration projects, a new systems wave was launched by other software companies. This new wave was the automation of activity management (PePPR) processes. Performance management, process management, project portfolio management, and risk management systems now promise to dramatically improve internal visibility, strategic alignment, corporate control, market flexibility, and competitive advantage. But can the installation of a new system truly transform an organization? Is business technology as "plug and play" to a company as a mouse is to a computer?

When operational systems are implemented, companies realize that major process changes are usually required for the new TLA glove to "fit." While this may lead to a lot of pain resulting from organizational change, the pain can become acceptable to the troops because they are told it is necessary to improve the success of the company. With PePPR management systems, on the other hand, the benefits to the company are harder to explain. Since the true beneficiaries of such systems are perceived to be management, the sales pitch for organizational change can be more difficult. This helps explain why cultural foundations are all the more critical to such system success. Many months of process reengineerings are the norm for successful TLA implementations. Many years of cultural change are the norm for successful enterprisewide activity management implementations. Motorola, Allied Signal, and GE spent many years implementing their Six Sigma process improvement initiatives; Harrah's [22] and Molson-Coors [23] took several years to instill a project management culture to support their project portfolio management initiative, and an innumerable number of companies still try to assure their employees that they will be rewarded, not fired, for identifying risks. If advanced systems are installed before a PePPR culture is created, users of the system will be less inclined to be thorough with their data entry because they just won't see the value-add to them. If such a system is installed that instead makes current processes more efficient (i.e., they are already implementing PePPR principles), then system embracement is much easier to achieve. That is, a culture of performance, process, project portfolio, and risk improvement needs to have been developed before a centralized PePPR management system may be embraced.

The early culture of a business is usually established by the personalities and actions of the organization's founders. If the leadership is sound, leaders' actions will usually map well to their words. With these actions, a company is born from the static pages of the business model. How the founders invest in new directions, how they direct the actions of the employees (processes), and how they respond to and track performance and risk all set the tone for action in a company. Eventually, managers keep track of their risks, performance statistics, project investments, and process improvements in lists or spreadsheets. As risks come and go, projects start and end, performance improves or slacks, and processes improve or deteriorate, these tracking spreadsheets get updated by hand. The manager pulls consolidated (or summary) information for reports that need to be passed up the chain of command. On their way up each successive rung of the ladder, PePPR reports are merged, prioritized, and summarized. A final report or set of reports is handed to the executives. This process of gathering data, feeding spreadsheets, generating reports, and iterating until management is satisfied can be excruciatingly inefficient; we'll refer to it as the PePPR grind. As a result, managers work hard to minimize this pain by finding ways to minimize this work. Transferring spreadsheets to small databases is one way to automate the report generation, but at the risk of losing the easily accessible formulas of a spreadsheet. Ultimately, managers are forced into purchasing a full-scale strategic management system once they reach some bottlenecks in their spreadsheets and rudimentary database systems.

The vendors of such PePPR management systems create database and multiuser versions of the spreadsheets typically used by managers to track performance and risk. These vendors then keep adding new bells and whistles so that their product glossies grow thicker than their competitors'. As PePPR vendors get heavy on functionality, they sell primarily to larger and larger companies that can afford such ever-costlier solutions. As it turns out, according to Nigel Rayner, author of Gartner's December 2006 Magic Quadrant for corporate performance management suites, "the sophistication of these systems is actually way ahead of what people are looking to buy, because most are just looking to replace an Excel-based planning system" [24]. Figure 1.11 shows how as staff effort and executive support increase on PePPR management activities (expanding PePPR culture), so does the need for bigger and better systems automation. But companies that buy a product before there is a need not only risk paying for unused functionality (i.e., lost value) but could be setting themselves up for cultural rejection of PePPR concepts. In Figure 1.11, a vertical gray bar represents a company that, for example, has some departments occasionally passing up risk performance reports and rarely improving processes or controlling projects. This company is applying little effort to advancing

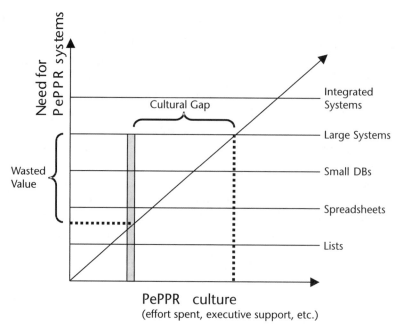

**Figure 1.11**   Culture versus systems gap.

activity management. Then, to continue the example, an executive feels that buying an enterprisewide system will bring staff up to speed on these important approaches. Training will need to be provided not only for the new system but also for the processes associated with integrated PePPR management. If this adds up to more work and less productivity than before systems installation, executives will end up with a rejected solution; their costly system will become a paperweight. To improve the odds of systems embracement and organizational excitement, be sure that automation purchases are aligned with the maturity of your organization.

## Support versus Control

According to Robert M. Grant, author of *Contemporary Strategy Analysis: Concepts, Technologies, Applications*, "The key to profitability is exploiting corporate differences" [25]. But according to Hiroyuki Itami, the key to long-term success is in the parallel development, not just exploitation, of the company's resources and capabilities. Itami refers to such ongoing attention to internal, aligned growth as "dynamic resource fit" [26]. As a company adapts to a changing industry with a flexible strategy, it should mold its capabilities to support such change. Otherwise, its strategy will be a slave to immovable (i.e., unsupported) capabilities. Training programs, organizational change initiatives, process reengineerings, reorganizations, outsourcing, mergers and acquisitions, and compensation changes are all ways that companies can coax, force, or guide internal capability changes. While some may mold their resources with strict discipline and control, others choose the empowerment and support route. In practice, however, managers tend to understand that different circumstances require different approaches. Achieving such a sensitive balance between discipline and support was the most elusive step for many companies Bartlett and Ghoshal studied. Nonetheless, Bartlett and Ghoshal found that successful entrepreneurial companies able to infuse the organization with self-discipline did so with "a supportive and nurturing management style." Employees are included in the design of metrics for performance management, empowered to make process improvement decisions, supported by management on their projects, and work in an open-book environment where risk identification is encouraged. The alternative is an authoritarian management style that leads to a garbage-in, garbage-out system of communication that can degrade executive visibility. Traditional activity management focuses predominantly on controlling mechanisms such as status and risk reports that percolate up. The PePPR model expands on this by also focusing on the support and inclusion mechanisms that expand downward. This combined approach of the PePPR model provides the control and support mechanisms to fit such dynamic internal events as staff turnover, management unpredictability, and executive churn to such dynamic external events as regulatory change, technology obsolescence, and globalization. Figure 1.12 expands on Figure 1.2 by illustrating how, through an integrated PePPR model, a company can establish a fit between the dynamics of its environment.

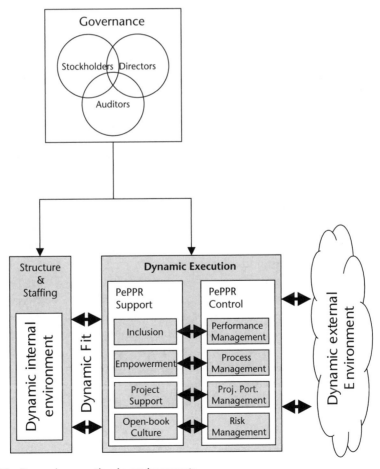

**Figure 1.12**   Dynamic execution in environments.

Part of the cultural development that exists over the years in mature organizations isn't just embodied in repetitive reports passing up the ladder; it is also the payback, or support, the troops get from implementing such processes. Poor performers should be provided with opportunities to improve (e.g., training), project managers should be provided with collateral from successful and failed projects (i.e., knowledge/document management), risk identifiers should be a part of the mitigation process (as a scriptwriter is on a movie set), and staff should be publicly rewarded for process improvement successes. A combined support/ control model not only improves a company's dynamic resource fit but improves the success rate of PePPR systems upgrades. If such support or recognition isn't part of the cultural fabric, then employees will extend their lack of support for PePPR processes to a lack of support for PePPR automation systems. If employees weren't entering and tracking PePPR data (i.e., living the PePPR grind of lists and spreadsheet reports) before with enthusiasm, they will be forced to do so with the installation of an enterprise solution. As we progress through the chapters, we will not only show how to implement the PePPR model, but we will also show how to implement it responsibly with systems, to fit it dynamically to your environments, and to balance it between support and control of the organization.

## Summary

According to Leibold, Probst, and Gibbert, the knowledge economy has led to a state in which corporate structure is just as malleable as corporate activities. That is, no longer can organizations expect to be sitting on firm ground when they try to hit the correct clay pigeon from among the thousands flying overhead. As with playing billiards on a speedboat, shooting trap on a trampoline, or juggling on a surfboard, precision moves on a moving foundation can be highly complex. Making a good choice and then executing well in today's market requires (1) an acute ability to prepare, adapt, and then commit, and (2) the ability to do so as a consolidated unit. The combination of these two traits (i.e., adaptive execution and systemic execution) is what we will refer to as dynamic execution. The key to executing successfully as intended in dynamic environments requires an ability (1) to see the terrain, understand your capabilities, and accurately predict the future, and (2) to operate dependably, change direction on a dime, and innovate relentlessly. The former we refer to as visibility management and address through risks (proactive visibility) and performance metrics (reactive visibility); the latter we refer to as execution management and address through processes and the project portfolio. The integration of these forms of strategic activity management will be called integrated PePPR management. The purpose of this book, then, is to introduce a maturity model, a framework, an organizational structure, and a rollout process for integrated PePPR management so that companies not only learn best practices but, through constant references to case studies, learn how to execute them.

# References

[1] Raynor, Michael E., *The Strategy Paradox*, New York: Currency/Doubleday, 2007.

[2] Trottman, Melanie, "Southwest's Fuel Hedging Yields Lower Prices, Savings," *Startup Journal—Wall Street Journal*, January 16, 2001, http://startup.wsj.com/forms/printContent.asp?url=http%3A//startup.wsj.com/columnists/challeng-ers/greatplains/20010116-trottman.html (last accessed on June 4, 2007).

[3] Carter, D., D. Rogers, and B. Simkins, "Fuel Hedging in the Airline Industry: The Case of Southwest Airlines," *Social Science Research Network*, July 2004, http://ssrn.com/abstract=578663 (last accessed on March 29, 2008).

[4] Bossidy, Larry, and Ram Charan, *Execution: The Discipline of Getting Things Done*, New York: Crown Business, 2002.

[5] Leibold, Marius, Gilbert Probst, and Michael Gibbert, "Frameworks for Systemic Strategic Management," in *Strategic Management in the Knowledge Economy*, by M. Leibold, G. J. B. Probst, and M. Gibbert, (eds.), New York, NY: Wiley, 2002, pp. 180–197.

[6] Bartlett, C. A., and S. Ghoshal, "Changing the Role of Top Management: Beyond Structure to Process," *Harvard Business Review*, January–February 1995.

[7] Rosenzweig, Phil, "The Halo Effect, and Other Managerial Delusions," *McKinsey Quarterly*, No. 1, 2007.

[8] Zadek, Simon, "The Path to Corporate Responsibility," *Harvard Business Review*, December 1, 2004.

[9] Coopersmith, Jonathan, "The Failure of Fax: When a Vision Is Not Enough," *Business and Economic History*, Vol. 23, No. 1, Fall 1994, www.hsofmich.org/~business/bhcweb/publications/BEHprint/v023n1/p0272-p0282.pdf (last accessed on May 18, 2007).

[10] Trimble, Vance, "A Review of Overnight Success: Federal Express and Its Renegade Creator," *Journal of Business Leadership*, 2000–2001, www.anbhf.org/pdf/reichert.pdf (last accessed on May 18, 2007).

[11] Perkins, Tom, "The 'Compliance' Board," *Wall Street Journal*, March 2, 2007, p. A11.

[12] ZoomInfo, The following key words were used to search a database of over 3.8 million companies for PePPR software vendors: process management: "business process management software"; project portfolio management: "enterprise project portfolio management software"; performance management: "operational performance management software"; risk management: "operational risk management software." See www.zoominfo.com/ (last accessed on June 3, 2007).

[13] Light, Matt, and Daniel B. Stang, "Magic Quadrant for Project and Portfolio Management, 2004," Garner, Inc., Stamford, CT, February 7, 2004.

[14] Gaughan, Dennis, and Carline Durocher, "AMR Research Report—IT Portfolio Management Software: Clear Benefits, Converging Marketplace," AMR Research, Boston, MA, June 1, 2004.

[15] "METAspectrum Market Summary—Portfolio Management Tools," META Group, Stamford, CT, May 24, 2004.

[16] "METAspectrum Market Summary—Project Portfolio Management Tools," META Group, Stamford, CT, February 18, 2004.

[17] Leibold, Marius, Gilbert Probst, and Michael Gibbert, *Strategic Management in the Knowledge Economy*, New York: Wiley, 2002, pp. 70–80.

[18] Senge, Peter M., and Goran Carstedt, "Innovating Our Way to the Next Industrial Revolution," *Harvard Business Online*, December 1, 2001.

[19] Johnson, Amy, "A New Supply Chain Forged," *ComputerWorld*, September 30, 2002, www.computerworld.com/industrytopics/retail/story/0,10801,74647p2,00.html (last accessed on May 15, 2007).

[20] Eckerson, Wayne W., "See It Coming," *Intelligent Enterprise*, Vol. 9, No. 2, February 1, 2006, pp. 25–29.

[21] Stodder, David, "Metrics through the Looking Glass," *Intelligent Enterprise*, Vol. 9, No. 2, February 1, 2006, p. 5.

[22] Melymuka, Kathleen, "Harrah's: Betting on IT Value," *ComputerWorld*, May 3, 2004, www.computerworld.com/managementtopics/management/story/ 0,10801,92759,00.html (last accessed on 6/24/2004).

[23] Bonham, Stephen, et al., "The Molson-Coors Operational Portfolio Architecture," CAIS, Communications of the Association of Information Systems, Vol. 18, December 2006.

[24] Smalltree, Hannah, "Corporate Performance Management Software: Gartner Study Says Competition Heats Up," SearchDataManagement.com, January 4, 2007.

[25] Grant, Robert M., *Contemporary Strategy Analysis: Concepts, Technologies, Applications*, 4th ed., Malden, MA: Blackwell Publishers, 2002.

[26] Itami, Hiroyuki, *Mobilizing Invisible Assets*, Cambridge, MA: Harvard Business Press, 1991.

## CHAPTER 2

# Maturity

For a small-town country store that has yet to experience a Wal-Mart invasion, times can be fairly comfortable, especially if there is high demand and there are no other stores around. If the owners are experienced in this line of work, they will know how to mitigate known risks (e.g., spoiled food, theft, potential competitors), track performance measures (e.g., delivery dates, daily sales, employee absenteeism), review and monitor new initiatives (e.g., a new coffee stand, new shelves, new cash registers), and improve processes (e.g., train employees, automate inventory work, improve the loading dock). With happy employees, loyal customers, dependable supply chains, reliable facilities, and disaster-recovery plans, the owners will feel that they've reached the top of the business maturity ladder. But once they decide to visit the big city or attend a trade convention, they'll start to question their business maturity level. The owners may see several organizations with five or more stores and a central office. While some may have implemented advanced process automation systems (e.g., enterprise resource planning, inventory control, and Web-based delivery systems), others will have automated some of the tasks normally done by management (e.g., performance, risk and project portfolio management). With more revenues, larger facilities, lower prices, faster processes, and more employees, other grocers may far surpass our small-town grocer in business maturity.

Such perceptions are common experiences that many small businesses face every day—that bigger is better. In reality, however, (1) bigger may not be better, and (2) to be better, bigger needs to be managed well. If the small-town grocer looked closer, he or she would see that some of the "more mature" companies had low margins, unhappy employees, inconsistent customers, shifting supply chains, and broken information technology (IT) systems. These larger companies may not have acted on "red-flag" risks, responded to lagging performance indicators, verified employee training, or controlled which projects they financed. These companies may have executed their strategies with little control or supportive direction. While these act as simplified generalizations, they illustrate that there can be very mature small companies and very immature large companies. We will use different models to help show which companies are mature and which are not.

As organizations have learned from successes and failures, researchers have developed best practice approaches to analyze the current state and determine the desired position of a company. These researchers, whether from academia, consulting companies, or internal staff, tend to package such best practices as maturity models. In this chapter, we will look at several models used to rate the maturity of a company. As we will see, younger companies work hard to achieve cash flow with little effort spent on planning. Once they've established themselves as dependably growing companies, portions of their initial business plans can become obsolete. From that realization onward, companies become gradually more mature in how they plan strategy and support its execution. That is, they learn how to develop actionable strategies. This will lead us into the second section of this chapter, which discusses the levels of maturity a company goes through in achieving dynamic execution, which we will label PePPR execution maturity.

## Corporate Maturity

This section looks first at the size of a company in the well-researched area of business lifetime. The three maturity models chosen then explain what processes a company should be engaged in and how a company should be structured for each model (i.e., first the size, then the approach). The first model uses five stages, the second model is more expansive with seven stages, and the third model goes down to four stages while also introducing five factors of maturity. After presenting these models, we'll have a foundation on which we can stack capability maturity models (CMMs) and then understand how an integrated PePPR execution maturity model should be applied to companies of differing maturity.

### STaRS

Michael Watkins, author of *The First 90 Days*, presents a model to help diagnose an organization's current position called the STaRS model (for Start-up, Turnaround, Realignment, and Sustaining Success) [1]. The central purpose for this framework is to help new leaders understand how to customize their leadership styles to companies in different stages of development. To better explain the four positions of STaRS, Watkins splits them into two groups: one that requires more doing than planning (referred to as a hunter management style) and one that requires more planning than doing (referred to as a farmer management style). In this model, start-ups and turnovers require more of a hunter style of management. With start-ups, the company is aggressively trying to build its resource base of cash, technology, and people to most efficiently launch a company, product, or project. With turnarounds, a company can be just as aggressively trying to fix problems to get its business, product, or project back on track. In contrast, sustaining successes and realignments require more of a farmer style of management. In a sustaining-success situation, the main challenge is to preserve "the vitality of a successful organization" and to take the company to the next level of success. In a realignment, the "challenge is to revitalize a unit, product, process or project that is drifting into trouble" [1]. While the hunter group tracks, finds, attacks, and kills the target, the farmer group grooms, plants, nurtures, and distributes its bounty. For example, while a turnaround may involve layoffs, relocations, and product discontinuations, a realignment may involve training, expansions, and product improvements; the turnaround attacks, the realignment nurtures.

These four STaRS positions act as stages in the maturity of a company. When the company starts, it is usually done so as a start-up lead by an entrepreneur. Over time, if it grows successfully, it reaches a state where management styles should change to best sustain the company's success. At this point, the company can diversify with more sub-start-ups or realign to accommodate unforeseen risks or unavoidable processes. If a realignment fails to fix corporate problems, then more drastic actions may be needed in the form of a turnaround. Figure 2.1 shows how if a company succeeds in either the start-up, realignment, or turnaround stages, it can end up in the sustaining-success stage. Then, if a company is successful at creating a stable growth environment, it can then launch other start-up ventures. The STaRS model shows that realignments or turnarounds are natural steps, not failures in business evolution, and that there are options available before a company goes from the peak of success to divestiture. Note, for example, that the path to shutdown is much shorter from a start-up than it is from a company with sustained success.

Companies that are in a sustaining-success or realignment phase rely more on the farming tools that activity management systems provide. Start-ups and turn-arounds, on the other hand, rely less on such tools and are instead hunting for sources of cash flow either by cutting costs or by gaining paying customers. Figure 2.1 shows this with the "More PePPR Reliance" and "Less PePPR Reliance" brackets. Turnarounds can be very chaotic and desperate experiences that result from unforeseen events, or blindsides. When they occur, crisis management super-sedes day-to-day management. Are the criteria for choosing projects correct, are the tracking metrics representative of true performance, have we discovered all possible risks, and are our competitors in fact improving their processes more quickly than we are? These are normal questions that should be asked by companies in a farming phase. Questions that would be asked by companies entering a turnaround via a blindside would include, can we recover from a felony conviction [2–4], can we reverse a crisis with an effective public relations campaign [5–7], or will we get our money back [8–10]? Addressing these latter questions shoot to the top of the prior-ity list for a company trying to survive. But once crisis is overcome, management can go back to asking the first set of questions typical of a healthy organization.

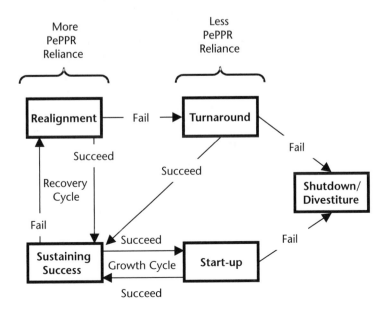

**Figure 2.1**   STaRS model.

Once you have determined your company's position, you will better understand whether rigorous strategic planning is a warranted enabler or a time-consuming constrainer. Does your company act on or yawn at the output of your planning sessions? While the STaRS model was primarily designed as an analysis tool, it can also serve as the foundation for understanding the amount of time that may have to be spent on strategic planning. This model will not help you eliminate planning in favor of doing (or vice versa); it will simply help you better balance the hunter versus farmer management styles when planning your strategy. Keep in mind that it is unlikely that your company will exactly fit the mold of any of the four STaRS situations. At the highest level, you may be able to summarize in one sentence a fit to one of them (e.g., "We consider ourselves a startup company"). "But as soon as you drill down, you will almost certainly discover that you are managing a portfolio—of products, projects, processes, plants, or people—that represents a mix of STaRS situations" [1]. A central drive to establish a culture of performance, process improvement, project success, and risk mitigation can help normalize such varying levels of maturity throughout your organization. An established PePPR culture will also help when a company needs to suddenly launch a start-up or initiate a turnaround. I once heard that the key to failure is resting on one's laurels of success. A company should take advantage of a sustaining-success position and wire itself to be well informed and well prepared for change. Integrated PePPR management will help establish such an environment so that when speed and winning choices are needed, it is second nature.

## The Pyramid of Organizational Development

Flamholtz and Randle define six areas of organizational development and their associated tasks that are necessary for a successfully growing company [11]. F&R present the tasks in a graphic they call the Pyramid of Organizational Development (Figure 2.2). The foundation of this pyramid is laid with the business concept or business plan. This is followed by a market analysis and, if possible, the creation of a niche. The products and services to be sold should be developed in Task 3, after the first two planning tasks are completed. Then, as the company grows, resources will need to be hired to allow the company to scale up (Task 4). Task 5 involves the introduction of systems to automate some operational tasks, such as human resources, accounting, inventory, supply chain, customers, and sales. Eventually, the entrepreneur or senior executive starts to experience an acute sense that things are out of control. No longer can he or she be everywhere and have input on everything. This person may have delegated tasks to lower-level staff by this stage, but providing input on high-priority/high-risk items and having a view into the status of the company is still critical. Also, executives realize the need to monitor operational performance and to influence new project investments. But with limited time, how do they know which investments to support to allow for maximum value-add to the organization? Also, with ever-decreasing visibility, how do they know that the performance metrics they hold management accountable to are accurate? Task 6 of F&R's model is where activity management systems are introduced to better formalize PePPR frameworks and to get executives back behind a functional helm.

**Figure 2.2**  Pyramid of Organizational Development. (*After* [11].)

The final task in organizational development is managing the corporate culture. If this is delayed too long, a company's culture will diverge from its initial goals, values, and mission. The culture will instead converge around the actions of the executives and management. The greater the difference between what executives dictate and what executives do, the greater the risk of corporate misalignment with strategy. To minimize this divergence, thus better influence its cultural development, a company should evaluate, early and often, how its staff is managed. Chapter 8 addresses some of the issues involved with cultural change while implementing integrated PePPR management.

With these core tasks of a growing company defined, F&R then came up with four stages in a company's maturity that can be reached while completing the tasks in the pyramid and three stages that can be reached once the pyramid has been completed. F&R also showed that the four growth stages could be mapped to the approximate organizational size (in sales) of both manufacturing and services firms (see Table 2.1).

### Stage 1: The New Venture

The launching of this stage can be the result of a brilliant, spontaneous idea or the output of many years of arduous research. Once an entrepreneur sets a direction, much effort tends to then be focused on growth. That is, the new venture identifies its market(s) and its product(s) and then works tirelessly to increase revenue so that it can meet and then exceed operational costs. Success in this stage requires an intense focus on execution. An everyone-does-everything approach is not atypical in the heat of such early battles in the history of a company. When a business enters this wilderness of unknown risks, instinct and experience are keys to survival so that the business can exit on the other side as a Stage 2 company. As a result, little atten-

**Table 2.1**   Stages of Organizational Growth

| Stage | Description | Critical Development Areas | Approximate Organizational Size (in Sales) | |
|-------|-------------|----------------------------|--------------------------|------------------------|
| | | | Manufacturing Firms | Services Firms |
| 1 | New venture | Markets and products | Less than $1 million | Less than $0.3 million |
| 2 | Expansion | Resources and operational systems | $1 to $10 million | $0.3 to $3.3 million |
| 3 | Professionalization | Management systems | $10 to $100 million | $3.3 to $33 million |
| 4 | Consolidation | Corporate culture | $100 to $500 million | $33 to $167 million |

*Source:* [11]

tion is paid to establishing repeatable processes, tracking performance metrics, or prioritizing projects to these metrics. When deciding on which projects to spend money, a shotgun approach is taken: if more than 50% of the pellets hit their target, it's a win.

## Stage 2: Expansion

In this F&R stage, a company can still consider itself in the STaRS start-up phase. Here, more effort is spent on acquiring the resources that will help grow a company beyond $300,000 for services companies and $1 million for manufacturing companies. Resources are no longer added just to maintain operations (e.g., a consulting contract, a restaurant, or a private bank); they are also added to expand operations (e.g., multiple contracts, additional restaurants, or new branches). Also, to support such increases in resources, operational systems are added (e.g., accounting, human resources, and inventory). While companies in Stage 1 may have implemented a suite of spreadsheets or simple databases to support early operations, Stage 2 companies not only build more advanced and dependable systems but delegate the maintenance of these systems from the founders or entrepreneurs to new resources. Whereas the business leaders were originally focused on their external environments to promote growth in Stage 1, they are now taking a more calculated focus on their internal environment (i.e., their growing capabilities).

Stage 2 companies are beginning to apply more well-rounded approaches to performance, process, and risk management. While not declaring these components of PePPR management as formal processes supported by costly systems, company leaders are nonetheless implicitly weighing and prioritizing their risks, investments, and financial targets. When financing new projects, they are starting to do so with a sniper rifle rather than with a shotgun. If they see their staff doing things inefficiently, they guide them in more productive processes. As customer needs become clearer, a better understanding of where and how quality can be added is realized. In short, a Stage 2 company has exited the chaos of the wilderness, is smoothing out its rough edges, and is becoming a more well-rounded organization—as seen both from the outside and the inside.

## Stage 3: Professionalization

At this stage, the sponsors of a venture realize that they can't just pump money, resources, and IT systems into the mix to support continued growth. They now need to develop management systems that help organize and plan the growth. Here, the F&R model begins to align with the sustaining-success phase of STaRS. "Until this point, it was possible to be more of a doer or hands-on manager than a professional manager" [11]. The professionalizing companies, from this point on, must become increasingly more adept at implementing such "farming" tasks as planning, motivating, leading, and controlling. Overzealous companies striving to become Stage 3 organizations can make the mistake of becoming over- controlling. As a result, a balance should be maintained that avoids creativity- stifling bureaucracy but also diminishes the chaos that can result from unchecked entrepreneurship.

Stage 3 companies, according to F&R, typically range from $10 to $100 million in sales for manufacturing companies. Coincidentally, this also falls smack in the middle of what Jay Ritter, Cordell Professor of Finance at the University of Florida, considers the point at which a company can consider going public. Specifically, he states that a company shouldn't even think about making such a move until they are realizing at least $50 million in revenue [12]. With the introduction of costly compliance requirements such as Sarbanes-Oxley, this can easily shift to the $100 million range. So, what happens just before companies register for an initial public offering? They start adhering to management control paradigms so that they survive not only the scrutiny of underwriting banks but also that of government regulators. This is the stage in a company where serious thought and execution go into formalizing performance, process, project portfolio, and risk management. If such early efforts are strong, companies will be better positioning themselves to launch new business units or to survive unforeseen turnarounds.

### Stage 4: Consolidation

Once a company reaches near the $100 million mark, it will have brought on several waves of employees. Many of them will be unfamiliar with the energy, desires, and vision of the original founders. As a result, the company can start to drift apart with different approaches to handling a market. This is seen most commonly when business units silo. Since such siloing can lead to undesirable approaches (i.e., unalignment), a company should do more than revisit and broadcast its mission, vision, and goals; it should evaluate the actions of management. Consolidation doesn't mean centralized planning and operational processes; it just means creating one strategic path and then holding business units accountable to it.

With a continued goal of not losing the entrepreneurial spirit, while also implementing centralized control systems, the corporation now needs to make sure that performance measurement, process standardization, project approval, and risk prioritization are all aligned with corporate strategy. Formal management control processes and deliverables were a good first step in a Stage 3 company. As the company silos (or "buckets") into larger business units, such formalization should have central guidance and follow-up.

### Stage 5: Diversification

A company that diversifies, or develops other products or services, is creating a scenario that mitigates the all-eggs-in-one-basket risk. Executives are exercising options that they hope will protect them against the uncertainties of the market (i.e., Michael Raynor's "strategic flexibility"). Businesses understand that a product or service has a lifetime before it loses its luster, is made obsolete, or becomes a commodity with consumers. Before reaching a point where revenues no longer support the infrastructure of a Stage 4 company, effort should go into creating new revenue-generating ventures. A company that is in the middle of such a process is considered a Stage 5 organization. Such diversification can occur through merger and acquisition (M&A) activity or through new product or market creation. When this happens, strategic business units (SBUs) are created that have responsibility for their own profit and loss. It is then common to provide these SBUs with additional authority to support their greater accountability. Such authority can come in the form of custom strategic plans and independent PePPR management activities. This stage and Stage 6 can be considered forms of realignment in the STaRS model.

## Stage 6: Integration

As with the consolidation in Stage 4 through culture management, so we have integration in Stage 6 through centralization of management systems and processes. Stage 6 companies can be seen as scaled-up versions of Stage 4 companies. The difference between the two lies in the complexity of the increased size of Stage 6 companies. In these larger corporations, different SBUs work on developing common, or standardized, operational and management control systems and informational communications systems. Many companies such as Cisco are M&A machines that maintain their Stage 6 statuses in real time. As they buy a new company (to further diversify or synergize), they immediately integrate their human resources, operational control, and management control systems [13]. Stage 5 companies, on the other hand, allow the new additions to continue to operate independently; Berkshire Hathaway, a financial holding company based in Omaha, Nebraska, is an example. A point that can be noted here, then, is that Stage 5 and 6 companies can be considered equally mature. In some cases, a mixture of both diversification and integration may prove to be the best approach based on how the executives perceive the future and interpret the past and present. Realignments can easily take such a mixed-bag approach to correcting problems. But how great does the problem have to be to cause a realignment to be labeled a turnaround?

## Stage 7: Decline and Revitalization

Where Stages 5 and 6 present two dimensions of the STaRS realignment level, F&R's Stage 7 is less about realignment and more about turnaround. That is, a Stage 7 company has reentered the level of action orientation more typical of a start-up. Less focus is on planning, leading, motivating, and controlling, and more focus is on execution. Corporate decline and the resulting need for revitalization can occur if, for example, projects or performance measures were aligned with out-of-date strategies, if processes began to lose focus on quality and efficiency, or if risks were not mitigated in a timely fashion. Revitalization or turnaround would look at all of these areas, as well as the company's markets and product lines, to maintain itself as an ongoing entity.

F&R's research has shown that growing companies go through the first four stages if they undertake the tasks in the Pyramid of Organizational Development. Very large companies will then experience the final three stages. Overlap occurs when companies implement components of later stages while labeled an earlier-stage company. For example, if a Stage 2 start-up decides to implement PePPR components, it can be considered "mature for its age." However, there is a difference between proactive (or early) maturity and losing site of immediate needs. If low-level PePPR applications are made in a young company, they should be done in such a way as not to distract the company from achieving the other tasks of a Stage 2 company first (e.g., resource hiring, product development, and operational support systems).

## A Business Maturity Model

In 2003, Deloitte consulting and Utrecht University of the Netherlands conducted a set of surveys "of around 1,000 manufacturers in North America and Europe" to understand what makes one business more mature than another. This resulted in the development of a business maturity model. With follow-up surveys in 2004 and 2005, the model was refined to reflect the increasing complexity of doing business internationally [14]. Specifically, the researchers found that because (1) more elements of production were being transferred abroad, (2) the number of markets was increasing, and (3) product life cycles were declining, greater demands were being placed on such business elements as logistics, marketing, and product development. The higher a company was graded by this model, the better it was at handling such new-economy complexities. The researchers referred to these companies as "complexity masters."

Rather than just grading a company as reaching a particular level overall, this model splits components of a business into five factors, or "pillars," as shown in Figure 2.3. The companies that took part in the survey were then graded for each pillar on a maturity scale of 1 to 4. This provided a better quantification of F&R's observation that different layers of an organization can be at different stages of maturity.

The first stage is reached when a company conducts some basic form of strategic analysis, implements repeatable processes, performs rudimentary risk and performance tracking, makes attempts to mold its culture, and deploys standard operational IT packages. When the majority of departments formalize these silos, the company starts to enter the second level of maturity. Documented, repeatable, and improving strategic planning, processes, risk monitoring, and performance management are indicators of a level 2 mature company. Companies at this level also show a continual effort to guide departmental cultures and to implement advanced, departmental IT systems. Companies that have reached level 3 have consolidated the best practices of each pillar from the different business units and departments to establish enterprise-level standard approaches. The highest maturity level is reached when a company extends each pillar out to partners, suppliers, and customers. While the highest levels may be achievable, this model allows them to be reached one pillar at a time. A pillar that is lacking in the model is the project portfolio pillar. Nonetheless, the authors did mention that projects are what allow a com-

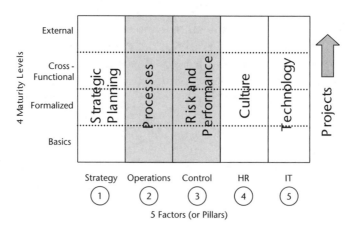

**Figure 2.3**   Author's interpretation of the Deloitte/Utrecht model's applicability to the PePPR model.

pany to advance to the next level. Below is a brief description of how a company matures in each and where in the book we will review them in more detail (also see Figure 2.4).

1.  *Strategy and policy formation:* As a company becomes more mature, it engages in more formal planning processes. A level 4 company continuously aligns its strategic plan not only internally with its business units but also externally with its business partners, supply chain companies, and industry network. We will take a look at how strategic planning maturity can improve in the next chapter.

2.  *Organizational and process:* More mature companies don't necessarily implement more formal process management approaches across the board and in one fell swoop; they just incrementally add structure to diminish

| | Strategy & Policy Formation | Organizational & Process | Organization Governance | People & Culture | IT |
|---|---|---|---|---|---|
| Level 4 Network | Network Strategy | Network Orientation | Chain Control | Human Capital Management | Network IT |
| Level 3 System | Integral Strategy | System Orientation | Management Control | Human Resource Management | Integral IT |
| Level 2 Process | Department Strategy | Process Orientation | Financial Control | Personnel Policy | Island IT |
| Level 1 Pioneer | Rudimentary Strategy | Functional Orientation | Cost Control | Personnel Management | Unstructured IT |
| | ① | ② | ③ | ④ | ⑤ |

**Figure 2.4**   Business maturity model. (*After* [14].)

chaos while allowing innovation. Level 4 companies involve the seniormost members of the organization to help centrally control such propagation of standards and processes while delegating responsibility to the organization. Chapter 5 will show how this process improvement can happen as companies mature.

3. *Organization governance:* Companies grow from central monitoring of financial metrics to a more delegated monitoring of both financial and nonfinancial metrics. Such monitoring includes performance indicators and risk flags. Chapters 4 and 7 show how performance and risk management, respectively, can be applied to organizations of different maturity.

4. *People and culture:* Maturity increases as companies focus more on the growth of their human capital through training, career paths, and knowledge management programs. Chapter 8 will go over the human factor when implementing PePPR components.

5. *IT:* Technology becomes less ad hoc and more aligned with the businesses goals. Also, as with the strategy-and-policy-formation pillar, external entities such as business partners and supply chain members can become better networked in with the level 4 company. We will refer to IT's role in activity management systems throughout the book, capping it off in Chapter 8.

The general conclusions of this study were two-fold: (1) more mature companies integrate components of each of the five pillars rather than treat them as pure silos, and (2) successful IT implementation takes place. The researchers found that enterprise performance doesn't necessarily improve when a company moves to a higher maturity level. Instead, they found that companies that improve each silo in parallel and with collaboration have a better chance at improving performance. For example, take an IT initiative (pillar 5) reviewed for alignment by an efficient approval committee (pillar 1). If the project sponsors communicated with the governance committee to integrate project risks with corporate risks (pillar 3), if other business units were included to smooth out any process-change effects (pillar 2), and if a project management certification and training process was established (pillar 4) rather than some project- or vendor-specific PM training, then the company as a whole would benefit. The alternative would be some siloed IT system and trained resources that solved the problems of one department at the expense of other departments. This example shows that integrated pillars (e.g., process, performance, risk, and strategy) are the causes, and successful IT implementations (i.e., projects) are the effects. Moreover, the authors of the Deloitte/Utrecht study felt that the ultimate effect is a higher rate of success in any endeavor, IT or not.

## PePPR Maturity

Evaluating a company for maturity can be a complex task given the sheer number of variables. As a result, corporate-level maturity models tend to be very broad and general. Since no one company can fit any mold perfectly, such models leave plenty of room for gray areas and interpretation. Models that get more detailed address specific corporate activities such as those found in performance, process, project portfolio, and risk management. Many maturity models can be found for each one of these activities. For example, Brett Champlin, president of the Association of Business Process Management Professionals, claims to have collected over 150 process management maturity models alone [15]. In each of the chapters that review the four PePPR management activities, we will dive deeper into some framework examples and draw the commonalities and the more astute perspectives from each. In this section, we will link PePPR maturity models (a special type of framework) to corporate maturity and understand the benefits of integrating the models between activity management types.

Parts of PePPR management may appear earlier for companies in certain industries: performance management in the luxury services industry, process management in manufactured goods industries, project portfolio management in the biotech industry, and risk management in the financial industry. Cultures are aligned around these specific PePPR management activities early in the history of companies in such industries. In general, however, since focus tends to be on growing the company in its early stages, integrated and balanced PePPR management doesn't typically occur until later. That is, executing for survival and validation takes precedence over establishing reliable, flexible, and integrated activity management models for Stage 1 companies. By the time a company is sustaining success as a Stage 3 and 4 company with a firm grasp of its processes, PePPR management implementations should be in place.

Figure 2.5 shows approximately how the three models map to each other. As can be seen, the business maturity model skips F&R's Stage 5 and any mention of turnaround or revitalization. Figure 2.5 also illustrates how PePPR management approaches start small (probably as lists and spreadsheets) and then expand rapidly into full-blown support systems. As companies experience the various stages of maturity thereafter, established PePPR management can ease the way.

### Model Dimensions

The common roots of PePPR maturity rest in a concept called capability maturity models (CMMs). The original CMM was developed by the Software Engineering Institute (SEI) in the late 1980s and early 1990s, and the concept has since been applied to PePPR components. The SEI described these models as "an evolutionary improvement path from ad hoc, immature processes to disciplined, mature processes with improved quality and effectiveness" [16]. The basic dimensions used in CMMs are stages of maturity (usually five) and proficiency to those stages. Over time, as more of these models were developed, more dimensions were used. In their paper "Towards a Business Process Management Maturity Model," Michael Rosemann and Tonia de Bruin researched a wide field of models and identified the following six dimensions [17]:

1. *Factors:* These are the independent variables that can each be tracked for maturity. Examples include culture, technology, strategic alignment, and governance.

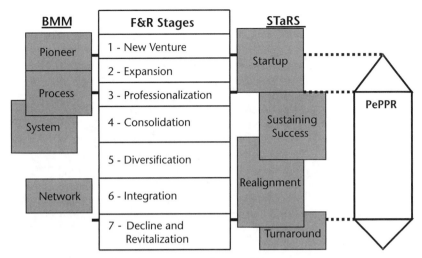

**Figure 2.5** Comparison of three business maturity paradigms.

2. *Maturity stage:* These are the levels of maturity each factor can attain. Examples include initial state, stabilized, repeatable, managed, and optimized.

3. *Time scope:* This dimension puts a timeline on when the organization plans on reaching the different stages of maturity.

4. *Organizational entity scope:* Which divisions, department, or business units are becoming more mature? This dimension allows management to be aware that factors may be at different maturity stages in different business silos. None of the PePPR maturity models we review in the next section use this dimension.

5. *Coverage:* Maturity models that take this approach will use such phrases as "business planning," "spreadsheets," "performance culture," or "integrated metrics." This dimension is a more detailed version of factors.

6. *Proficiency:* This dimension adds some meat to the coverage dimension by actually testing an organization to make sure it is proficient in the coverage it has declared and that action is being taken on its strategies. Phrases could include "business plans are required for all initiatives," "spreadsheets are being used effectively," "a culture of performance is so great that all new metrics were generated by lower management," and "metrics are integrated and used consistently by executives."

Rosemann and de Bruin represented these in the multiple dimensions shown in Figure 2.6. Such a complex model is rarely seen in maturity models as a common goal is to keep them simple so that they will be adopted and become standards. Since most models will pick and choose just a few of these dimensions, it can be difficult to line models up side by side to compare them. Nonetheless, before presenting an integrated PePPR maturity model, we will look at several CMMs for each PePPR component.

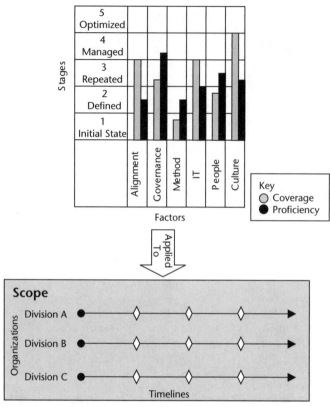

**Figure 2.6** CMM dimensions: how stages, factors, coverage, and proficiency should be evaluated for different organizations periodically. (*After:* [17].)

## Capability Maturity Models

While these models primarily focus on how to improve a company's maturity for each PePPR component separately, all but two of the models go beyond this narrow view and reference the need to integrate with one or more of the other PePPR components. As we build an integrated PePPR model in the next section (referred to as the "Execution Maturity Model"), we will reference these CMMs using a hyphenated abbreviation. The letters to the left of the hyphen refer to the component type ("PO" for portfolio management, "PE" for performance management, "PS" for process management, and "R" for risk management). The right side of the hyphen refers to the specific CMM referenced. We will also be referencing the feeds in the PePPR model, represented by the block arrows that connect performance, process, project portfolio, and risk management in Figures 2.7 to 2.10.

### Performance Management

1. *INPHASE Software:* This is one of the few performance management software companies that has made its maturity model available to the public (Table 2.2). Its model is very simple and supports performance management trends by recommending technology implementation sooner rather than later (common among performance management CMMs). A unique feature

**Table 2.2** Performance Management Maturity Model Comparisons

| | INPHASE (PE-IN) | AMR (PE-AM) | Deloitte (PE-DE) |
|---|---|---|---|
| *Stages* | 1—Disparate uncoordinated approach<br>2—Systematic performance measurement<br>3—Effective performance reporting<br>4—Performance management<br>5—Performance culture | 1—Operating<br>2—Integrating<br>3—Optimizing<br>4—Innovating | 1—Nonexistent<br>2—Developing<br>3—Defined<br>4—Advanced<br>5—Leading |
| *Factors* | | Initially technology driven<br>Ultimately technology and philosophy driven | 1—Processes<br>2—Performance measures/data<br>3—Organization alignment<br>4—Technologies and tools |
| *Process Groups* | | 1—Plan<br>2—Set goals<br>3—Monitor execution<br>4—Measure actuals to targets<br>5—Conduct performance notification<br>6—Resolve and close loop | |
| *Proficiency (Progress)* | X | X | X |
| *Time* | X | | |

of this model is the inclusion of time as a dimension, along with the basic five-stage and proficiency dimensions [18].

2. *Deloitte survey of Dutch manufacturing:* Deloitte's Integrated Performance Management Capability Maturity Model was presented to Financial Executives International, a trade group for chief financial officers. The model uses five stages and four factors that separate technology, organizational effects, and processes from the core performance management factors (e.g., measurement and data) [19].

3. *AMR Research:* The authors of this model believe that a strong technical focus should exist in the earlier stages but should not be led by IT departments; such approaches, they contend, usually fail. This model uses four stages and six process groups [20].

## Process Management

1. *Curtis et al.:* This is a simple model because only proficiency and stages are used (Table 2.3). While the model doesn't list out common processes that improve with each stage, it does list out different processes that are specific to each layer [21].

**Table 2.3**   Process Management Maturity Model Comparisons

|  | Curtis (PS-CU) | Rosemann (PS-RO) | Stemberger (PS-ST) |
|---|---|---|---|
| Stages | 1—Initial<br>2—Managed<br>3—Standardized<br>4—Predictable<br>5—Optimized | 1—Initial state<br>2—Defined<br>3—Repeated<br>4—Managed<br>5—Optimized | 1—Initial<br>2—Defined<br>3—Linked<br>4—Integrated<br>5—Extended |
| Factors |  | 1—Strategic alignment<br>2—Governance<br>3—Methodologies<br>4—IT<br>5—People<br>6—Culture |  |
| Proficiency (Progress) | X | X | X |
| Time |  | X |  |

2. *Rosemann and de Bruin:* These authors' paper lists most of the dimensions that can be used, culminating in the dimensions shown in Figure 2.6. However, their final model only presents three dimensions (stages, factors, and proficiency) and leaves detailed descriptions of the proficiencies open for further research [17].

3. *Stemberger et al.:* This is another simple model with no reference to a factors dimension. However, a framework is provided to help guide business process change initiatives [22].

## Project Portfolio Management

1. *The Center for Business Practices (CBP):* A part of PM Solutions, Inc., this organization published a book that lists two dimensions, stages and factors (Table 2.4). Their model is referred to as the project portfolio management maturity model [23].

2. *Bryan Maizlish and Robert Handler:* These two wrote the book *IT Portfolio Management*, which presents a maturity model specifically for IT organizations. While the model also uses five stages and six factors, they are slightly different from those used in CBP's model. For example, Maizlish and Handler's model starts from a Stage 0, where no project portfolio management (PPM) processes are in place, and works its way up to a Stage 4 of maximum maturity [24].

3. *The Project Management Institute (PMI):* The PMI, a standards-setting company for project managers, developed the Organizational Project Management Maturity Model (OPM3) to supplement their enormously popular standard on project management (the project management body of knowledge [PMBOK]). In an attempt to address as many scenarios as possible, the model tends to be very high level. Rather than using factors, this model uses what it refers to as domains and process groups [25].

**Table 2.4**  Project Portfolio Management Maturity Model Comparisons

|  | CBP (PO-CB) | Maizlish and Handler (PO-MH) | PMI (PO-PM) |
|---|---|---|---|
| *Stages* | 1—Initial process<br>2—Structured process and standards<br>3—Organizational standards and institutionalized process<br>4—Managed process<br>5—Optimizing process | 0—Admitting<br>1—Communicating<br>2—Governing<br>3—Managing<br>4—Optimizing | 1—Standardize<br>2—Measure<br>3—Control<br>4—Continuously improve |
| *Factors* | 1—Portfolio governance<br>2—Project opportunity assessment<br>3—Project prioritization and selection<br>4—Portfolio and project communications management<br>5—Portfolio performance management<br>6—Portfolio resource management | 1—Projects<br>2—Applications<br>3—Infrastructure<br>4—People<br>5—Processes<br>6—Information | |
| *Coverage (Domains)* | | | 1—Projects<br>2—Programs<br>3—Portfolios |
| *Process Groups* | | | 1—Initiate<br>2—Plan<br>3—Execute<br>4—Control<br>5—Close |
| *Proficiency* | X | X | X |

### Risk Management

1. *McConnell:* This author develops his own maturity model, compares it to the enterprise risk management (ERM) standard developed by the Committee of Sponsoring Organizations of the Treadway Commission (COSO), and then describes applicability to Basel II for financial institutions (Table 2.5). The McConnell model has five stages that he suggests be applied to the eight "components" (factors) of the COSO ERM model. However, details are not provided on how this would be done [26].

2. *Treasury Board of Canada:* The authors of this report don't label their proposal as a maturity model; they refer to it as an integrated risk management framework. Nonetheless, they do spell out four stages of implementation where each stage reflects a greater maturity level than the previous stage [27].

3. *Deloitte:* The foundation of this "Risk Intelligent Enterprise" model is that in lower stages, risk identification and mitigation activates are not rewarded. As the company matures through the stages, rewards are applied to such risk activities. The basic five-stage dimension is used, and the proficiency dimension is mapped to a company's custom risk profile [28].

**Table 2.5**  Risk Management Maturity Model Comparisons

| | Deloitte (R-DE) | McConnell (R-MC) | Treasury Board of Canada (R-TB) |
|---|---|---|---|
| Stages | 1—Tribal and heroic<br>2—Specialist silos<br>3—Top-down<br>4—Systematic<br>5—Risk intelligent | 1—Initial<br>2—Managed<br>3—Defined<br>4—Quantitatively managed<br>5—Optimized | 1—Developing the corporate risk profile<br>2—Establishing an integrated risk management function<br>3—Practicing integrated risk management<br>4—Ensuring continuous risk management learning |
| Factors | | (From COSO)<br>1—Monitoring<br>2—Information and communication<br>3—Control activities<br>4—Risk response<br>5—Risk assessment<br>6—Event identification<br>7—Objective setting<br>8—Internal environment | |
| Proficiency | Mapped to custom risk profile | X | X |

### Execution Maturity Model

For each of the four stages of PePPR execution maturity, we will provide a companion illustration that shows how the execution maturity model evolves. In each accompanying illustration, you will see integrating components wrapped in a bold box and nonintegrating components in italics below the bold box. These nonintegrating components are meant to show how individual PePPR components need to evolve in their stage to support the integrating components of the next stage. This same illustrative approach is applied to all stages until Stage 4, where no nonintegrating elements are needed for future stage development (i.e., you'd be at the highest stage possible). The elements of each of these stages were placed in their locations based upon not only where they generally appear in the other siloed CMMs but also how several companies have implemented them. In this chapter, we will focus on the contributions of the maturity models. Then as we dive deeper into each of the PePPR components in later chapters, you will be able to see how other companies have implemented stages of the PePPR execution model.

### Stage 1: Ad Hoc (Nonintegrated) Execution

Ad hoc is a well-used description for this layer among the different maturity models (Figure 2.7). PO-CB uses it to describe how all PPM processes are implemented, and R-MC and R-DE use it to describe how risks are handled at their earliest stages. In describing a company's core processes, PS-CU explains that at this early stage, such processes are moving an organization forward in an inefficient manner. Product development, service delivery, and supply chain management are just a few example

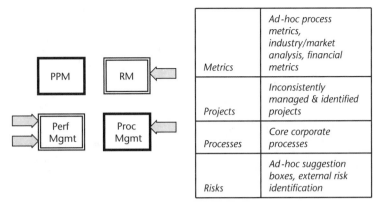

| | |
|---|---|
| Metrics | Ad-hoc process metrics, industry/market analysis, financial metrics |
| Projects | Inconsistently managed & identified projects |
| Processes | Core corporate processes |
| Risks | Ad-hoc suggestion boxes, external risk identification |

**Figure 2.7**  Stage 1 of PePPR execution maturity.

process categories that could be delivering inconsistent results. PE-AM explains that companies at this stage are simply grabbing "the low-hanging fruit, allowing them to realize benefits quickly" at the expense of long-term strategic gain; the prime example would be a strict focus on financial metric improvement [20]. Though companies at this level may claim that they've implemented PePPR components, such control is thin. For example, functional units may claim success at one moment but be unable to duplicate past successes predictably. A risk is delivered here, a performance metric is reported on there, one project finishes on budget, and some process recently demonstrated improved quality. To get to the next level, key functional units should not only establish consistent and ongoing siloed PePPR component success but also demonstrate the beginnings of an integrated model. Multiple identified risks should influence project selection, and multiple performance metrics should provide for actionable process improvement steps.

### Stage 2: Controlled Execution

Stage 2 companies have consolidated the metrics required to monitor the company's processes (Figure 2.8, feed 4). The PE-IN model shows this in its second stage as "key performance data collected efficiently" [18]. But the main push in this stage is to spend money on projects that improve process (feed 7) and mitigate risks (feed 8). This allows companies to better align their project portfolio with their process productivity strategy and risk profile. PS-ST hints at process improvement projects as activities that begin to occur in this model's second stage and then result in measurable customer satisfaction by its third stage. R-TB hints at launching risk mitigation projects in this model's second stage when the authors highlight the need to integrate risk management with the strategic objectives of the company.

*Nonintegrating Factors*    There are also three main nonintegrating activities that occur at this stage in preparation for the integrating activities of Stage 3. Before a company can get a good handle on the aggregate health of its project portfolio (in PePPR Stage 3), projects need to be providing statuses up to the program level. The PO-MA model has this occurring in its Stage 3, and the PO-CB model has it occurring in Stage 2. Also, before a company can get a good handle on the aggregate

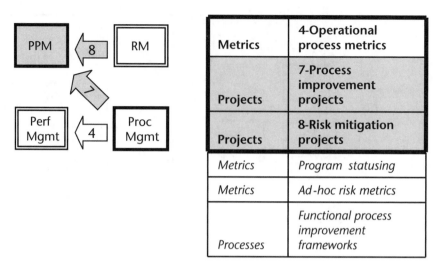

**Figure 2.8**   Stage 2 of integrated PePPR maturity.

risk level of its projects and processes, key risk indicators should be established and fed by a bottom-up culture of risk identification. Such a feed of risks usually starts at this level with data focused on financial and compliance risks (R-DE Stage 2). Finally, as process improvement projects may have already started, companies at this stage start to understand the value of implementing a standard process improvement framework (any of the Deming-based, International Standards Organization, or Office of Government Commerce approaches would work). So, before a methodical approach to *improve* enterprisewide process performance metrics can start, steps should be put in place to *create* a culture around such a framework, as seen in Stage 3 of the PS-CU model.

## Stage 3: Integrated Execution

PePPR Stage 3 is noteworthy for its extreme improvement in corporate visibility by gathering metrics that accurately grade the health of the project portfolio and that accurately map all corporate risks to the risk profile (Figure 2.9, feed 1). While Stage 2 companies focus primarily on process metrics to feed their performance management systems, Stage 3 companies also allow for risk metrics (R-DE level 4, R-TB levels 2 and 3, and R-MC level 4) and project portfolio metrics (PO-MH levels 3 and 4 and PO-CB level 5) to feed these systems (feeds 5 and 6). R-DE refers to this integration as "performance-linked metrics." Specifically, R-TB writes that reporting on risk metrics should take place through such normal reporting channels as performance reporting, and PO-MH writes that reporting on project portfolio metrics should be integrated with other portfolios, such as process, risk, and product portfolios. According to PO-CB, such integration of project portfolio metrics doesn't occur except in the most mature companies (i.e., at this model's Stage 5). In general, such extreme integration of the PePPR components for improving the visibility of the company starts in CMM Stage 3 and continues through to Stage 5. Ultimately, PE-IN refers to this heightened level of visibility in its Stage 5 as a "Performance

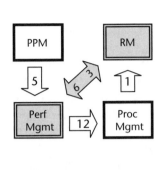

| | 5-Portfolio statusing |
| Metrics | metrics |
| Metrics | 6-Consolidated risk metrics |
| Processes | 12-Engrained performance improvement processes |
| Risks | 1-Identify and report on process risks |
| Risks | 3-Metrics scrutinized/audited |
| Risks | *Functional risk cultures* |
| Processes | *PPM control and support processes started* |
| Risks | *Consolidated project risks* |

**Figure 2.9**  Stage 3 of integrated PePPR maturity.

Culture." Besides just providing a more robust set of data to the performance management system, Stage 3 companies also develop standard means (or processes) for improving not only the metric results (feed 12) but also the metrics themselves (feed 3). That is, the metrics are also continuously reviewed and audited to ensure alignment with the ever-changing direction of the company. PE-DE accomplishes such an auditing function (feed 3) by requiring companies to show a clear linkage between performance measures and "organizational success (i.e., operating measures support financial results)" [19].

*Risks and Processes (Nonintegrated)*     Besides accomplishing these integrated PePPR activities, companies at this level of maturity also develop (1) risk cultures specific to the different functions, (2) processes to support and control the project portfolio, and (3) methods for consolidating project risks. Before a single, standard way of managing risks can be implemented across the organization, companies at lower levels of maturity usually first see such development among different functions, such as manufacturing and finance (R-MC believes such siloed cultures occur at a lower level, its Stage 2). At Stage 3, the project portfolio office begins to evolve around a framework of supporting projects for success, as well as controlling projects through statusing software, as seen in Stage 3 of PS-CU's process maturity model. Finally, while Stage 3 companies are primarily focused on passing process-level risks up to the performance dashboards, they are also beginning to consolidate their project risks in the project portfolio so that a complete picture of operational risks can be available. PO-CB mentions the need for this activity in Stage 3 of its model, which can, in turn, act as a prerequisite to support PePPR feed 2 in Stage 4 companies of our execution maturity model.

## Stage 4: Culturalized Execution

This is the stage where integrated PePPR cultures start to crystallize with strong focus on PePPR process standardization. The Treasury Board of Canada's Secretariat refers to a company that "practices integrated risk management" as one where such risk processes are integral to the core processes of a company at Stages 2 and 3 of its model (Figure 2.10, feed 10). R-DE waits until what is believed to be a more realistic maturity, Stage 5, where [28]: "risk management is everyone's job." With the project portfolio, PO-MA's model continues to support an "integration" of portfolios at Stage 4, and PO-CB's model refers to project portfolio processes as organizationwide by its Stage 3 (feed 11). With the integrated PePPR model, we will opt for complete cultural buy-in of risk and project portfolio management at Stage 4, or the highest maturity level. PE-AM's performance model has companies "adjusting their model to shifts in a dynamic market," [20] and PE-IN's performance model has companies engaged in continuous improvement at Stage 5 (feed 9). That is, metrics should constantly be reviewed for alignment to the shifting strategy and market. Investments in projects that help with such improvements of the performance management system tend to be found in companies that are at a Stage 4 maturity in the integrated PePPR model. R-TB's model states that at Stage 3 a company should be feeding project portfolio risks to the risk portfolio (feed 2). This is substantiated by R-DE's Stage 5, where risk has become part of the company's "decision-making" process (e.g., as in determining which projects to keep or to cancel).

## PePPR and Corporate Maturity

Table 2.6 shows where the stages of the nine CMMs are applied in the PePPR execution maturity model. PS-RO and PO-PM are the only two CMMs that made little or no mention of integration with other PePPR components. Nonetheless, this table clearly shows how many maturity models require companies to integrate PePPR components before movement can be made up their respective maturity ladders. Some of these models are spread out widely in the PePPR model (e.g., PE-AM), some are compressed (e.g., PE-IN), some are spread evenly (e.g., R-DE), and some are spread inconsistently (e.g., PO-CB). The main reason for this slight inconsistency is due to how the PePPR execution maturity model was designed. Besides trying to

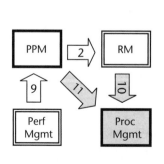

| | | |
|---|---|---|
| Processes | | 10-Engrained risk mitigation processes |
| Processes | | 11-Engrained PPM processes |
| Projects | | 9-Metric improvement projects |
| Risks | | 2-Project risks fed to risk portfolio |

**Figure 2.10**   Stage 4 of integrated PePPR maturity.

**Table 2.6**   Capability Maturity Model Stages Distributed Throughout the PePPR Maturity Model

|          | Ad hoc | Integration | | |
|----------|--------|------------|-----------|-------------|
|          |        | Controlled | Integrated | Culturalized |
| PE-AM    | 1      |            |           | 3           |
| PO-CB    | 1      | 2          | 3, 5      | 3           |
| PS-CU    | 1      | 2          | 3         |             |
| R-DE     | 1      | 2          | 4         | 5           |
| R-MC     | 1      |            | 2, 4      |             |
| PE-IN    |        | 2          | 5         | 5           |
| PO-MH    |        | 3          | 3, 4      | 4           |
| PS-ST    |        | 2, 3       |           |             |
| R-TB     |        | 2          | 2, 3      | 2, 3        |
| PE-DE    |        |            | 4, 5      |             |
| PS-RO    |        |            |           |             |
| PO-PM    |        |            |           |             |

align the PePPR model as closely to these CMMs as possible, two other considerations were used: (1) alignment with first-hand corporate experiences, and (2) mutual consideration for the needs of each component's maturity. As we drill deeper into the different PePPR components in later chapters, we will evolve our understanding of how the integrated PePPR model is implemented in organizations at different maturity levels (see Figure 2.5).

## Accountability

Where in the organization do these strategic PePPR processes reside? Are certain members of the company more involved with risk or process management than others? Figure 2.11 illustrates where each PePPR process tends to mature. The chart also aligns the PePPR processes with corporate operations and with two levels of strategic development. We can see that while the board can get involved with the long-term strategy (usually by guiding and approving only), it is very interested in enterprisewide operational risk and performance measurement. Since risk mitigation and strategic performance improvement are how the board guides and grades executives, the executive staff is also involved with these two activities to improve visibility. This, in turn, helps executives better influence capital project approvals, project portfolio status reviews, enterprisewide process improvement frameworks, and large-scale process change efforts. The greatest overlap of all four PePPR activities occurs at the middle management level. Not only does this level of the organization contribute to the long-term strategy, but it also creates its own functional strategies and guides the operations of the company. Middle managers ensure accurate reporting on the status of the project portfolio, the performance of the entire company, and the identification of risks. If process improvement standards are required, middle management makes sure they are implemented completely. Finally, we show the line staff as the primary workhorses behind implementing such enterprise process improvement frameworks as Six Sigma, Kaizen, and the Information Technology Infrastructure Library (ITIL). To a lesser degree, they are involved with the reporting of risks, performance, and project health. According to our

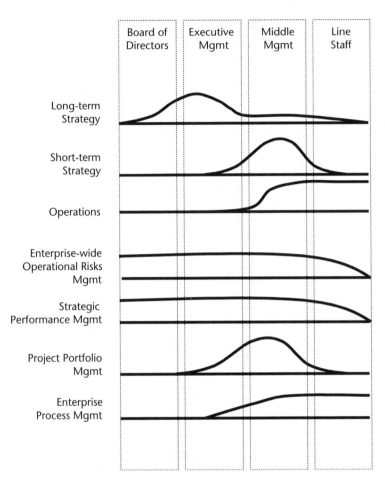

**Figure 2.11**   Strategy and PePPR responsibilities.

model, a healthy company will have developed a culture in which line staff identifies and broadcasts risks and performance improvement ideas without fear of reprisal, where middle management is empowered to develop strategies and mold the project and process portfolio, and where executives monitor and actively guide process improvement and project portfolio processes. Accountability for execution is spread throughout the organization with integrated guidance provided by what we will describe next as the virtual strategic management office (VSMO).

## The Virtual Strategic Management Office

External environments with globalization, regulations, and innovations are becoming more dynamic, and internal environments with communications technology, personnel lawsuits, and cultural mergers are becoming more complex. So, given such turbulent and complex environments, what kind of structure would best implement PePPR management throughout the enterprise? Should it be a single matrixed office, or should it be an executive order adopted by the current hierarchical structure? Lee G. Bolman and Terrence E. Deal, authors of *Reframing Organizations:*

*Artistry, Choice and Leadership*, feel that "if an environment is stable, tasks are well understood and predictable, and uniformity is at a premium," then a vertical, or hierarchical, structure is preferred [29]. But in a turbulent environment, lateral communications work best. That is, Bolman and Deal feel that cross-functional, or matrixed, structures best provide the communications necessary to handle rapid change. If a business unit was unaware that a product may become obsolete, it would want its marketing department to notify it; if a regulation was about to get passed, the various business units would want to be in the legal loop; and if a competitor was able to drastically improve its performance through some innovative approach to processes, then your business units would like to know if a sister business unit has figured it out. These are all examples of why companies would want to break down communication walls and avoid the horse blinders of siloed business units.

Marius Leibold, Gilbert Probst, and Michael Gibbert, in their article "Frameworks for Systemic Strategic Management," claim that systemic strategic management requires "a radical shift in [the] strategic management mindset." Rather than discarding current organizational models, Leibold, Probst, and Gibbert suggest creating a "shadow organization" to initiate, experiment with, and develop business models *alongside* traditional business models [30]. According to a survey by Alexander Kandybin and Martin Kihn, authors of "Raising Your Return on Innovation Investment," the most efficient companies "were lean, with strong cross-functional teams" [31]. Such organizations are what Robert Grant refers to as "parallel structures" [32]. These structures can exist as cross-functional tiger teams that break the isolation of marketing and R&D during product development, as cascading project portfolio management offices in projectcentric organizations, or as communities of practice that help develop "organizational capabilities, promote innovation and instill flexibility" [33]. Such parallel structures can be managed by what Robert S. Kaplan and David P. Norton, authors of *The Strategy Focused Organization*, refer to as the "shared services group" [34], or what we will refer to as the strategic management office (SMO). An SMO would provide support to business units in strategy development, risk management, project portfolio management, strategic process management, and performance management.

Often, a corporate office for strategy will focus on strategy development and strategic alignment. The IT organization, on the other hand, will then run PePPR management systems that can feed the strategy office with the information it needs to ensure alignment. As the flow of strategic information increases into such an office, so does the need for data analysis, as well as the size of the office. An alternative to this ballooning bureaucracy would be a virtual strategy office that spreads the ownership of PePPR management throughout the organization. As a cost center, a strategy office tends to be a clear target during budget cutbacks. So, if this office creates value-add by acting as a critical center for communications, corporate control, and organizational support, while also maintaining a small footprint, then the risk of cuts can decrease. The key is that executives will see a virtual SMO as an office that provides a great deal of visibility into the organization; thus, they will perceive such a large task as being accomplished by a large office. In reality, the virtual SMO will be a small organization that leverages the strengths of reporting processes that are already in place. The resulting perception of divisions and departments will more closely mirror the reality that the SMO is a small but effective organization.

Would a company delegate responsibility for risk and performance management to an SMO even if risks were already handled by the functional divisions? Would an SMO manage the process portfolio even if the departments and divisions were best positioned to recommend improvement initiatives? With a VSMO, the answer would be no on both counts. A small, central SMO office can however support the normalization of risk and process measuring across the company, the consistent reporting of risks and metrics up through the company, and the balanced inclusion of performance, process, project portfolio, and risk during strategic review of the company. Departments or divisions know their processes and should be responsible for improving those processes to reduce costs and improve output quality. A corporate process management office, on the other hand, should be responsible for educating and auditing departments on the application of an enterprisewide process improvement framework such as Six Sigma, Lean, Kaizen, Critical Chain, or ISO9000. This same division of labor can also be used when implementing performance and risk management. The functional organization will be held accountable for the implementation of such risk management frameworks as Turnbull or COSO, and such performance measurement frameworks as Balanced Scorecard, Performance Prism, or the European Network for Advanced Performance Studies (ENAPS) model, while the central office ensures such common frameworks (industry standard or custom) are executed throughout the organization.

Kaplan and Norton wrote a paper in 2005 entitled "Creating the Office of Strategy Management" (OSM). In this OSM, they propose consolidating "nine key strategy management processes," which include scorecard (performance) management, best practices sharing (e.g., process quality programs), initiative management (i.e., project portfolio management), and ongoing strategy reviews (which can include risk management). Organizations they sighted as having successfully implemented their OSM model include Chrysler, Grupo Nacional Provincial, the U.S. Army, and the Canadian Blood Service. In these implementations, a goal was to avoid creating another bureaucratic, matrixed organization. Instead, "most organizations have 10 or fewer people working in their OSM" [34]. We will build on this concept of a VSMO (eventually to be named the Integrated PePPR Management Office, or IPMO) that both controls and supports the goals of the company through PePPR management in the final chapter.

## Summary

It is fairly well known that achieving the highest level in most maturity models ends up requiring more resources than it's worth. Also, even focusing too heavily on one model can cause a company to barrel down an improvement path at the expense of other areas. There are so many dynamics in a company that different models should be chosen for different conditions, business units, or activity management types. Before adopting models, however, we presented another area of model-adoption scrutiny: the maturity of the organization as a whole. We found that if your company is in the frantic stages of a start-up or the desperate stages of a turnaround, performance, process, project portfolio, and risk management can justifiably take a second seat to cash flow. But when a company is achieving sustainable financing, it can then focus on those tasks that give it sustainable competitive advantage. The STaRS model, F&R's model, and the Business Maturity Model all provided next steps for companies in any of these stages of maturity. From here, we were able to draw on the knowledge provided by nine strategic activity maturity models to develop our own consolidated execution maturity model that fit to the varying levels of organizationwide maturity. A key theme to this model was, as the Deloitte/Utrecht study found, that companies that integrate their evolution of the four PePPR silos improve better than those that focus just on siloed maturity in performance, process, project portfolio, or risk management. This integration occurs most strongly with the group of individuals who are the most difficult to convince of the values of integrated PePPR management: middle managers. But if ownership for integrated PePPR is delegated to different support groups in the company (e.g., human resources, IT, finance) and supported by a central virtual strategic management office, middle managers will perceive less "turf" loss. Such a VSMO, to be referred to in Chapter 8 as an integrated PePPR management office, can be a part of a core strategy office, or it can report directly to the executive staff. Either way, it can act as the facilitator and driver for the integration and evolution of enterprise-level PePPR management.

## References

[1]    Watkins, Michael, *The First 90 Days*, Cambridge, MA: Harvard Business School Press, 2003.

[2]    Squires, Susan E., et al., *Inside Arthur Andersen: Shifting Values, Unexpected Consequences*, Upper Saddle River, NJ, FT Press, 2003.

[3]    "Top 100 Corporate Criminals of the Decade," *Corporate Crime Reporter,* Vol. 21, No. 1, May 24, 1999, www.corporatecrimereporter.com/top100.html#Annotated (last accessed on April 3, 2007).

[4]    "Top 100 Corporate Criminals of the Decade," *Corporate Crime Reporter,* Vol. 9, No. 3, March 4, 1996, http://www.corporatecrimereporter.com/top100.htm (last accessed on April 3, 2007).

[5]    Agovino, Theresa, "US: Merck Steps Up Public Relations Campaign after Recall," Spinwatch.org, November 24, 2004, www.spinwatch.org/content/view/531/9 (last accessed on April 3, 2007).

[6]    Nwazota, Kristina, "Jayson Blair: A Case Study of What Went Wrong at the *New York Times,*" Online NewsHour, December 10, 2004, www.pbs.org/newshour/media/media_ethics/casestudy_blair.php (last accessed on April 3, 2007).

[7]    Greyser, Stephen A., "Johnson & Johnson: The Tylenol Tragedy," Harvard Business School Case 583043, October 12, 1982.

[8]    Landon, Thomas, Jr., "The Winding Road to Grasso's Huge Payday," *New York Times*, June 26, 2006, www.iht.com/articles/2006/06/26/business/web.0626grasso.php (last accessed on April 3, 2007).

[9]    Allen, Linda, "Losing Your Tail on the Repo Market: The Story of Robert Citron," *Arbitrageur,* 1998, www.allbusiness.com/arbitrageur/19980322/3025220-1.html (last accessed on April 3, 2007).

[10]  Strom, Shelly, "Crisis Management: Some Companies Seek Help; Others Deal Internally," *Portland Business Journal*, July 5, 2002, www.bizjournals.com/portland/stories/2002/07/08/focus2.html (last accessed on April 3, 2007).

[11]  Flamholtz, E. G., and Yvonne Randall, "Growing Pains Transitioning from an Entrepreneurship to a Professionally Managed Firm," San Francisco, CA: Jossey-Bass, 2000.

[12]  Crane, Mary, "Are You Ready to Go Public?" Forbes.com, November 13, 2006.

[13]  Rifkin, Glen, "Growth by Acquisition: The Case of Cisco Systems," Strategy + Business, Second Quarter 1997, www.strategy-business.com/press/16635507/15617 (last accessed on January 19, 2007).

[14]  Scheper, W. J., W. V. Bertoen, and C. G. Rexwinkel, "Mastering Complexity Using the Business Maturity Model," Deloitte, May 1, 2005, www.deloitte.com/dtt/research/0,1015,cid%253D83748,00.html (last accessed on January 19, 2007).

[15]  Spanyi, Andrew, "Beyond Process Maturity to Process Competence," BPTrends, June 2004, www.bptrends.com.

[16]  Chrissis, Mary Beth, Mike Konrad, and Sandy Shrum, "Introduction to CMMI," Boston, MA: *CMMICRJ Guidelines for Process Integration and Product Improvement*, Addison-Wesley, July 11, 2003.

[17]  Rosemann, Michael, and Tonia de Bruin, "Towards a Business Process Management Maturity Model," 13th European Conference on Information Systems, Regensburg, Germany, May 26, 2005, is2.lse.ac.uk/asp/aspecis/20050045.pdf (last accessed on June 20, 2007).

[18]  "Performance Management Maturity Model," InPhase Software, 2002, som.cranfield.ac.uk/som/research/centres/cbp/pma/PM_Maturity_Journey.ppt (last accessed on June 20, 2007).

[19]  Deloitte Development, LLC, "Integrated Performance Management," Financial Executives International, 2005, www2.fei.org/rf/download/Integrated_Performance_Management.ppt (last accessed on June 20, 2007).

[20]  Durocher, Carline, and John Hagerty, "A Maturity Model for Enterprise Performance Management," AMR Research, April 15, 2007, is2.lse.ac.uk/asp/aspecis/20050045.pdf (last accessed on June 20, 2007).

[21]  Curtis, Bill, John Alden, and Charles V. Weber, "Overview of the Business Process Maturity Model (BPMM)," Object Management Group, September 2006, www.omg.org/docs/bmi/06-09-01.pdf (last accessed on June 20, 2007), pp. 119–133.

[22]  Stemberger, Mojca Indihar, Andrej Kovacic, and Jurij Jaklic, "A Methodology for Increasing Business Process Maturity in Public Sector," *Interdisciplinary Journal of Information, Knowledge, and Management*, Vol. 2, 2007.

[23]  Pennypacker, James S., (ed.), *Project Portfolio Management Maturity Model*, Center for Business Practices, 2005.

[24]  Maizlish, Bryan, and Robert Handler, *IT Portfolio Management, Step-by-Step, Unlocking the Business Value of Technology*, Hoboken, NJ: Wiley, 2005.

[25]  "Organizational Project Management Maturity Model," Project Management Institute, Inc., Newton Square, PA, 2003.

[26]  McConnell, P. "Measuring Operational Risk Management Systems Under Basel II," Continuity Central, April 20, 2005, http://www. continuitycentral.com/feature0197.htm (last accessed on January 5, 2008).

[27]  "Integrated Risk Management Framework," Treasury Board of Canada Secretariat, April 1, 2001, www.tbs-sct.gc.ca/pubs_pol/dcgpubs/RiskManagement/rmf-cgr_e.asp (last accessed on April 15, 2006).

[28]  Layton, Mark, and Rick Funston, "The Risk Intelligent Enterprise," Deloitte Development LLC, 2006.

[29]  Bolman, Lee G., and Terrence E. Deal, *Reframing Organizations: Artistry, Choice, and Leadership*, 3rd ed., New York, NY: Wiley, 2003.

[30] Leibold, Marius, Gilbert Probst, and Michael Gibbert, "Frameworks for Systemic Strategic Management," in *Strategic Management in the Knowledge Economy*, by M. Leibold, G. J. B. Probst, M. Gibbert, (eds.), New York, NY: Wiley, 2002, pp. 180–197.

[31] Kandybin, A., and Kihn, Martin, "Raising Your Return on Innovation Investment."

[32] Grant, Robert M., *Contemporary Strategy Analysis: Concepts, Technologies, Applications,* 4th ed., Malden, MA: Blackwell Publishers, 2002.

[33] Wenger, E. C., and W. M. Snyder, "Communities of Practice: The Organizational Frontier," *Harvard Business Review*, January–February 2000.

[34] Kaplan, Robert S., and David P. Norton, *The Strategy Focused Organization*, Cambridge, MA: Harvard Business School Press, 2001.

[35] Kaplan, Robert S., and David P. Norton, "Creating the Office of Strategy Management," Cambridge, MA: Harvard Business School Press, 2005.

## CHAPTER 3

# Strategy

## A Brief Introduction to Strategy

How is the first day of a new business determined? Is it the day an idea was born, the day of incorporation, the day of discharge from bankruptcy, or the day a new strategy was finalized? Legally, of course, it is when the business is registered with a government agency as a partnership, nonprofit, or corporation. But in the minds of the business's leadership, the first day can very well be the day of birth or rebirth. That birthing process for smaller companies can be idea-to-cocktail-napkin, cocktail-napkin-to-e-mail, then e-mail-to-associates. In other words, in the first stage of a company, "strategic planning will probably be a very informal, even intuitive process" [1]. This method of strategic development and deployment is common among entrepreneurs, where its major strength is its speed of application. On the other hand, if a new venture has more than one sponsor, team scrutiny can slow the birth of a company. For example, what market and industry research was conducted that led to the cocktail napkin? What can cause the proposed approach to fail? How will we know we are successful? How do we achieve that success? If we plan on maintaining the success, how will we do so? As the business plan becomes more elaborate, founders may refer to the birth of the company in terms of its first weeks or months rather than its first day.

Things get complicated when there is more than one person with ownership of, or responsibility for, a new venture (either a company or a unit of an existing company). If one person is allowed to control all decisions, every other stakeholder could be left out in the cold if the venture fails. As a result, those who have a stake in a venture tend to require that some controls be wrapped around those decisions that can directly lead to either success or failure. How are risks being mitigated to prevent failure, and how is performance being tracked to ensure long-term success? These are the two core, controlling objectives of owners who govern the health of a company. Depending on the market winds, the risk aversion of different owners, or the company's industry (as mentioned in Chapter 1), may be focused more on risk management than on performance management. For example, when Sarbanes-Oxley (SarbOx) deadlines are nearing, corporate leaders tend to frantically zero in on risk management at the expense of performance dashboards. Once the dust settles and SarbOx compliance processes are second nature, a more balanced governance is reestablished through performance management. While there may be other strategic swings, such as productivity versus growth, such swinging usually occurs around some high-level strategy that includes a vision and a set of goals.

## What Is Strategy?

In *On War*, Carl von Clausewitz claims that strategy defines the location where, the moment when, and the force with which a battle will be fought [2]. Other famous strategists, such as Sun Tzu, Napoleon Bonaparte, and George Patton have provided their input on the definition of strategy, but in sum, it comes down to being the plan on paper that guides the participants in a competition. In the corporate world, Eric G. Flamholtz and Yvonne Randle explain in their book *Growing Pains* that "strategy consists of where (in what markets) a firm chooses to compete and how it will compete in its chosen markets in order to achieve the best results" [1]. The union of the military view and this corporate view gives us the "where, when, and how" actions that will be taken to ensure achievement of strategic goals. Therefore, strategy is defined by a set of goals and instructions on their execution. Robert Grant agrees with this but then adds analysis activities as necessary steps to successfully realizing a strategy. He refers to his approach as the four basic factors of strategic success (shown as bold boxes in Figure 3.1).

1. *External analysis:* Have a profound understanding of the competitive environment.
2. *Internal analysis:* Achieve an objective appraisal of the company's resources.

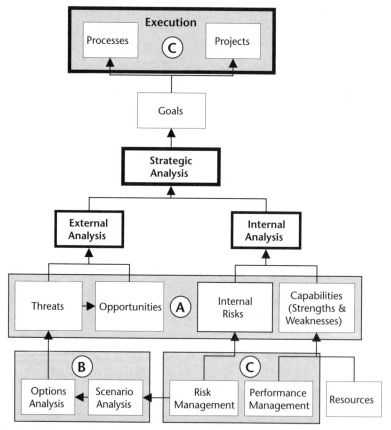

**Figure 3.1** (a) PePPR management integrated with (b) classic and (c) modern analysis techniques.

3. *Goals:* Establish goals that are simple, consistent, and long term.
4. *Execution:* Ensure effective implementation.

Combining these four factors then leads us to the core task of business strategy: "to determine how the firm will deploy its resources within its environment and so satisfy its long-term goals, and how to organize itself to implement that strategy" [3].

As we will see, modern strategic analysis relies heavily on two extensions of external risk management called scenario analysis and options analysis. These processes assess threats to the current direction and opportunities of the company using a concept known as game theory. Risk management, along with performance management, also finds application in the internal analysis processes of a strategic review. Figure 3.1 shows how these two PePPR components support the need for increased visibility during strategic reviews. This figure also shows how the output of strategic analysis (i.e., goals) then sets the stage for execution of the strategy. As has been shown, execution is made up of a series of both processes and projects. Overall, the figure illustrates how old-school techniques [Figure 3.1(a)] and contemporary techniques [Figure 3.1(b)] integrate with activity management components [Figure 3.1(c)].

## From Goals to Action

How resources are deployed can be documented as the action plans of the strategy. Should heavy equipment be used to build a bridge, or should it be used to build a skyscraper? Should the staff be used to implement Six Sigma and improve processes, or should it be used to implement a new project and contribute to growth? Should cash be used to acquire a new company, or should it be distributed as dividends? The question then becomes, should such action plans be part of the strategy or part of the operational plans (i.e., tactics). Grant attempts to help with this by separating goals, which should be a part of the corporate strategy, from the action plans by asking two questions: what business or businesses should we be in, and within each business, how should we compete [3]? The answer to the first question describes the corporate strategy of the company (goals); the answer to the second describes the primary themes of business strategy (strategic action plans). An example of an answer to the first question would be, we are a bridge-building, process-improvement-focused company that plans to grow through acquisitions. The when, where, and how answers to such questions lead to the business strategies. Going even deeper, what separates business strategies and their actions plans from operational plans? The main difference between the how-to action plans in the business strategy and those in operational plans can be embodied in one world: control [4]. While strategic action plans are high level, they also act as categories (or buckets) for lower-level actions (or tactics) that (1) are documented in operational plans and (2) involve contact with resources, customers, suppliers, or various environments.

Such separation of goals, strategic actions, and tactics can be considered one step toward delegating responsibility for strategic development to business units. It can also be a way to more clearly separate strategic actions from tactical actions. For example, improving customer service survey results by 2%, reducing inventory levels by 25%, decreasing employee turnover rates by 10%, and increasing the return on investment (ROI) of all capital-intensive projects by 15% are all examples of goals that could go into a business strategy plan. Table 3.1 shows how strategic actions (also listed in business strategies) and tactics (listed in operational plans) can result from one of these examples. This chart is also a short example of how companies can trace, map, or align operational activity back up to the strategy. Brian Huffman, author of "What Makes a Strategy Brilliant," does a good job of putting this in the context of competition by stating, "Tactics are 'strategy-in-process.' If we have the initiative, our tactics are generally slave to our strategy; if the enemy has the initiative, our tactics are generally slave to his strategy" [5]. Sure, there are times when a company must react to a competitor's moves, but generally you want them to react to your tactical moves that are aligned with your corporate strategy through goals and action plans. Unfortunately, a company can still be aligned, even if the strategy becomes a slave to its tactics; we'll call this reverse alignment.

This book focuses on strategic action items (or business strategies) and the feedback loops that can be linked to tactical actions. As processes are applied, projects are realized, performance is monitored, and risks are identified and mitigated, these feedback loops can mold the business strategies. This is where care must be taken to avoid reverse alignment. While the flexibility that results from constant reassessment of business strategies is important in today's fast-paced market, it should be balanced with a corporate strategy that provides a dependable compass heading when in stormy seas.

As a company grows, the mappings shown in Table 3.1 become more and more detailed. As the complexity mounts, entrepreneurs or intrapreneurs (as Flamholtz and Randle (F&R) refer to new-venture sponsors in existing companies) begin to realize the need to organize or plan. So, how much time should be dedicated to strategy for your specific company? How much effort should be put into risk and performance analysis to support strategic planning efforts? It all depends on where you sit in a given maturity model. The previous chapter introduced corporate and PePPR maturity; here we will show how strategic planning fits into the mix.

**Table 3.1**   Strategies versus Operations Using a Goals, Actions, Tactics Example

| Corporate Strategy (Strategic Goals) | Business Strategy (Strategic Actions) | Operational Plan (Operational Tactics) |
| --- | --- | --- |
| Improve customer survey results | Liberalize return policy | Outsource returned inventory |
| | | Retrain return-desk clerks |
| | | Market new policy heavily |
| | Increase communication | Follow up on calls |
| | | Sponsor neighborhood charity events |
| | | Have management staff call centers |
| | Improve customer contact tracking | Implement a customer relationship management system |
| | | Create simple, automated interfaces |
| | | Segment follow-up communications |

## Strategic Planning

At the highest level, a business is defined by its inputs, outputs, and internal components. For any particular company, these internal components are first framed by some chosen business model and then evolve though some chosen strategic model. Figure 3.2 shows the basic inputs of a business as financing and supplies and the basic output as products, services, or both. Elements that define the business include its structure and staffing model, its internal and external environment, and the way it conducts itself (i.e., its processes). This sample will find itself documented in business models that include such details as its marketing approach, its exit plan, and its competitive analysis. In the early stages of a business, the vision and mission of the company can derive from the strategic portions of the business plan. But as the company grows and industries evolve, strategic plans take over. Like the initial business plan, strategic plans are how a company views the future and how it will get there, given its capabilities.

A strategic plan should address what Kenichi Ohmae refers to as the three Cs: the company, its customers, and its competition [6]. When planning strategically, executives will try to mold each of these three Cs to better advance the health and prospects of the firm. Unfortunately, as change is applied to one, the other two Cs will react, many times unpredictably (Figure 3.3). So, regardless of how much effort is applied to improving customer satisfaction or training up the staff, if competition reacts more than any of these first two Cs, then customer interest can shift, and staff training can become obsolete on a dime. How change in any one of these three Cs affects a company isn't as much a function of effort applied as it is of reaction realized; increasing the customer base can be like banging on a brick wall, while surpassing the competition can be a cake walk. Not only can it be difficult to know which is an easier hurdle (so that resources can be *allocated* appropriately), but it can be difficult to know how two Cs will react to major change in any one (so resources can be *reallocated* appropriately). The ability to react quickly provides a competitive advantage that comes from the combined attributes of 20/20 vision and speed of execution, the two attributes that are strengthened with integrated PePPR management. Rather than constrict the natural oscillation of the triad, PePPR management allows for dependable flow of motion.

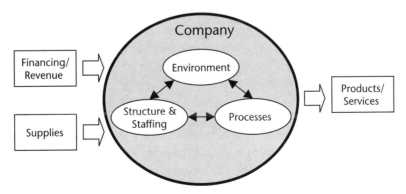

**Figure 3.2**   Core components of business models.

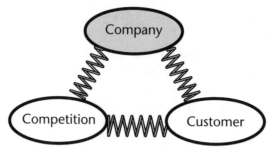

**Figure 3.3**   Spring loading Ohmae's three Cs.

### Planning Maturity

Each of the maturity models in Chapter 2 touched on the concept that a company's strategic planning process becomes more structured as it matures. Evidence of such structure with planning in a younger company would include the creation of meeting schedules, agendas, goals, attendee lists, documentation tasks, schedules, and deadlines. But beyond these basic administrative tasks, how formal, exclusive, and frequent should the planning process become? Sure, the addition of formal processes can be critical in a chaotic environment, but must the processes be relegated only to executives who exclude staff members? What about planning frequency? Does a company that is trying to shape an industry require more planning sessions than a company that is preparing to adapt to unforeseen market forces?

As economies have changed recently, so have the approaches to planning. Where once it was acceptable for executives to lock themselves in a room and develop a grand plan, now it is becoming understood that this may not be the best approach. More dynamic marketplaces are leading to more dynamic planning processes and more adaptable (or flexible) strategic plans.

The need for integrated, rather than siloed, PePPR management processes is growing stronger. In a world of rapid change, clarity and resilience become crucial. If these mechanisms don't support an efficient planning process, then the resulting dust cloud will lead a company on a blind, hacking journey. Risk managers, project portfolio directors, performance systems sponsors, and process improvement tiger teams can't be battling each other for resources or strategic vision. Mutual understanding and support for their contributions to dynamic execution should be crystal clear; they need to operate as a single entity. In this section, we will start off with a review of some newer contributions to strategy theory and how it might impact planning. We will then go through other planning approaches until we culminate with our conclusion that actionable stratgies require openness and cooperation in the planning process.

### Shape versus Adapt

Whenever a large ship enters a port, events can get fairly chaotic on the bridge: depths change and buoys approach quickly, fog forces the crew to go to radar, sailboats cross the bow, other ships try to communicate with you, and line handlers and anchor details need to maintain their timing. A company steaming through a newly chaotic marketplace experiences the same kind of information overload. A ship's crew reacts to such a scenario by slowing down, staying alert, and taking more frequent navigational fixes. A truly proactive navigator will lay alternative courses in case problems occur as the ship enters a tight spot. Such an approach allows the captain of a ship more time and options to alter course and avoid disaster. At the same time, a balance must be monitored to prevent the ship from going too slowly, or it could end up in an uncontrolled drift. While both a ship and a company can run aground from their current momentum, a ship has the rigidity to respond to commands. A company can only respond uniformly to directional changes with similar rigidity if its culture is *aligned* with a strategy of *flexibility*.

Like a ship entering port, the more complex the business plan and the more tumultuous the environment, the more there is a need for strategic options that ready a company for unforeseen risks. Any company that is in such a scenario should be constantly measuring its performance and risk levels so that it can prepare and then react before disaster occurs. With frequent analysis, planned alternatives, and a staff that can easily adapt to change, a company will be well positioned for the current marketplace dynamics. But does a dynamic marketplace, full of uncertainties, mean that a highly adaptive strategy with multiple goals and directions needs to be maintained? Or should a company throw flexibility to the wind and focus on a single goal with the hope of shaping a particular industry? Contemporary strategists are taking lessons learned from the information technology (IT) wave of the 1990s and coming up with some new ideas on planning. Such recent publications as Phil Rosenzweig's the *Halo Effect* [7], Michael E. Raynor's *The Strategy Paradox* [8], and Marius Leibold, Gilbert Probst, and Michael Gibbert's *Strategic Management in the Knowledge Economy* [9] refer to a shape-versus-adapt trade-off.

Choose a direction and put all of the company's resources into achieving a goal, or hedge the company's bets by supporting multiple goals. Does the company want to survive unpredictable turmoil, or does it want to shape an industry and become its leader? One would think that a company that is the leader of a fairly stable industry should stick to its guns and continue to march ahead. But look at what is happening to record industry giants now that music has been digitized online [10] or to film and camera companies now that photography has been digitized [11]. Hugh Courtney, author of "Making the Most of Uncertainty," believes that the best scenario to develop an adaptive strategy is one where a company perceives stability or where it feels uncertainty is low [12]. In contrast, Courtney also believes that the best time to settle on one shaping strategy is when there is a lot of turmoil in an industry. Examples of success in this area include Yellow Tail in the wine industry, Google in the online search industry, and Apple in the digital-music industry. In the recording and film industries (those that should have adapted), there was a perceived level of certainty. With the wine, search, and digital music industries (the shapers), the industries were full of uncertainties, new, or both. Therefore, according to Courtney, when deciding to be an industry adapter or shaper, the level of uncertainty with the market should be a prime consideration. In short, a company should adapt to industry changes "when key sources of value creation are relatively stable or outside the company's control" [12]. A company should shape an industry when the key sources of value creation in an industry are unstable yet within the company's control (e.g., price versus quality and application of technology).

Nonetheless, shaping strategies tend to be the norm. For example, as uncertainty increases, adaptive strategies can be less preferable because a company will never know if it has covered all options. In fact, a great number of companies can only afford the time, money, and resources to focus on one goal rather than many, regardless of the uncertainty in their marketplaces. Unfortunately, according to a study of several thousand companies by Michael Raynor, "organizations pursuing the most commitment-intensive strategies generate the highest returns, but they also suffer the highest mortality rates" [8]. If your company were fortunate enough to reach a state of sustained success, then according to a McKinsey study of companies between 1985 and 1995, you would join 86% of the other successful companies that chose a "shaper" strategy. This leads us to an empty conclusion: shaping strategies are (1) good for those who succeed, (2) bad for those who don't, and (3) most common among all.

So, if a company wants to both shape an industry and be adaptive to blindsides, what basic activities should it focus on? How can integrated PePPR management help? According to Courtney, "Successful adapters tend to focus on continuous experimentation" or innovation [12]. Examples would include any company with a well-funded R&D department staffed by creative, passionate, and diligent workers. A fully adaptive strategy should be chosen as a means to finding successful shaping strategies, not as a fallback plan when an industry shaper is deemed too formidable (e.g., Yellow Tail, Google, or Apple). Such an overly adaptive approach could lead to passivity. In fact, implementing a highly flexible strategy, particularly in an uncertain environment, is "hardly passive and hardly easy for many companies"; it requires "real up-front commitments—financial and human"[12]. With PePPR management, the commitments will be primarily human. Establishing cultures of bottom-up risk and performance management support and top-down process and project portfolio control will help keep the corporate, business, and operational links tight—tight enough to support long-term commitments to a shaping strategy while also supporting short-term flexibility.

Peter M. Senge and Goran Carstedt provide a way to look at a corporate strategy through three dimensions: its context, its content, and its process. Traditionally, a strategy is viewed through the context lenses of internal or external analysis. But this section has just presented strategy in the context of dynamic execution. How can strategies be implemented in extremely dynamic conditions? Should the company be adaptive, or should it "stick to its guns" through thick and thin? The next few sections expand on this context by looking at strategy content and processes.

## Basic Planning

More times than not, a company founder will have a vision, a set of goals, and a plan to achieve his or her vision and goals. Then, as the company grows, it runs into the inevitable speed bumps (e.g., litigation, international taxes, employee benefits) and unwanted boundary conditions (e.g., regulations, natural disasters, employee churn). These basic elements of business act as lessons learned that ultimately cause executives to rethink how they manage their businesses, both strategically and operationally. When entrepreneurs progress from Stage 1 to Stage 2 companies, they may feel that they can no longer rely on intuitive or implicit strategic planning. Ultimately, the founder may realize (e.g., when the company reaches Stage 2) that one way to better run their operations would be by first running repeatable planning sessions that result in executable strategies. We will first show a simple planning approach, then a more detailed approach, and conclude with a planning model that supports speedy results for large companies.

Strategic planning sessions tend to involve the combined efforts of the leaders of the business. Executives start with an open-ended dreamscape of where they see their company several years in the future: the vision. They continue squeezing their creative juices until they come up with one or two approaches to achieve their vision, the output of which is documented as the strategic mission. Somewhere in this process, taglines, mottos, values, and goals may also result as the first components of a complete strategy. In support of this process, executives also apply the constraints of their chosen industry, the capabilities of their organization, and the laws of the land. While the initial components of the strategy look more into the future (vision, mission, goals), the latter components look at the past (e.g., resource experiences and industry research), present (e.g., resource capabilities and regulations), and future [3]. Once the higher-level strategic foundation is laid, a more thorough strategic analysis can be done. Such an analysis will review past mistakes made by other companies, the current industry environment, and the alignment of the company's objectives to its corporate vision. Ultimately, after all this research, a strategy can be documented and communicated to the rest of the organization.

Figure 3.4 shows a basic strategic planning process where a mission leads to a set of goals, strategies, and action plans. A more mature process would also include monitoring capabilities to ensure accountability for execution and feedback loops to help improve upon not only the goals' strategies and action plans but, in the rare case, the mission. Until recently, such planning processes and their associated feedback loops were seen primarily as a set of goals that supported a common, long-term direction. However, now the strategy is seen as a set of goals that can support a range of directions, both long term and short term; that is, "plans have now come to be seen not as descriptions of future performance, but as a basis for initiating flexible and speedy responses to a changing present" [9].

## Extended Planning

As the company grows and complexity expands, executives will find that more controls and more structured processes can be used to develop sound, flexible strategies. Figure 3.5 shows how more analysis would be added, risk reviews would be integrated, and budget and operating plans would be linked [13]. The figure shows that not only are risk management and performance management fed by operational activities such as processes and projects, but these two activity management components also support the development of the strategic plan through various forms of analyses.

*Extended Analysis*    Rather than glancing cursorily at the industry you are entering, the regulations that exist, the capabilities of your team, and the robustness of your other resources (e.g., cash, IT, equipment, facilities, or reputation), extended analysis would go into more detail in each of these areas. Luckily, many methods

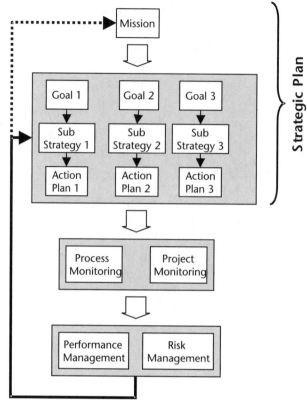

**Figure 3.4**   Basic strategic planning model.

and models developed by industry and academic experts will help with this. The next section presents some classic examples just to get you started. Not only would more formal models be used for more complex corporate scenarios, but they would be used iteratively during the planning process. As will be seen, they can be used first to help map the mission, vision, and goals to the changing demands of the market. Then, the models can be used to help map execution plans to the strategic goals.

*Risk Management and Strategy*   With basic strategic planning, the components of the resulting strategy (e.g., mission, values, goals, execution plans) are more influenced by reactions to issues as they occur. A looming regulatory deadline may cause human resources to be reallocated, production-line equipment breakdown may lead to unrelated project cancellations, and international conflict may force rejection of expansion plans. On the other hand, the strategic components of companies with more robust strategic planning approaches will be influenced more by proactive risk management processes. Risks will be mitigated by (1) accommodating regulatory changes far earlier than when they are due, (2) replacing equipment that has reached its recommended lifetime before failure, and (3) understanding potential conflict early so that expansion plans can target other locations. As with strategic planning models, scenario and option methods have

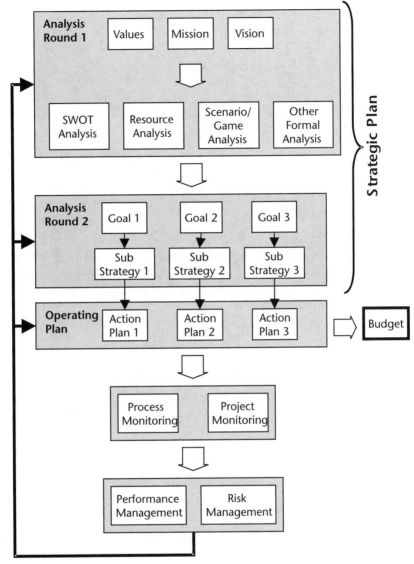

**Figure 3.5**   Control planning approach.

been developed that can help transition a company to such a proactive strategic environment. Chapter 7 will go into more detail on risk management to show not only how to integrate it with the other PePPR components but also how to use it to support strategic planning.

*Linking Operating Plans*     As strategic planning becomes more formal, it has a tendency to also become more hierarchical. Executives see the process as a way to regain control over an organization that has turned into a crazed octopus of initiatives and processes (e.g., Stage 3 and 4 companies). In extreme cases, a strategic management office will direct operational decisions not just through budget approvals but also through operational plans. It has been seen in the faster industries, on the other hand, that such evolving hierarchical control can have restrictive consequences on flexibility, creativity, and responsiveness to the market. As a result, new strategic methods have been introduced that involve, rather than direct, operational units on strategy planning. This "open-book" planning approach is becoming more and more popular as companies are realizing how much operational momentum can influence strategic design. According to Nick Demos, Steven Chung, and Michael Beck, authors of the 2001 article "The New Strategy and Why It Is New," "Operational decisions and transactions can often redefine the company's strategy and thus alter the path forward"[14]. The section in this chapter on open-book planning will go into more detail on how this relates to operational plans.

### Planning for Control

Before looking at how some strategic control can be delegated to the business units, let's first understand just what is required for such control. According to Robert Grant, beyond strategic planning systems, three management systems are critical to gaining control: financial systems, information systems, and performance measurement systems [3].

### Financial Systems

At the center of financial planning and control is the budgetary process. Budgets are split into the capital expenditure budget (or as Robert S. Kaplan and David P. Norton call it, the strategic budget) and the operational budget [15]. The capital expenditure budget develops from the strategy formulation process. That is, the strategy will forecast capital expenditures and set performance guidelines for the resulting projects in a given year. The operating budget, on the other hand, "is a pro-forma profit and loss statement for the company as a whole, and for individual divisions and business units for the upcoming year." Like the capital budget, it is part forecast and part performance target, but unlike the capital budget, it sets performance targets more on processes than on projects. While smaller projects tend to sprout within business units under the umbrella of the operational budget, larger projects are allocated to the capital expenditure budget. It is through this latter budget that executives are better able to control the flow of money to ensure new and ongoing projects are mapped to their strategic desires. Executives are less able to exercise immediate control over the operational budget since it is usually associated with the fixed costs of keeping the business running.

### Information Systems

Along with controlled cash flow, there is the need for accurate information flow. Systems that manage finances, the customers, operating equipment, human resources regulations, and performance metrics are some of the major examples in today's corporations. Unfortunately, if the information management capabilities of a company are fraught with problems, then executives begin to lose control. They end up basing strategic decisions on flawed or untimely data. As Jim Collins, author of *Good to Great*, explains, such systems should be transparent to the operations of the business [16]. None of Collins's "good-to-great" companies began their extended growth periods with revolutionary technology. In fact, "fully 80 percent didn't even mention technology as one of the top five factors in [their] transformation." In great companies, while technology is key to success, it should be subservient to the core values (i.e., strategy + culture) of the company. That is, information systems are critical to adequately controlling complex organizations; they just better run correctly.

### Performance Measurement Systems

With a sound strategic planning process, reliable financial controls, and complete yet transparent IT systems deployed, a performance measurement system can be leveraged. It is with such a system that executives can link custom key performance indicators (KPIs) to the strategy and thus ensure complete organizational alignment. For example, the chief executive officer (CEO) may want to monitor the goal of maximizing shareholder value, the chief financial officer may watch average cost of capital, and divisional managers may look at more specific goals, such as maximizing return on capital employed and project ROIs. Further down the totem pole, we may find department heads monitoring certain operational indicators. Examples could include sales per square foot for retail managers and cost of goods per sales for purchasing managers. The real value from such measures comes not just from improving KPI values over time but from maintaining their link to the strategy. If the strategy changes, executives may end up monitoring the wrong metric; they would be navigating dangerous waters with out-of-date charts. Kaplan and Norton refer to these ever-updating charts of metrics and strategic links as the "strategic architecture" [15].

As entrepreneurial cultures enter a state of high growth, a risk evolves that the company can become overly chaotic with little control over the direction of the business or division. On the other hand, the intent of control structures "is not to control people's behavior in predefined ways but to influence them to make decisions and take actions that are likely to be consistent with the organization's goals" [1]. Companies that have built such control structures to better manage their strategic plans are typically at an F&R Stage 4. After piecemeal control mechanisms were implemented by business units in Stage 3, corporate leaders are now trying to centralize such mechanisms. Besides the administrative tasks mentioned earlier, another mechanism to help control strategic planning is the frequency with which planning occurs. If the company strives to be a shaper, it should be resolute on a plan that requires less second-guessing. Organizations that hope to include adaptive elements in their plans, however, should be prepared to review their strategies more frequently. For example, Kaplan and Norton feel that in rapidly changing industries, strategic reviews should occur every quarter [15]. Nonetheless, from a general perspective, Stage 3 management should be investing "the equivalent of at least one week per year on planning." Then, in Stage 4, planning sessions (with equal frequency) should have become institutionalized and advanced [1].

## Planning for Execution

The first planning session will usually be lengthy due to the fact that no prior planning work can be leveraged, and the planning process hasn't been streamlined for that particular corporate culture. The frequency and duration of subsequent planning sessions will then be based mostly on how uncertain the industry is and how much of an adapter the company wants to be. Sure, executive personalities may cause some exceptions to this, but, in general, industries with high volatility (or change) tend to necessitate a more flexible planning process. That is, planning sessions will be frequent and short. Since larger companies tend to have more moving parts and dimensions to consider, planning sessions can lengthen and occur less frequently. As a result, larger companies can have a tendency to "miss the boat" when market demands shift on a dime. To combat this, large Stage 4 and higher companies will delegate strategy planning to their business or strategic business units so that such lapses in visibility can be avoided.

Figure 3.6 illustrates how the strategic analysis can move to these business units while the monitoring and values/vision/mission stay with the executive office. This will allow executives to be less distracted and more focused on the stronger controlling structures of PePPR management. Nevertheless, Flamholtz and Randle believe that such delegation should occur whenever a company starts strategic planning (typically Stage 2 companies and up). "Unless the plan is 'owned' by line managers, it will tend to get ignored." If the strategy is ignored, unalignment will propagate through projects and processes.

Paul F. Kocourek and Paul Hyde, authors of "The Model 2 Organization, Making Your Company Safe for Zealots," claim that most organizations adopt business models that primarily differ by how much analysis responsibility is owned by functional or business units and how much is owned by the executives [17]. Such a separation of responsibility tends to be more apparent among companies that have business units that can operate fairly independently. Companies differ on how many support units these self-sustaining business units control (e.g., human resources, IT, finance), but they basically share a common theme of controlling their own profit and loss. More independent versions of these are referred to many times as strategic business units (SBUs). If SBUs interact with other businesses, strategic business networks (SBNs) or strategic business systems (SBSs) interact with multiple networks [18]. In SBNs or SBSs, executives can delegate the strategic analysis process to consortium review committees or partner conferences.

If a company doesn't have more than one SBU, it makes sense for the central office to develop the corporate strategy and then support its implementation. If no SBN or SBS exists, then there is no need to include "outsiders." This more self-contained, undelegated approach is more common due primarily to the greater numbers of small and mid-sized companies. But as complexity increases with corporate growth, executives would do a service to budding new SBUs if the corporate house were first in order. This would allow SBUs to leverage the strengths of being a part of a growing concern. Such an approach allows for accountability and tracking mechanisms to be in place before strategic processes are delegated. Well-implemented activity management tracking systems shouldn't allow executives to micromanage the contact points of business (e.g., customers, suppliers, employees, environments); rather, the systems should provide executives the freedom to control

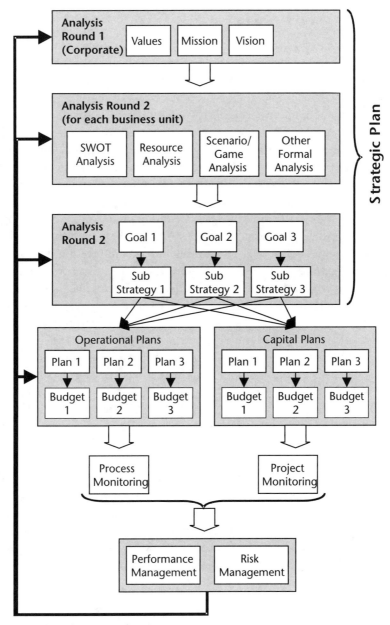

**Figure 3.6** Distributed strategy planning.

the company's future and to support resolution of inter-SBU friction as more business units come on line.

With delegated (some refer to it as organic) planning, executives will direct and guide, but employees will share responsibility for strategy planning. In fact, according to McKinsey and Company, there appears to be a trend toward involving employees and customers in the strategy planning processes [19]. While McKinsey noted this recently (September 2006), others have pushed for it since the 1990s. To put such open-book strategic planning into context, let's draw on open-book project planning as an analogy.

### Open-Book Project Management

The planning process adopted can affect not only what the company executes but how it does so. As mentioned in Chapter 1, if employees see a link between executive talk (planning) and executive walk (execution), cultures can start aligning with strategies. For example, a closed-door, exclusive planning process that generates a plan to promote teamwork, innovation, and rapid growth could result in rejection and complacency. On the same note, an open-door, inclusive planning process that generates a plan to promote realignment, cost reduction, and rapid consolidation without explaining that jobs are safe could result in panic and premature exodus. Either way, if past actions don't fit the words, confusion can end up being the least of your problems.

For example, a common tactic among managers of IT projects is to offer train-the-trainer programs for the end users of their IT project deliverables upon project completion. Some even combine project marketing with such training in the hopes of passing passion for the deliverable on to the trainers. In essence, train-the-trainer programs try to pass ownership and knowledge of, as well as passion for, a project deliverable onto "trainers." Unfortunately, usually only knowledge gets passed on: passion and sense of ownership depart with those who built the system. The problem here is that since the end users aren't impassioned by the value of a new project deliverable, they tend not to use it to its fullest potential. In many cases, these users will enter erroneous data into the new system or even revert to using their legacy system.

Another approach to project rollout can reduce the odds of end user rejection and ultimate ROI disaster. Rather than lumping all organizational change processes into the project rollout phase (e.g., in a train-the-trainer approach), project managers can get their customers involved with the project in the beginning. Open-book project management isn't just about allowing access to budgets, costs, and forecasts; it is also about involving project stakeholders in several aspects of the project, for example, many of the tasks of a project can easily involve untrained users. Such tasks could include requirements gathering, test-plan development, user proto-typing, training documentation, quality assurance, marketing, and long-term ROI audits. By getting users involved early and often, organizational change hurdles can be significantly reduced [20].

### Open-Book Strategy Planning

This same approach can be taken to help ensure the success of strategic formulation and rollout. W. Chan Kim and Renee Mauborgne, authors of *Blue Ocean Strategy*, feel that those strategies formulated using "fair-process," or open-book, strategy planning are effectively building "execution into strategy making from the start" [21]. Just as in IT projects where you wouldn't have end users design or build a system, you probably wouldn't have employees balance the company's books. However, employees can be involved with front-end mission/vision/values development, as well as with back-end goal mapping, documentation, and rollout of the strategy. By getting end user stakeholders involved early and often in IT projects, I have found there to be a higher chance of deliverable embracement. By getting employee stakeholders involved early and often in strategy management via open-book strategy planning, Kim and Mauborgne have found there to be a higher chance of successful strategy execution.

While getting all stakeholders to embrace and execute a strategy is a strong benefit of open-book strategy planning, some amount of corporate control should also be implemented. Along with getting buy-in from staff, a company should establish incentives and penalties "that encourage individuals to subjugate their goals and desires to those of the organization" [3]. The strategic planning, or formulation, process is thus multifaceted. It is both about encouraging employees to adopt the strategic principles through participation and about establishing controls to monitor the achievement of these principles through enforcement. A company should both build consensus around long-term goals and create structure around the resulting business initiatives, metrics, processes, and risks. Robert S. Kaplan and David P. Norton refer to this as resource-based strategy formulation, where goals and measures of accountability are introduced by line staff as well as executives [15]. A company that takes this approach "realizes that a strategy of flexibility and innovation must be influenced by bottom-up as well as top-down ideas, decisions and actions.... Building execution into all levels of strategy is critical to success given that 70–90% of strategic plans fail to succeed or build momentum" [15].

## Model 2 Organizations

Kocourek and Hyde have created just such a structure that also allows for open-book strategy planning. They present their framework in the context of four models that, as mentioned earlier, differ by how much executives empower their business unit managers. Kocourek and Hyde show that these differences in how responsibilities are distributed "reflect fundamentally distinct philosophies about how and where value is created" [16]. This is more than just a strategic-level approach to the old-school concept of delegation; their model refers to structure and culture that should also be in place to successfully delegate planning. As a result, executives who are successful at it spend more time fulfilling their job description; those who aren't spend more time fulfilling subordinate job descriptions.

*Model 1* Financial holding companies serve as a good example of companies that fit this mold. Executives of these firms have little interest in running the companies they own. Rather, they make a point of buying healthy ventures they know can run independently; proven track records make delegation a low risk. Liberty Media, Berkshire Hathaway, Hanson Trust, and Kohlberg, Kravis, Roberts, and Company all fit this mold.

*Model 2* As the corporate core, or the executive team, becomes more involved in developing a common strategy for all of its business or strategic business units, it becomes more of a Model 2 organization. General Electric (GE), Boeing, and Proctor & Gamble all have central organizations that propagate and hold SBUs accountable to them. Some of them, such as GE, also use their centralized control structure to propagate strategic management frameworks, such as Six Sigma process management. Kocourek and Hyde characterize this model as "strategy and oversight."

*Model 3*    In Model 2 companies, once direction is given, units are then tracked for compliance with that direction. In Model 3 organizations, executive teams do more than just track strategic alignment; they also become involved with business unit decision making processes. While this level of executive involvement is usually seen in less mature organizations, it can also be seen in larger organizations where risk management is critical. Examples include banks, stock trading companies, and mining companies.

*Model 4*    Characterized by Kocourek and Hyde as "command and control" companies, these types of organizations "believe the head office contributes significant value by being actively and heavily involved in decision-making at the operational level. This model is frequently found in simple single-line businesses such as the Chevron Corporation and Emerson Electric Company, or those that have been under regulatory control, such as utilities" [16].

While less mature companies (e.g., Stage 1 and 2) tend to follow more of a Model 4 approach, more mature companies can fall into any of the four models. Traditionally, the larger a company gets and the more decoupled its business units become, the more a company migrates from a Model 4 to a Model 1 type of governance. To better understand when and why it should move to a new model type, a company should be in tune with its priorities. With a PePPR architecture in place, processes are prioritized for their critical impact on the business; performance metrics and risks are identified and prioritized to align with critical processes and the strategic goals; and initiative proposals are listed and prioritized to advance performance goals, mitigate risks, improve processes, and support the strategic goals. These prioritized lists of PePPR elements are then consolidated from each business unit by a central office.

Kocourek and Hyde believe central, strategic, or head offices fall into two categories: those supporting the "linkages" between business units and those supporting the business units. Those engaged in business-support activities should delegate such activities to a *shared services organization*. Besides such traditional shared support functions as human resources, finance, and IT, there is a growing trend toward the creation of what we referred to in Chapter 2 as shadow organizations. Besides prioritizing PePPR elements across business units, these "shadow," or matrixed, offices can also be instrumental in creating such controls as performance management systems, risk management systems, and program management systems [17]. Kocourek and Hyde go so far as to say that these structures and systems are prerequisites to moving to Model 2 status.

In 1983, Jack Welch dismantled his planning department of 200 senior managers. He felt that the outflow of performance and forecasting binders prevented his best and brightest from focusing on new markets and competitive advantage. They were too focused on the details at the expense of the big picture. The value in this action was slowly realized by other industries over the next couple decades. Not only was responsibility for strategic planning distributed among the business units, but when a central corporate strategy needed to be refined, some involved many representatives of the company. "J. M. Smuckers Co., the Ohio-based maker of jams and jellies for example, enlisted a team of 140 employees—7% of its workforce—to devote 50% of their time for six months on a major strategy exercise." "Instead of having just 12 minds working it, we really used the team of 140 as ambassadors to solicit input from all 2,000 employees," says President Richard K. Smucker. "It gave us a broader perspective, and it brought to the surface a lot of people with special talents" [22]. When the Nokia Group realized it was time to review its strategy after its explosive 70%-per-year growth, it enlisted 270 employees in 1996. "By engaging more people, the ability to implement strategy becomes more viable," says Chris Jackson, head of strategy development at Nokia [22].

Involving many in the strategic planning process should not preclude executive involvement, however. According to Howard Muson, author of "Strategic Planning for the Time-Challenged," a common reason strategic planning sessions fail is lack of CEO support. "Many chief executives make the mistake of delegating the planning to a committee. Unless employees know that it's a high priority for the boss, forget it, they'll pursue their own agendas." The balancing force to this potential mistake is an overinvolvement by the CEO—specifically, if the leaders engage in "analysis-paralysis." This occurs when "they develop overly ambitious objectives, or too many of them, then despair when they can't make progress on all of them" [23].

In the middle, we have the committee of 6 to 10 key people (in GE's case they had 12 to 20 executives or business unit leaders) led by a mediator and including the CEO. Before such high-level planning sessions, strategic ideas can be solicited from key representatives of the entire company—as J. D. Smuckers and Nokia did. Then, once the strategy and all the associated goals and measurement objectives have been defined, a strategy communication plan should be developed. Staff should see the results of their input, but by the same token, corporate secrets should be protected. Develop high-level, detailed, and timed versions of the strategy that are segmented to different logical groups in your organization. If communication of strategic details is segmented, be sure interbusiness collaboration needs aren't sacrificed. This is why great care and attention to detail must be taken when a strategy, for reasons of security, cannot be completely open book. "The board of directors and senior managers have to see the whole thing, but lower level employees may need just a summary of objectives and what's most relevant to their work" [23]. In short, understand your business boundary conditions and then push for more and more of an open-book approach as found in a Model 2 organization.

This brings us back to our Chapter 1 topic of support versus control. For integrated PePPR management to work, it needs to be accepted and implemented throughout the organization. For plans to be executed, not only do they need to be embraced and implemented by the entire organization, but they need to be implemented well. Integrated PePPR management ensures that the visibility available to the frontline workers is efficiently passed up to the executives. The executives guide their staff on designing strategic plans that address scenarios offered by such visibility. Then, the organization needs to efficiently execute the plans. Open-book cultures, staff inclusion, project support, and organizational empowerment are all methods that can help with this by removing communication brick walls and instilling engines of passion (see Chapter 1, Figure 1.12). Getting everyone involved in strategic planning and integrated PePPR management takes its physical form as a matrixed virtual strategic management office (see Chapter 2). Aided by robust IT systems to support PePPR deployment, Model 2–type companies are ideally positioned to experience the dynamic execution abilities typical of the sailboat racing and emergency room teams mentioned in Chapter 1. In essence, such companies aren't planning because it's just another process required of executives; they are planning for execution because it's a passion of the company.

## Planning Methodologies

In the early days of a company, just about all of its focus is on establishing itself as a viable business. Activities can include fine-tuning its offerings to maximize revenue, hunting down quality problems, and financing payroll. One of the last things such start-up companies are worried about is applying a methodology to strategic planning. They need to prove they can hit one target before they formalize the process of aiming and shooting out other targets. As mentioned earlier, their first strategic plan is very likely documented and updated via an e-mail stream. Over time, once a company has realized it can hit targets, it will probably want to consistently hit other targets. The way to achieve consistency is to document and implement some "aiming" process. That is, the company should develop a consistent method for planning and revisiting its corporate strategy. We will review three such methods that all share the common theme of iteration, or revisiting and refining, the strategic plan: one formal, one small customization, and one large customization.

### Hoshin Kanri

Invented and applied in Japan, Hoshin Kanri is a framework derived from the evangelism of W. Edwards Deming's TQM revolution in the 1950s. Loosely translated, *hoshin* means "compass," and *kanri* means "managing to long-range goals." That is, Hoshin Kanri is a strategic planning framework that helps companies set direction and manage for long-term results. The framework provides a method for constant and iterative improvement of the company's processes and projects by cycling on the four phases of Hoshin management: set, deploy, monitor, and diagnose. Then, to ensure the strategy is propagated out to all corners of the business, departments and divisions are required to go through the same strategic cycling process. This leads to a suite of lower-level strategies that are influenced by both the needs of the market and the goals of the corporate strategy.

   The overall approach is illustrated in Figure 3.7, which was drawn from Michael Cowley and Ellen Domb's popular book on the subject, *Beyond Strategic Vision*. With Hoshin Kanri, before determining a vision (Step 2), the organization must first understand its current situation, both in terms of resources available and the external environment (Step 1). Once the vision is created, "breakthroughs," or projects, need to be identified to advance components of the vision, or vision elements (Step 3). Breakthrough activities are those directed at achieving significant improvement in operational performance. Specifically, they are activities typically directed at resolving issues the business "will face in the next two to five years" [24]. Risk management and project portfolio management are integrated with the strategy-formulation process to help set the goals. At Step 4, two things occur: plans are created to improve the project success (risk mitigation and project support plans), and processes are identified that support normal, ongoing operations (early process

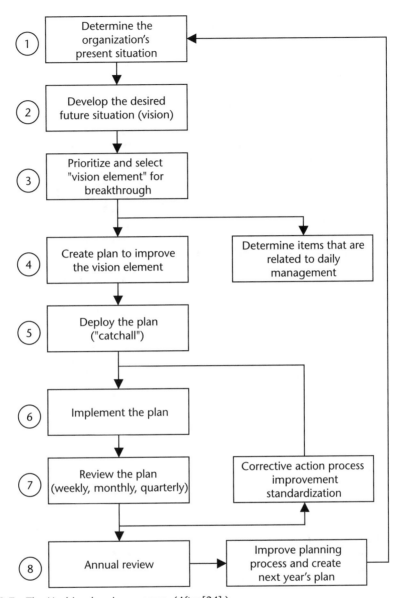

**Figure 3.7** The Hoshin planning process. (*After* [24].)

management). Once plans are implemented (Steps 5 and 6), Hoshin recommends weekly, monthly, and quarterly reviews, which allow for near-real-time corrective actions to be applied (Step 7, performance management framework). The goal here is to minimize reactive management techniques and to promote proactive mitigation of risks. The final step (Step 8) is the annual review of the plan and the resulting improvement recommendations. More than just corrective actions to projects, processes, or both, these annual recommendations are meant to be improvements to the strategy [25].

If we look at the Hoshin planning process through PePPR lenses, we end up with Table 3.2. The Hoshin steps and their associated descriptions are pulled from Figure 3.7 and filled into the first two columns. Then we describe how the PePPR

**Table 3.2** Integrated PePPR Mapped to the Hoshin Planning Process

| Hoshin Step | Description | PePPR Feeds (Identified in Parentheses) |
|---|---|---|
| 3 | Prioritize and select "vision elements" to support breakthroughs | Projects are selected to dramatically improve the performance metrics of the company (9). Examples of such projects include new product development, process improvements (7), and risk mitigation projects (8). |
| 4, 5, 6 | Create plans to improve the vision element and then execute on the plans | Project portfolio management provides frameworks to improve project success rates. Such frameworks allow for smooth flow of project portfolio risks to a corporatewide risk management coordinator (2). Allowing for such frameworks to become a normal part of business processes ensures continually high project success rates (11). |
| 7 | Regularly review the plan and implementation (weekly, monthly, quarterly) | As projects are implemented, review the support mechanisms that were put into place to ensure project success. That is, constantly review such components of the project and process portfolios as strategic alignment, risk balancing (6), metric maximization (4, 5), resource utilization, and quality. Continuous reviews would effectively help risk (1, 10), project portfolio management (PPM), and process improvement activities become part of the everyday "culture" of the company. |
| 7A | Take corrective action, implement process improvement, and standardize | The output of the reviews should lead to a validation of the metrics being monitored (3), a process that allows for ongoing metric improvement (12) and a set of processes that can be improved (7). |

feeds (in parentheses) map to these Hoshin steps. This shows that the Hoshin methodology considers not just the components of PePPR but also their integration.

Figure 3.8 shows the three-step process for strategy planning and execution. Three sources of information feed the "set" phase: past data (e.g., process and project metrics), future data (scenario and options analysis), and current environmental data (industry analysis and corporate capability reviews). The data gathered from these three categories feed the annual Hoshin strategy sessions. The output of this process is defined as five key elements of these sessions (Steps 1 to 4 of Figure 3.7): the goal statement, defined metrics, target values, deadline dates, and strategies to accomplish [26]. While a goal statement is classic strategy planning, metrics, targets, and deadlines add specifics to the goals typically not seen until the operational plans are developed. This shows that the Hoshin framework attempts to integrate strategy execution into the planning process. Besides just setting ethereal goals, such as improved sales, better inventory turnover, and lower cost of goods sold, a Hoshin strategy requires that the "By how much?" and "By when?" questions be answered in the published strategy document. Along with links to execution, other distinguishing characteristics of Hoshin strategy planning are strategy cascades, project-versus-process considerations, and continuous improvement.

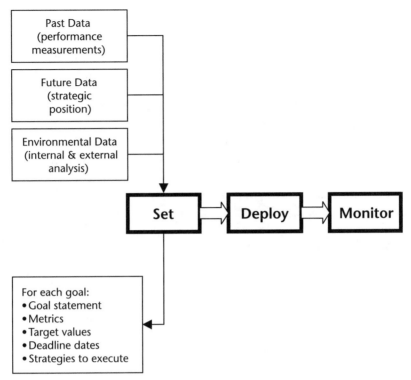

**Figure 3.8**   The Hoshin Kanri three-step strategy planning and execution process.

- *Strategy cascades:* Once the central strategy is developed, business units and departments are required in turn to develop their own strategies. Each level of these should comprise the same five elements of Hoshin planning, just in greater detail. To ensure alignment throughout the organization, the desired outcomes (deadlines and target values) of an upper level become the feeders into the strategy plan of the lower level.

- *Project versus process:* With Hoshin, a clear distinction is made between operational processes and the project portfolio. To best capture the essence of a company, both of these need to be considered, but they should be considered separately. The main reason for their distinction is the need for different types of metrics, goals, and improvement feedback loops. While Chapters 5 and 6 will cover process and project portfolios in greater detail, this book, as a whole, highlights the areas where process and project portfolio management can be integrated.

- *Continuous improvement:* In order for a project team to know that it can do a better job at delivering on its goals, either it needs to be able to compare current-state metrics to some original benchmarks or it needs input from some external auditing body. Either form of feedback would allow it to improve upon its processes. For processes not associated with a project (i.e., operational processes), continuous improvement can be realized by implementing formal frameworks, such as Critical Chain, Lean, Kaizen, TQM, or Six Sigma.

If a Hoshin Kanri consultant came into my company and recommended that I review my strategy for improvement every week or month, I'd laugh him or her out of my building. But if he or she recommended that weekly or monthly status reports include both goals and accomplishments, require a couple sentences linking goals to corporate strategy, and provide a section for recommended changes, then I'd start to see the picture. Hoshin Kanri doesn't require formal group meetings every week; it just requires incremental improvements on aligning the strategy and that those improvements be sewn into the culture of the organization (PePPR feeds 3, 9, and 12). Hoshin management covers more than just strategy planning; it addresses how a company should operate and grow. Planning frameworks that focus on both project support and process improvement are common. But frameworks that include department cascading and clear execution steps aren't so common. The next two strategic planning processes are examples of frameworks that, like Hoshin, include processes to support continuous feedback and improvement.

## City of Woodland

Organizations should not feel required to fit the mold of any particular strategic planning framework. Rather, they should adopt the core components of proven frameworks and fit them to the culture of the organization. One such example is the City of Woodland, California, which came up with a simple process, derived from various other frameworks, that showed links to execution, included improvement steps, and accommodated projects and processes. Missing from such a simple approach, however, are steps for continuous improvement between annual strategy-review sessions.

Governments tend to set strategies when elected officials come to office every four years. Then, if some major event causes voters to demand change at midterm, strategic reviews may occur reactively. Hoshin provides for proactive improvements through risk and performance management so that surprises are minimized at annual reviews. Less-structured organizations, on the other hand, end up making larger, annual course changes after strategic executions have wandered off course. This can be a trade-off some are willing to make in favor of having the organization adopt and use the framework. Complex strategy planning processes with required new tasks and organizational change are notorious for their intimidation and ultimate rejection. The City of Woodland appears to have realized this and chose to develop a framework that fit its culture (Figure 3.9).

## Exxon-Mobil

While a much larger organization may need to put more controls in place than the City of Woodland, it still may need to customize a planning process to its needs. Exxon-Mobil found that since there was increasing turbulence in its market, it couldn't be constrained by a purely centralized planning process. Rather than go with a strict Hoshin model that allowed for cascading strategic development, it opted for a similar decentralized approach. The company also wanted its approach to be "less formalized and more flexible" [3]. Figure 3.10 shows how the flow of Exxon-Mobil's strategic planning process starts with business units' submitting

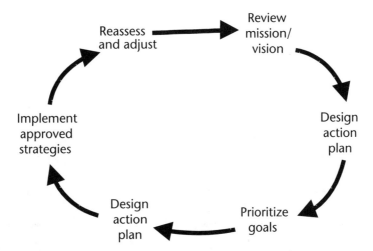

**Figure 3.9** City of Woodland strategic planning methodology. (*After* [27].)

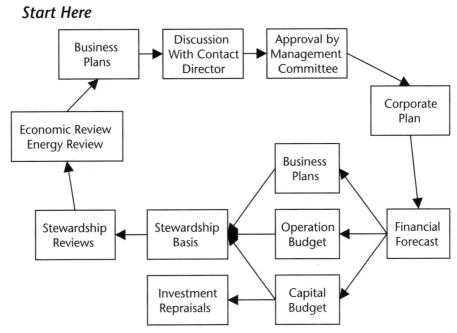

**Figure 3.10** Strategic planning at Exxon.

business plans to a management review committee. This "ground-up" approach shifted strategic planning from a "control perspective, in which senior management used the strategic planning mechanisms as a means of controlling decisions and resource deployments by divisions ... towards more of a coordination perspective, in which the strategy process emphasized dialog involving knowledge sharing and consensus building" via business plan reviews [3]. The role of a central strategic planning staff was diminished in favor of planning groups controlled by each business unit. That is, the company adopted the strategic planning methods of a Model 2 organization. This provided the flexibility for change these business units needed to more effectively shift their strategic directions to the market.

Once they had a set of approved business plans, the executives were able to develop a corporate plan that allowed them to comprehensively forecast financial returns. Then, since their business plans included operational (or process) improvement projects, senior managers were able to create both operational and capital expenditure budgets. The process improvement efforts and adherence to business plans would be monitored following a "stewardship" model (or oversight committee or individual). The new projects, on the other hand, would be audited periodically through "investment appraisals." Finally, reviews of internal planning and the external environment would precede a new round of business plans. Like Hoshin, execution, improvement, and process-versus-project differentiation is central to the Exxon-Mobile strategic process. But unlike Hoshin, the company's planning process cascades up to the corporate plan, not the other way around. Also, besides monitoring for adherence to the business plan, midstream reviews of the monitoring process itself embed the continual-improvement concept of Hoshin. The approach taken at Exxon is executives' reaction to a frustration being felt across many industries: how can long-term decisions and forecasts be made if the demands of each market are no longer stable. As Exxon has shown, Model 2–like approaches to strategy formulation (such as providing flexibility to those more in touch with market demands) may need to be developed [28].

## Strategic Analysis

So far, we've looked at different approaches to strategic planning that aid how PePPR management integrates. Once it has been determined that an internal or external analysis is worthwhile, however, what techniques can be used? How should techniques be chosen that fit the core goals of the company? Where planning looks at a bigger process picture of when and how time should be allocated to strategy, analysis drills deeper in the how side by providing techniques, tools, and concepts. Let's start with how techniques can be chosen to best fit the goals of the company.

Examples of such tools include political, economic, social, and technological (PEST) analysis, strengths, weaknesses, opportunities, and threats (SWOT) analysis, Porter's Five Forces, and Porter's value chain analysis. Examples of concepts include the resource-based view, game theory, and the innovation-based view. Figure 3.11 shows these in relation to the two general environments that influence a company: its internal and external environments. With the exception of SWOT and value chain analysis, each tool or concept has a primary environment of focus. In general, however, each technique ultimately influences its nonprimary environment. For example, while PEST analysis lists out external variables, it also guides a company on how to address these variables internally. It is what Eric D. Beinhocker, author of "Strategy at the Edge of Chaos," refers to as an "outward-in" approach. A common approach to using such tools for strategic analysis is to choose a set that provides a

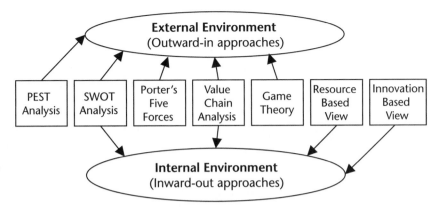

**Figure 3.11**   Framework support for internal versus external corporate environment analysis.

balanced view of the corporate environments [29]. If too much of a prolonged inward focus is used, a company risks limiting its "opportunity horizon and introduces resistance to change" [9]. On the other hand, if too much of a prolonged outward focus is used, a company risks making commitments that it can't fulfill due to limited capabilities. To provide a balanced analysis of a company, usually several of these tools and concepts are used. The resulting strategic analysis then provides a sense of completeness because of its multidimensionality.

### Classic Analysis

According to Beinhocker, many of these strategy tools "owe their origins to ideas developed in the 1950s in a field known as the theory of industrial organization. Industrial organization theory, which is concerned with industry structure and firm performance, is in turn based on microeconomic theory" [29]. The timeline shown in Table 3.3 is a generalized view of when strategic analysis tools and concepts were introduced and when they were most popular. Leibold, Probst, and Gibbert broadly label these four resulting "eras" as planning, balancing, positioning, and resources and capabilities [9].

### Planning

During the 1950s and 1960s, there was a ground swell in understanding the need for planning. This planning focused primarily on budgetary needs and financial ratios (i.e., classic performance monitoring). It was felt that the plans for the future of the company could be made based on the financial results of various components of the business and the industry. If making money should be the primary goal of a company, it was believed, then maximization of shareholder value should be the primary financial subgoal. While cash flow can be tracked by dollars transacted, different methods are used to track shareholder value. Some examples include return on net assets, earnings before interest and taxes, return on capital employed, and net profit margin. By quantifying their forecasts with shareholder value metrics, companies felt that their crystal ball was a good compass for strategic analysis.

**Table 3.3** History of Strategic Analysis

| Issue/Period | Planning/ 1950–1960s | Balancing/ 1970s | Positioning/ 1980s | Resources and Capabilities/1990s |
|---|---|---|---|---|
| Dominant Focus | Business and budgetary planning | Optimizing corporate entities and functions | Market "adapting" and unique "fit" | Resource-based view |
| Main Concerns | Planning growth, budgeting, financial control | Balancing a portfolio of SBUs/firms/products, developing synergy of resources and functions | Market niches, environment adaptation | Internal competitive advantage, responding to hypercompetition |
| Principal Concepts and Tools | Investment planning, financial budgeting, economic forecasting, linear programming | Portfolio planning matrices, SWOT analyses | Industry analysis, competitor analyses, value chain analyses, profit impact of market strategy (PIMS) analyses | Resource analyses, core competency analyses, capability analyses |
| Organizational and Implementation Issues | Formal structures and procedures, predominantly financial management | Multidivisional structures, diversification, quest for market share growth | Industry restructuring, value chain configuration, positioning evaluations | Restructuring around competence, core competencies, outsourcing, alliances |

*Source:* [9].

## Balancing

In the balancing era, a lot of focus was on the delegation of workloads among functions and businesses. This is when the M-form, or SBU-based, corporate structure evolved. But besides structure, strategists also looked at balancing the analysis between internal and external environments to create actionable goals. The more famous tool that evolved in this time frame was the SWOT analysis. Developed in the 1960s, SWOT analysis is a way to better understand a company's internal and external environments by reviewing its strengths and weaknesses (e.g., capabilities and risks) and its industry's opportunities and threats (e.g., possible investments and risks).

## Positioning

While it is difficult to actually differentiate and understand the company's strengths and weaknesses, achieving such an understanding is important to guide a company to long-term success. Self-awareness prevents companies from (1) engaging in unfamiliar areas, and (2) reacting to ill-conceived strategies. In analyzing a company's external environment for opportunities or threats, some companies have turned to the Porter's Five Forces framework. One of Porter's key points is that "competitive strategy is about being different—it means deliberately choosing a different set of activities to deliver a unique mix of value" [9]. This concept, along with such tools as competitor analysis, market analysis, value chain analysis, and profit impact of market strategy, or PIMS, analysis, formed the basis of the "positioning era" of the 1980s.

### Resources and Capabilities

This era saw a shift from taking more of an outward-in view of the company to taking more of an inward-out view. Gary Hamel, author of "The Challenge Today: Changing the Rules of the Game," summarized this shift in thinking clearly when he explained that companies of previous eras defined themselves by "what they do: we are a bank, we are an airline, we are a car company, etc. You see new opportunities when you can escape a product- or service-centric definition of a company, and see it in terms of what it knows—its core competencies" [30]. According to C. K. Prahalad and G. Hemel, authors of "The Core Competence of the Corporation," these core competencies are fundamental to a firm's performance and strategy [31]. They are to be differentiated from what Robert Grant refers to as distinctive competencies, or "those things that an organization does particularly well relative to its competitors" [3]. The combination of this competency analysis with such overlapping approaches as resource analysis, capability analysis, and business process reengineering, became known as the resource-based view. According to Leibold, Probst, and Gibbert, this is also when strategic theories of hypercompetition and high-velocity strategies were born [9]. These theories contended that one firm will outperform another if it more efficiently disrupts a current situation through unconventional capabilities (i.e., by "repeatedly forming new, albeit temporary, competitive advantages based on different resource combinations than those of the existing pattern") [9].

## Modern Analysis

Through the history of strategic analysis, the constant goal was to better forecast events so that a company could position itself to best overcome them. Nonetheless, Michael Raynor shows that a growing consensus feels the forecasting capabilities of classic strategic analysis tools aren't achieving their advertised purposes. He argues that if a random sampling of companies that used such tools were compared to an equal random sampling of those that didn't, there would be no difference in the number of successes or failures. Specifically, "due to the disruptive impact of networking technologies, speed of globalization, and rate of product and industry innovation, environmental forecasting and prediction are impossible in many, if not most industries" [8]. Leibold, Probst, and Gibbert back this up by stating that "plans have now come to be seen not as descriptions of future performance, but as a basis for initiating flexible and speedy responses to a changing present" [9]. Brian Huffman also cites several authors who subscribe to an evolutionary, or "learning," school of thought which holds that strategy should be more a result of insights, states of mind, and intuition than of "rigorous analysis or some rote process" [5]. In short, though classic approaches may provide better insight for companies in stable environments, Huffman feels that for highly dynamic environments, "strategies generated by strategic paradigms are predictable, and predictable strategies are bad."

Thus, we return to the concept of flexibility and adaptability that we referenced in Chapter 1. This heightened need for flexibility does not preclude the need for long-term commitment to a vision. Companies that end up shaping industries are ones that set a course and do not deviate despite the challenges. Nucor took about

40 years to take over the U.S. steel market in the face of imminent bankruptcy and small economies of scale, and Toyota took about 60 years to become the number one auto maker in the face of trade barriers, prejudices, and powerful competitors. They weathered storms and stuck to their core visions of improving customer satisfaction and ensuring high quality. But such visions were over landscapes they knew had little likelihood of changing. Nonetheless, while maintaining commitments to such long-term visions as customer- or quality-centricism, businesses should still "adapt to an economy of constant change in the short term" [32]. Nucor can react to customer demands very quickly with their low-cost, thin-slab technology [33], and Toyota's production system can switch auto-type production output within an hour [34]. These two companies have innovated their way to being on the starting lines of several races. If the gun goes off for any of the races, they are ready to capture the lead quickly.

## Scenarios and Options

In contrast, if a company changes course too often for the sake of flexibility, it will miss the opportunity to shape an industry. But if a company is not flexible, it can become a slow-moving behemoth that gets steamrolled by a changing industry. Michael Raynor believes that the best way to handle such a paradox is to improve the visibility of the business environment through two tools common to risk managers called scenario planning and options analysis [8]. To take advantage of the opportunities offered by the uncertainties of fast markets and to become industry shapers, Leibold, Probst, and Gibbert also recommend that companies "reinvent their strategic planning processes" to include such tools as game theory (a superset of scenario planning) [9]. These forms of critical thinking don't necessarily improve a company's ability to forecast; instead, they improve its positioning for unknowns (Flow 1 in Figure 3.12). Katsuhiko Shimizu and Michael A. Hitt, authors of "Strategic Flexibility: Organizational Preparedness to Reverse Ineffective Strategic Decisions" substantiate this by suggesting that to maintain flexibility, a company should, in essence, adopt an open-book risk management (improve visibility) and implement efficient project portfolio management (improve execution) [35]. Specifically, he believes that a company should focus on three capabilities:

1. Paying attention to negative feedback (i.e., open-book risk identification);
2. Collecting and assessing negative data objectively (i.e., risk management);
3. Initiating and completing change in a timely fashion (i.e., efficient project portfolio management; Flows 1 and 2 in Figure 3.12).

Coming full circle, Alexander Kandybin and Martin Kihn, authors of "Raising Your Return on Innovation Investment," explain that companies with the greatest project ROI use more than just a mix of such project portfolio approaches as strategic fit, risk-adjusted net present value (NPV), new product portfolio balance, and prioritization; they also apply advanced valuation methodologies "such as decision trees, simulation, and real options" [36] (Flow 3 in Figure 3.12). In summary, a belief is growing that for a company to best position itself for rapidly changing environments, it should support its project portfolio and strategy planning process by

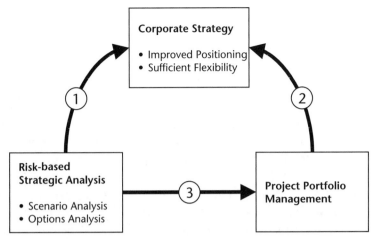

**Figure 3.12**   Risk and project portfolio management integrated with modern strategic analysis.

identifying risks through scenario analysis and understanding risk consequences through options analysis. Johnson & Johnson has incorporated such an approach into its standard strategic planning process. Figure 3.13 shows that this company creates scenario simulations (or a "range of possible futures") in its "Anticipate" step, creates options (or "contingents") in its "Formulate" step, supports the strategic goals chosen (or "commits") in its "Accumulate" step, and then tracks (or "monitors") performance in its "Operate" step. Each step involves more than just an awareness of options; actions are taken to make sure the options can be implemented if the primary actions (e.g., strategic initiatives) don't meet performance thresholds. Johnson & Johnson's model also appears to resemble the Hoshin Kanri

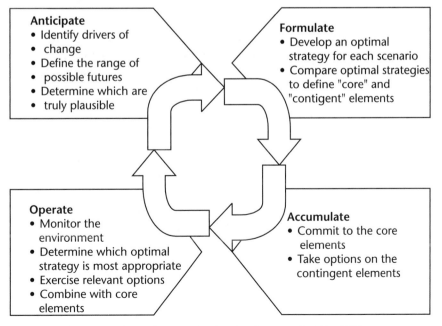

**Figure 3.13**   Johnson & Johnson's strategic planning framework. (*After* [8].)

strategic execution model of "develop desired future," "create plan to improve," "deploy and implement the plan," and "review the plan and process."

## Innovation

Any particular company that is mature enough to conduct strategic planning sessions should choose those classical or modern frameworks that best suit its internal and external environment. During the 1990s, strategic thinkers viewed the technical revolution with an interest that resulted in a wave of innovation-focused literature (e.g., Tom Peter's *ReImagine*, Kim and Mauborgne's *Blue Ocean Strategy*, and Clayton M. Christenson's *The Innovator's Dilemma*). As the "bubble" burst at the turn of the millennium, there was a renewed focus on the importance of innovation centers within companies; R&D labs, employee education programs, collaboration systems, and academic consortium memberships are all examples. While the 1990s zeroed in on start-up and technology-based companies as the center of the innovation universe, strategists now feel that such organizations are losing their exclusive claim to innovation as their fundamental source of competitive advantage.

Companies such as Nucor in steel, Starbucks in coffee, Yellow Tail in wine, and JetBlue in airlines have all become enormously successful by following what Kim and Mauborgne refer to as "value innovation" strategies [21]. These companies didn't just focus on value-add activities, such as growth projects and process improvements; they did so in creative and market-changing ways.

According to Kim and Mauborgne, "Value without innovation tends to focus on value creation on an incremental scale—something that improves value but is not sufficient to make you stand out in the marketplace" [21]. Achieving large returns, rather than just incremental value, requires a company to take huge gambles on the unknown outcomes of innovation efforts. Flamholtz and Randle expand on this by framing innovation differently for companies at different levels of maturity. For example, start-up companies have less to lose and are willing to bet the farm. On the other hand, Stage 3 and higher companies "tend to be oriented more toward incremental innovations. They are less likely to bet the company, and they often spread their risk among a portfolio of products or projects" [1]. So, to avoid incremental value-adds and see large value returns from activities and outputs, their activities and outputs should be innovative. But as a company gets larger, such innovation tends to occur incrementally to better mitigate risks.

To show how the maturity of an organization can affect the way it embraces risky innovation, let's look specifically at the project types that can get funded. Figure 3.14 shows how, over time, new companies tend to enter the market with new product ideas (product innovation curve). Once their products become successful, they alter designs for different customer segments, add features so they can add "new and improved" taglines, and ultimately start lowering prices as competition develops. All this is done to best squeeze all the dollars out of a product idea. As the company moves on, other product ideas may sprout, but if an idea incubator isn't a part of the company (e.g., raw R&D as found in biotech firms), reliance on product innovation diminishes over time. As the company tries to squeeze every last pound, ruble, or yen out of its product, it also modifies business processes to do so (process innovation curve). For example, supply chains are tightened, marketing approaches are modified, and product development processes are reengineered.

Over time, as product innovation lessens, the company relies more on business process innovations. Looking at it from the standpoint of how the company invests in new projects, fewer initiatives are approved for product improvements, and more are approved for process improvements. Ultimately, a company turns to strategic innovations to maintain maximum shareholder value. Kodak switched to digital imaging, Hewlett-Packard dove into printing, IBM focused on professional services, and Tom Hanks became a full-time actor. All of these ventures made substantial strategic shifts (or innovations) that launched them into higher levels of return. By investing capital, changing processes, and developing new products, their central sources of profits changed from their traditional sources of film, electronics, computer servers, and stand-up comedy. Since strategic innovations require such immense change and commitment of resources, they are usually seen as efforts of last resort. Figure 3.14 shows the cycle of innovation types that can occur in a company that fails to constantly produce new innovative products and processes. Examples of companies that have succeeded at this include Sony, Apple, and Google, all famous for their incessant stream of product innovations.

Care must be taken, however, when a company decides to invest highly in "innovation" activities. For example, Kandybin and Kihn conducted a study of global personal-care and consumer health-care companies and found that there was "no clear correlation between R&D spending as a percentage of sales and growth in revenues or profitability." They also cited a 1997 study by Christoph-Friedrich von Braun, *The Innovation War*, which found, after analyzing 30 Global 500 firms, that "no correlation between increased R&D spending and improvement in profitability" existed [36]. Kandybin and Kihn concluded that profitable innovation cannot be bought. Instead, they referred to building an innovation capability around an innovation value chain [36] made up of four components: ideation, project selec-

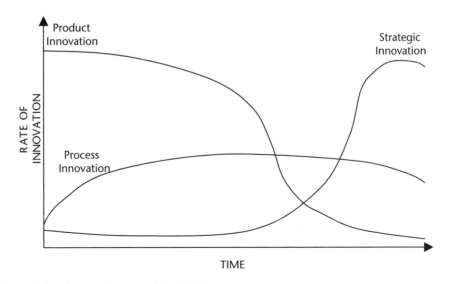

**Figure 3.14**   Innovation types. (*After* [3].)

tion, development, and commercialization (Table 3.4). This process guides the creation of the project portfolio to improve the performance, or value-add, of the organization through innovation.

## PePPR Analysis

In modern strategic analysis, an understanding is growing that new techniques are needed to accommodate new market speeds. Risk-based analyses like game theory, scenario analysis, and real options are methods for planning and improving forward visibility that have become more popular than traditional strategy tools. Robust project portfolio management is a method for improving flexible execution that has become more popular than ad hoc project management. These two methods support improved visibility and execution by looking at both external environments and internal capabilities. However, these two methods alone don't provide the complete input needed for a well-balanced strategic review; enterprisewide performance management and process management are also needed. For example, scenario analysis should include performance metric goals, and options analysis should include current process capabilities. Figure 3.15 builds on Figure 3.12 by adding these latter two components of PePPR management and shows more clearly how risk management is linked to scenario analysis. Basically, Figure 3.15 illustrates how PePPR management integrates to support modern strategic analysis. For that matter, this chapter has attempted to show how integrated PePPR management not only enhances the competitive advantages of a company (as shown in Chapters 1 and 2) but improves coordination during the strategic analysis process. Positive interaction among the PePPR components, rather than siloed conflict, can act to improve the probability of strategic realization through improved positioning and the right amount of flexibility. Such positive interaction is, in turn, possible through open-book visibility and delegated (or organic) execution through the ranks.

**Table 3.4**   Innovation Value Chain

| Ideation → | Project Selection → | Development → | Commercialization |
|---|---|---|---|
| New product and technology ideas | Strategy and new product linkages | Disciplined and effective stage/gate process | Marketing and investment planning |
| New business concepts and opportunities | Governance of new initiatives | Time to market | Consumer profiling and segmentation |
| Consumer insights | Tracking and definition | Bottleneck elimination and identification of project "congestion" | Competitive response and timing |
| Trend analysis and anticipation | Project-approval decision-making processes | Parallel planning of work steps | Advertising and promotion decision making |
| New-to-the-world ideas and extensions of existing ideas | Use of advanced valuation methodologies | Resource allocation | Product tracking |

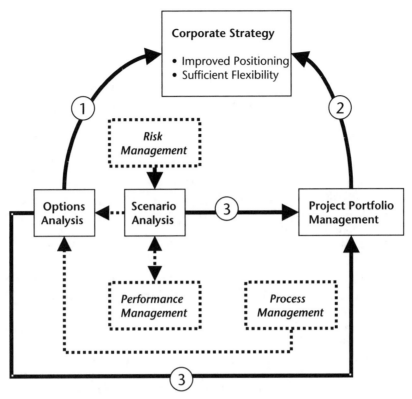

**Figure 3.15** PePPR integrated with modern strategic analysis.

## Summary

While strategy is a concept that has been around for centuries, new concepts have blossomed recently to support the increased speed of market dynamics. Open-book strategic execution, shape-versus-adapt approaches, options and scenario analyses (e.g., game theory), and extended strategic design (e.g., with partners, consortiums, value systems, or a combination of the three) are some of the new planning and analysis techniques. Enterprise-level performance, process, project portfolio, and risk management are some of the new execution techniques that have exploded in response. In this chapter, we first looked at the classic analysis techniques and then showed how the newer techniques evolved from these. Once the broader organization is included (with some security constraints considered), mature strategic planning goes from being a controlling exercise to one linked to execution. Kim and Mauborgne's "fair-process" and Kocourek and Hyde's "Model 2" organizations support the experiences seen at Smuckers and Nokia: including staff in strategic design leads to impassioned delivery of that strategy. Combining this powerful technique for strategic execution with the supportive elements of integrated PePPR management (see Figure 3.15), companies now have the tools to better anticipate and navigate the new market storms.

# References

[1] Flamholtz, Eric G., and Yvonne Randle, *Growing Pains*, San Francisco, CA, Jossey-Bass, 2000.

[2] von Clausewitz, Carl, *On War*, Nwe York, NY, University Press, 1976.

[3] Grant, Robert M., *Contemporary Strategy Analysis: Concepts, Technologies, Applications*, 4th ed., Malden, MA, Blackwell Publishers, 2002.

[4] Michaelson, Gerald A., *The Art of War for Managers*, Avon, MA, Adams Media Corporation, 2001.

[5] Huffman, Brian, "What Makes a Strategy Brilliant?" in *Strategic Management in the Knowledge Economy*, by M. Leibold, G. J. B. Probst, and M. Gibbert, (eds.), New York, NY, Wiley, 2002, pp. 106–117.

[6] Ohmae, Kenichi, *The Mind of the Strategist: The Art of Japanese Business*, New York: McGraw-Hill, 1991.

[7] Rosenzweig, Phil, "The Halo Effect, and Other Managerial Delusions," *McKinsey Quarterly*, No. 1, 2007.

[8] Raynor, Michael E., *The Strategy Paradox*, New York, NY, Currency/Doubleday, 2007.

[9] Leibold, Marius, Gilbert Probst, and Michael Gibbert, *Strategic Management in the Knowledge Economy*, New York, NY, Wiley, 2002, pp. 70–80.

[10] Meza, Phillip, "Hollywood's New Romance with IT," *Optimize Magazine*, No. 22, March 1, 2007.

[11] Agence France-Press, "With Film Dying, Fuji Photo Targets Women's Beauty Products," Inquirer.net, September 12, 2006, http://newsinfo.inquirer.net/breakingnews/ infotech/ view_article.php?article_id=20575 (last accessed on June 14, 2007).

[12] Courtney, Hugh, "Making the Most of Uncertainty," *McKinsey Quarterly*, No. 4, 2001.

[13] McNamara, Carter, "Basic Overview of Various Strategic Planning Models," Authenticity Consulting, LLC, 1997.

[14] Demos, N., S. Chung, and M. Beck, "The New Strategy and Why it is New,"*Strategy and Business*, October 1, 2001, http://www.strategy-business.com/press/16635507/14254 (last accessed on January 8, 2007).

[15] Kaplan, Robert S., and David P. Norton, *The Strategy Focused Organization*, Cambridge, MA: Harvard Business School Press, 2001.

[16] Collins, Jim, *Good to Great*, New York, NY, Harper Business, 2001.

[17] Kocourek, Paul F., and Paul Hyde, "The Model 2 Organization, Making Your Company Safe for Zealots," Strategy + Business, January 1, 2001, www.strategy-business.com/ press/16635507/10797 (last accessed on January 8, 2007).

[18] Senge, Peter M., and Goran Carstedt, "Innovating Our Way to the Next Industrial Revolution," Harvard Business Online, December 1, 2001.

[19] McKinsey and Company, "Improving Strategic Planning: A McKinsey Survey," *McKinsey Quarterly*, September 1, 2006 (last accessed on December 25, 2006).

[20] Bonham, Stephen S., "People Are the Key to Systems Success," Frontline Solutions, Vol. 2, No. 1, Duluth, MN, January 1, 2001.

[21] Kim, W. Chan, and Renee Mauborgne, *Blue Ocean Strategy*, Cambridge, MA: Harvard Business School Press, 2005.

[22] Byrne, John A., "Strategic Planning," *Business Week*, 1996, www.businessweek.com/ 1996/35/b34901.htm (last accessed on December 23, 2006).

[23] Muson, Howard, "Strategic Planning for the Time-Challenged," The Conference Board, May 1, 2004.

[24] Kenyon, David A., "Strategic Planning with the Hoshin Process,"QualityDigest.com, May 1997, www.qualitydigest.com/may97/html/hoshin.html (last accessed on December 6, 2006).

[25]  Cowley, Michael, and Ellen Domb, *Beyond Strategic Vision: Effective Corporate Action with Hoshin Planning*, Burlington, MA, Butterworth Heinemann, 1997.

[26]  Shiba, S., T. Pursch, and R. Stasey, "Introduction to Hoshin Management: Achieving Alignment at Analog Devices and Teradyne," *Center for Quality Management Journal*, Vol. 4, No. 3, 1995, pp. 22–33.

[27]  City of Woodland, California, "Technology Public Session, Strategic Planning Methodology," City of Woodland, California, 2006, www.cityofwoodland.org/feature/techplan (last accessed on December 6, 2006).

[28]  Harnel, Gary, *Leading the Revolution*, Cambridge, MA: Harvard Business School Press, 2000.

[29]  Beinhocker, Eric D., "Strategy at the Edge of Chaos," in *Strategic Management in the Knowledge Economy*, by M. Leibold, G. J. B. Probst, and M. Gibbert, (eds.), New York, NY, Wiley, 2002, pp. 159–167.

[30]  Hamel, Gary, "The Challenge Today: Changing the Rules of the Game," in *Strategic Management in the Knowledge Economy*, by M. Leibold, G. J. B. Probst, and M. Gibbert, (eds.), New York, NY, Wiley, 2002, 198–209.

[31]  Prahalad, C. K., and G. Hamel, "The Core Competence of the Corporation," *Harvard Business Review*, May–June, pp. 79–91.

[32]  Bossidy, Larry, and Ram Charan, *Execution: The Discipline of Getting Things Done*, New York: Crown Business, 2002.

[33]  Brown, Stuart F., and Alicia Hills Moor, "Steel Technology Is Red Hot Speedier, Simpler Production Methods That Looked Economically Dicey a Few Years Ago Have Put America's Metal Melters Back on the Map, Quality Is Up and the Innovation Isn't Over," *Fortune Magazine*, May 13, 1996.

[34]  Abbott, Ashok, "Strategic Flexibility and Firm Performance: The Case of US Based Transnational Corporations," Global Institute of Flexible Systems Management, Vol. 4, New Delhi, India, January–June 2003.

[35]  Shimizu, Katsuhiko, and Michael A. Hitt, "Strategic Flexibility: Organizational Preparedness to Reverse Ineffective Strategic Decisions," *Academy of Management Executive*, Vol. 18, No. 4, 2004.

[36]  Kandybin, Alexander, and Martin Kihn, "Raising Your Return on Innovation Investment," Strategy + Business, May 11, 2004, www.strategy-business.com/resiliencereport/resilience/rr00007?pg=0 (last accessed on June 2, 2007).

## CHAPTER 4

# Performance Management

Throughout history leaders have sought information to help them make better decisions. Kings and generals have deployed diplomats, spies, and scouts to gain ever-needed advantages. Gathering information on the status of their domains was their way of gauging the performance not only of their enemies and competitors but also of themselves. Some notable advances in information gathering include the sultan of Syria's messenger pigeons, Genghis Khan's horse-bound (and pigeon-based) communication networks, and Abraham Lincoln's Balloon Corps. Performance measurement became performance management when these leaders used their information-gathering tools also as information-dispersion tools.

With the advent of the information age in the 1960s and 1970s, decision-support systems were developed for business leaders. These systems required manual entry of business unit performance statistics that were then summarized for executives; spreadsheet macros were some of the later implementations of these. Then, in the late 1980s and 1990s, executive information systems (EISs) were deployed. These applied some of the lessons learned from custom and ad hoc reports and spreadsheet macros to more customized applications, first as mainframe-generated green screens and dot-matrix reports, then as client server applications with graphical user interfaces (GUIs). However, some problems with many EIS systems caused performance management to fall out of favor. Sure, performance reports continued to evolve, but real-time metric updates in GUIs (e.g., dashboards) hit a wall. EIS dashboard projects tended to follow old-school development methodologies that spit out results 6 to 12 months after executive requirements were written. For example, rather than releasing some subset of functionality using an iterative development methodology, end users would have to wait longer for all functionality, while the project used a "waterfall" development methodology. By the time the EIS systems were completed, market forces had caused executives to look at other key performance indicators (KPIs) in the business. Not only did resulting EISs not meet final needs (though they sometimes met initial requirements), but they were very difficult to modify. In short, "most of these implementations were technical successes, but business failures" [1].

As EIS experiences mounted, a small movement started to look at how the performance of an enterprise could be measured flexibly in real time. From the demand side, enterprise resource planning (ERP) systems have pushed executives toward a technical business mindset, and regulatory compliance has pushed operational reporting to new levels of scrutiny. From the supply side, EIS-like technology and performance measurement frameworks have evolved dramatically [2]. Eventually labeled enterprise performance management (EPM), this concept was expanded by H. Spangenberg in 1994 beyond just performance management to include performance planning, performance control, and performance rewarding [3]. At about this same time, "scorecarding," a name for enterprise-level metric tracking, evolved, and Robert Kaplan's Balanced Scorecard became the most popular method. It wasn't until after the 3 to 4 year technology slump at the turn of the millennium that we started to see new definitions for performance management. In 2003, the Gartner Corporation referred to it as corporate performance management (CPM). Gartner claimed that CPM was "an umbrella term describing the methodologies, metrics, processes and systems used to monitor and manage an enterprise's business performance" [4]. Then, in 2006, the Cognos Corporation provided a more technology-based view that enterprise performance management referred to the integration and automation of:

- Scorecarding;
- Business intelligence (BI), or decision support, including financial reporting and consolidation;
- Planning.

Eventually, International Data Corporation referred to EPM as business performance management (BPM) [2]. While Cognos focuses primarily on BI integration, Gartner doesn't. Instead, Gartner believes that several "systems" are needed to support performance management. Gartner also expands Spangenberg and Cognos's "planning" into methodologies and processes, as shown in Figure 4.1.

To better understand Gartner's process-centric approach to performance management, let's look at Figure 4.2, which illustrates how enterprise performance management is influenced top-down by the corporate strategy (Figure 4.2, no. 1) and bottom-up through the analysis of current processes (Figure 4.2, no. 2). Bottom-up business process analysis (BPA) is based on analysis-results-action, where actions can take the form of new projects (Figure 4.2, no. 3). Gartner argues that not only do the analysis-results-actions affect business processes, but that they ultimately also affect the corporate strategy (i.e., bottom-up strategic design). However, as Figure 4.2, no. 4 illustrates, defining objectives and their associated metrics from the strategy is outside Gartner's definition of performance management. EPM "as a concept does not provide the goals and the metrics" [3]. What is included in performance management, however, is the information technology (IT) architecture necessary to manage all the reporting data generated by processes and projects. Such data management and data "warehousing," in turn, needs to be supported by data analytics engines and reporting systems (Figure 4.2, no. 5). Before going into the details of the system side of performance management, let's dig deeper into its foundation: performance measurement frameworks.

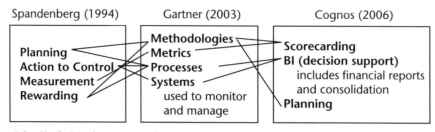

**Figure 4.1**  Similarities between performance management frameworks.

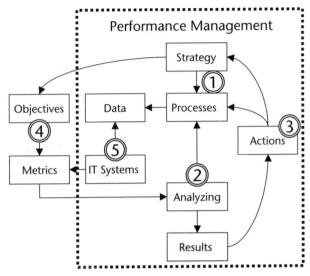

**Figure 4.2** Gartner's view of enterprise performance management.

## Performance Measurement Frameworks

Performance measurement has been around since the industrial age in the form of financial measurement. It wasn't until the mid-1980s that academics and consultants started hearing executives complain that financial metrics didn't provide the complete picture on their companies. As a result, several approaches started to get published in the late 1980s and early 1990s to provide executives with a more balanced view of their organizations (see Figure 4.3).

Among the first to tackle this problem were D. Scott Sink and T. C. Tuttle in 1985 and 1989 [5, 6]. Their model "claim[ed] that performance of an organizational system is a complex interrelationship between the following seven performance criteria" [6]:

1. *Effectiveness:* This refers to actual output versus expected output.
2. *Efficiency:* This refers to expected resource consumption versus actual resource consumption.

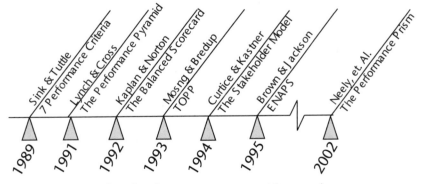

**Figure 4.3** Summary timeline of performance measurement frameworks.

3. *Quality:* This refers to very subjective measurements that can be made at six checkpoints: upstream systems, inputs, value-adding processes, outputs, downstream systems, and the quality management process.
4. *Productivity:* This refers to output versus input.
5. *Quality of work life:* This is measured via surveys of employees.
6. *Innovation:* This refers to patent counts, project proposal numbers, process improvement numbers, and so forth.
7. Profitability/budgetability: This refers to revenues, earnings before interest and taxes, and budget process duration.

Sink and Tuttle also urged companies to address the following four performance-based tasks:

1. Performance improvement planning;
2. Performance measurement and evaluation;
3. Performance improvement and control;
4. Cultural support systems.

Of the seven criteria, only one is directly associated with finances. This was the earliest attempt to show how to use multiple dimensions to frame the metrics chosen. Sink and Tuttle then went on to explain that measurement is only one of four tasks that should be completed to manage a company's performance. Besides planning and improvement, they looked at the need to address organizational change and cultural support issues, an approach rarely found in performance measurement frameworks. After Sink and Tuttle released their two books, others began to enhance their ground-breaking efforts. Figure 4.3 presents the timeline of some of these evolutionary approaches to performance measurement frameworks.

### Balance

In 1991, R. L. Lynch and K. F. Cross introduced a way to measure performance using a hierarchical paradigm. They used a pyramid to represent the concept of when and where it would be best to extract certain performance measures (Figure 4.4). While executives outlined their objectives through the development of a strategy, the resulting measures that tracked those objectives cycled (and were summarized) back upwards to the executives. As those objectives were applied more deeply in the organization, the metrics chosen applied to different parts of the Performance Pyramid framework. For example, metrics used to measure quality, delivery, cycle time, and waste tended to be used more at the departmental level, and metrics used to measure market shifts and financial returns tended to be used more at the business's executive level [7].

Kaplan and Norton then introduced the Balanced Scorecard in their famous *Harvard Business Review* article of the same name in 1992. Their approach simplified the frameworks of past attempts by categorizing performance measures into one of four perspectives: financial, internal business processes, customers, and innovation and learning. Within each of these perspectives, goals (or objectives) would

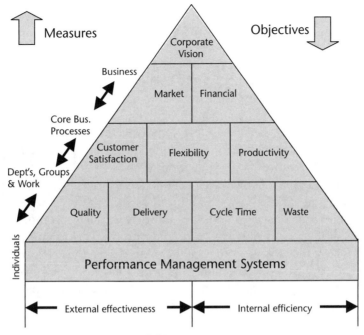

**Figure 4.4** Performance Pyramid. (*After* [7].)

need to be set and tied to the corporate strategy. Then the metrics that were to be used to measure progress toward those goals would be defined (see Figure 4.5).

The Balanced Scorecard tried to elevate nonfinancial metrics up from the operational level and into the executive suites. As companies grow, cultures get watered

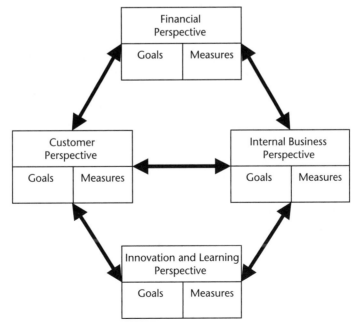

**Figure 4.5** Balanced scorecard (*After* [8].)

down, siloed units evolve, and unaligned IT chaos spreads; looking only at financial metrics is akin to a lifeguard's wearing horse blinders. The Performance Pyramid addressed this, but it wasn't until the advent of Balanced Scorecard that accountability for balance was escalated to the executive level.

Many companies don't want to balance; they just want the money. For smaller companies that need the cash flow from sales to survive, such sentiments can be understandable. But as companies grow and gain access to alternating sources of cash flow, balance becomes more important for long-term growth and survival. However, "identifying, quantifying and monitoring balanced measures is easier said than done. It requires an organization to get very sober about assessing its performance beyond the income statement and stock price. It requires the organization to look long and hard at how it does business and the outcomes it needs to produce to sustain growth consistent with the culture it wants to promote" [9]. Do executives want a prioritized balance as promoted by the Performance Pyramid (explained later) Or are they focused on the stakeholders, as in the Performance Prism? Do they prefer an industry-specific model as with Quint Studer's model (also, explained later) Or do they prefer a custom approach as countless companies and governments have implemented? Choosing the right measurement framework to start a performance management initiative should accommodate both best practices and the company's culture.

With smaller companies, the culture of balance can shift vertically in the organizational chart. According to Schachar Feldman, vice president of professional services at NICE Systems, performance metrics tend to become more balanced the further down in the organization one goes. At his company, executives focus primarily on financial metrics. In contrast, a more balanced view is used at the divisional level. For example, besides following profit and loss (P&L) KPIs, Feldman also looks at other process-centric metrics (Figure 4.6, feed 4), such as the number of training sessions given (employee growth), utilization rates, travel times (business processes), and the number of cases opened (customer satisfaction). Based on the driving forces of pre–level 4 companies (e.g., financial return and market differentiation) such as NICE Systems, the Performance Pyramid may be an easier cultural fit if balanced measurements are desired.

At smaller companies, strategic metric balancing will tend to be more uneven, and strategic metric automation will tend to be less available. This isn't to say that operational performance management is lacking, however. The operations department at nLight Corporation, the Vancouver, Washington–based maker of laser components, which is responsible for such divisions as manufacturing, IT, and facilities, monitors a rather robust set of metrics. Database analysts assigned to this department pull the data from different systems and present it in a reporting services application. The majority of the metrics are operational and strive to present a balanced view of the organization. Such metrics are reviewed weekly by operations management and then quarterly by the nLight executive team, various managers, and other key contributors. The few financial metrics that result from this process (the prime metric being cash flow) are reviewed monthly with the executive team. So, instead of a real-time dashboard that executives can access anytime, nLight depends on the reporting services application for its performance management processes. This can be sufficient for smaller companies since the paths of communica-

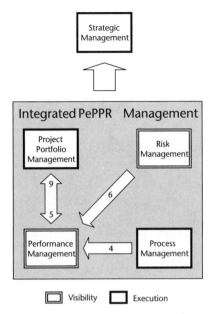

**Figure 4.6** Performance-based integrated PePPR.

tion are fewer. But as companies grow past a Flamholtz and Randle level 3 maturity, and the need to consolidate many operational metrics into a few strategic metrics reaches critical mass, performance reporting automation becomes more valuable. Otherwise, a small army of staff will develop that focuses primarily on developing manual reports for executives.

## Processes

In 1992 and 1993, SINTEF, Scandinavia's largest independent research organization at the time, partnered with the Norwegian Institute of Technology, the Norwegian Federation of Engineering Industries (TBL), and 56 participating enterprises to develop TOPP. This consortium created another framework by focusing on three dimensions that crossed the four perspectives of the Balanced Scorecard. TOPP designers felt that corporate performance is a function of how effectively and efficiently the company meets its goals and how flexible it is to changing market demands (Figure 4.7).

With TOPP, you would try to improve the effectiveness of the four Balanced Scorecard perspectives by first looking at business processes. Figure 4.8 shows how TOPP framed a base set of "primary" processes, a second set of "support" processes, and a third set of "development" processes. The creators of TOPP felt that their three dimensions of performance could then be best applied to this process framework.

The next year, SINAF, the originator of TOPP, cooperated with four other research partners (CIMRU, BIBA, GRAI, and TUE) to work with five industrial partners (TBL, AMT, Volkswagen, AUGRAI, and ITC) in Norway, Ireland, Germany, France, and the Netherlands, respectively. They created a new model that evolved partly from TOPP called the European Network for Advanced Performance

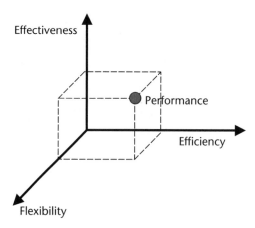

Figure 4.7   TOPP performance dimensions.

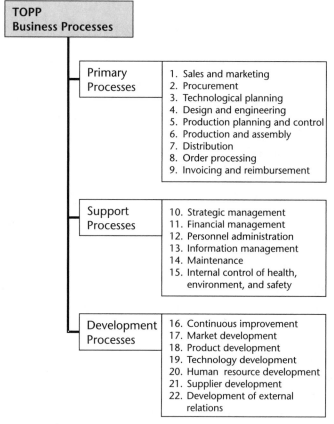

Figure 4.8   TOPP process hierarchy. (*After* [10].)

Studies (ENAPS) model. While ENAPS continues to evolve, it originally came up with 117 generic performance measures. These measures give an overview of the size and financial position of an enterprise. The "Process Level" performance indicators are used to determine the performance of the processes defined in the ENAPS framework. This process framework separates processes into two categories: business processes and secondary processes (Figure 4.9).

TOPP and ENAPS attempted to provide more specifics on how to measure performance. This approach follows a trend found in how U.S.-based and European-based modeling differ. The Project Management Institute's project management body of knowledge (PMBOK) (U.S.-based) versus the Office of Government Commerce's Prince2 (British-based) in project management methodologies, and the United States' Sarbanes-Oxley versus Europe's Basel II in operational risk regulations, are examples of where the U.S. models were written vaguely so as to allow implementation to be customized to a wide range of industries. The European models (ENAPS, Prince2, and Basel II) were all written with much more detail and with a focus on implementation speed. That is, less customization would be required before the framework could be applied. See Chapters 6 and 7 for more on these models.

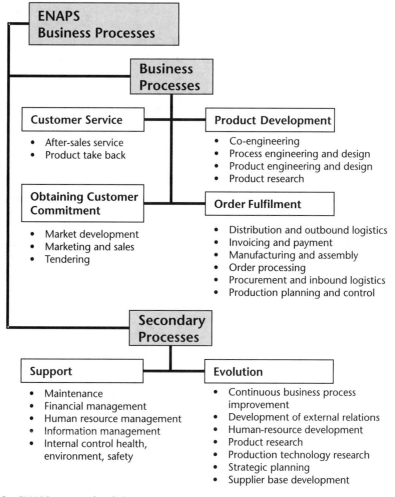

**Figure 4.9** ENAPS process-level view.

## Stakeholders

A couple of models were introduced that looked at performance measurement from a stakeholder's perspective. This perspective claimed that a company should architect its performance improvement approach based on the perceptions of its suppliers, customers, employees, management, and owners. For example, if customers feel a company is performing poorly, they will go elsewhere; if employees are disgruntled, they may leave; if suppliers are unsatisfied with pricing, they may forsake quality; and if management and owners are uncomfortable, realignments and turnarounds can occur. The first of these models was introduced by R. M. Curtice and G. T. Kastner in 1994 shortly after the advent of the Balanced Scorecard and TOPP. The second was introduced more recently as the Performance Prism by A. Neely, C. Adams, and M. Kennerley (Figure 4.10). They felt that by looking at metrics through stakeholder touch points, performance accountability could be better traced to its roots [11].

## Custom Integration: A Case Study

Porter General is a 369-bed tertiary care hospital in Denver, Colorado. It supports a wide array of services, such as open-heart surgery, pancreas transplants, joint-revision replacement, subspecialty retina surgery, and gastrointestinal surgery. This wide range of offerings causes the chief medical officer, Dr. Diane McCallister, to juggle the conflicting objectives of different "customer" groups.

### Performance and Strategy

All "customers" are ultimately interested in patient care, but they also have secondary goals that can conflict with the each other. When such customer groups are brought together to define the strategic direction of the hospital, disagreement is common. For example, while administrative staff is interested in business sustenance and growth, doctors are interested in best-of-breed tools. While medical support staff is interested in avoiding understaffing and burnout, patients are interested in uninterrupted attention. To help develop a common ground, McCallister turned to a performance measurement framework developed by the guru of healthcare strategy, Quint Studer. In his model, each department should develop substrategies

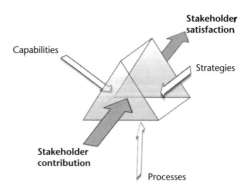

**Figure 4.10**  Performance Prism.

around five pillars, which McCallister customized to her organization by adding a sixth pillar (see Figure 4.11). After prioritizing the pillars from left to right, metrics were then linked to each of them. In this way, McCallister was able to quantify and balance the application of resources to each customer set. This, in turn, allowed executives to more clearly communicate the strategy as one that respected the needs of all parties (i.e., conflict was reduced).

### Performance, Risk, and Strategy

When creating performance measurement metrics, Porter focuses initially on the first two pillars (quality and service) and afterwards on financial metrics. This is in contrast to a typical for-profit company, which almost always puts financial metrics first on the priority list. Porter, as a not-for-profit (NFP) organization, believes that if the first two pillars are successful, good financial health will follow. For example, by tracking and reporting on a NFP regulation of providing free community services, Porter feels it can attract the kind of employees it wants. Moreover, it believes that contributing a certain number of defibrillators to the community or providing a certain amount of charity care per year are examples of metrics that will improve its reputation (and thus business) with the community. In fact, Porter contributes and provides up to four times the requirements as a way to proactively prepare itself for unexpected regulatory scrutiny (strategic risk management), but also because it is also just sound business. By focusing so heavily on performance metric improvement, the hospital has positioned itself to be more adaptive to the risks of a regulatory environment.

### Performance Metric Validation

One particular difficulty Porter is having in developing representative performance metrics is in proving the validity of the metrics to medical staff. Holding administra-

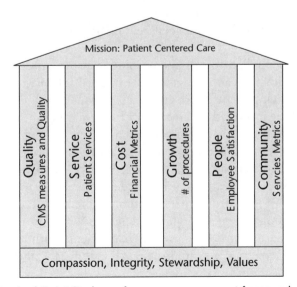

**Figure 4.11**  Customized Quint Studer performance measurement framework.

tive staff accountable to metric thresholds is one thing, but holding doctors to similar metrics is another. For example, the care of a patient can't occur until a doctor orders it; yet, it is the hospital that is measured for performance. McCallister is well aware that Porter will only be able to hold doctors accountable to performance goals by appealing to their respect for evidence-based medicine. This approach to driving performance metrics also works well for achieving regulatory compliance among the doctors. Because research tends to outpace the physicians' ability to keep up with it, the hospital acts as a prime source of summarized information. If Porter administrators can prove how regulations are based on valid research, the doctors will enthusiastically step in line. The data that results from this research not only improves the visibility of internal risks but also feeds such productivity metrics as patient turnover rates and cost-of-safety programs. In summary, for metrics to be embraced by a scrupulous organization, the metrics must be vigorously and publicly validated.

## Performance Metric Improvement and Risk Mitigation

Another set of customers that Porter must cater to are what McCallister refers to as regulatory customers. Since the hospital is constantly at risk of violating such regulations as those set by the Centers for Medicare and Medicaid Services, the Health Insurance Portability and Accountability Act (HIPAA), and the Joint Commission on the Accreditation of Healthcare Organizations (JCAHO), there is an incessant drive for a culture of risk mitigation. Therefore, as the strategy was developed and all associated processes were redesigned around the performance measurement framework, risk mitigation approaches were tightly integrated. One common requirement of many of the regulations is to provide strict reports on how well the hospital adheres to safety and handles documents. After assessing its ability to meet these requirements, the staff realized that it had been conducting risk reporting and performance management manually. This, in turn, led to a drive to implement a computerized information system (CIS). This CIS would allow the hospital to better track risks and performance metrics associated not only with regulatory compliance, safety data, and document management but also with quality of patient care.

The CIS would also help the hospital improve productivity by linking business processes with clinical processes. For example, if consistent processes were applied to heart attack patients, both costs and patient health would be improved. In this case, if a patient entered the emergency room in acute cardiac arrest, he or she would have a much better chance of survival and going home early if within 90 minutes both an aspirin (1) and a beta-blocker (2) were prescribed and the patient was sent for cardiac catheterization (3). All three metrics would be tracked to ensure patient survival (4) and reduce patient bedtime (5). Metrics 1 to 3 would track the clinical process of curing a cardiac arrest victim, and metrics 4 and 5 would track the business process of patient throughput. The CIS would produce metric reports, dashboard summaries, or both, showing that patient death risks were being reduced as cardiac arrest metrics were improving, all within McCallister's custom performance measurement framework.

## Automated Enterprise Performance Management

As mentioned, performance management provides a framework not only for information acquisition but also for business improvement (or optimization). One model that addresses both sides of this EPM coin was introduced by Rolstadas Asbjorn [12]. He proposed that for EPM to be effective, both a framework and a unique IT systems architecture must be in place. For example, if a business has established a scenario modeling framework, it also needs systems to implement the scenarios. However, in order for such system-level activities to be effective, company data needs to be gathered and analyzed. More specifically, Greg Taylor [13] claims that the basic components of an EPM system should include "reporting and analysis, reference data, source systems, and applications, all linked via an information hub or data warehouse" [13].

Most of the time, when implementing a new IT system, companies find that such systems can't run independently. These systems need data fed into them, data retrieved from them, external monitors to track their performance, and support systems to keep them running. Considering the data input/output (or flow), systems rely on more than just humans; they rely on other systems. For example, if a salesman needs resources to make a sale, he or she will enter forecast information into a sales force automation (SFA) system. Once a sale is made, this SFA system will trigger a receipt in an ERP system and a customer detail record in a customer resource management (CRM) system. Such triggers can be either by (1) database entries or (2) interprocess communications (see Figure 4.12).

To help automate performance management processes through process-based triggers, a technology called enterprise application integration (EAI) systems hit the market in the mid-1990s. Then, as EAI systems evolved, EAI vendors introduced the ability to control these process triggers with business rules. This led to the industry

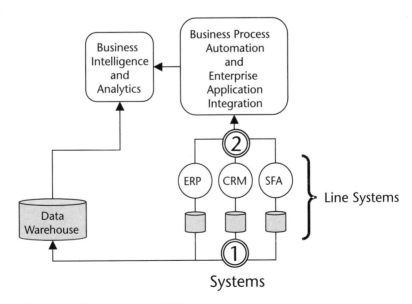

**Figure 4.12** Integrating systems and EPM.

standard term *business process automation*, or BPA. The system-specific databases and trigger information from EAI systems both feed another type of system spawned in the mid-1990s called a data warehouse (DW). By unloading information into a DW, IT organizations were able to maintain their line systems without compromising their performance due to report generation and data analysis. Also, metrics could now be centralized to help with performance reporting.

## Data Warehouses

While the siloing of business units can make enterprisewide business process engineering difficult, separate IT systems can make interdivisional data integration just as tricky. Such fragmentation of company data in turn makes consolidated performance reports less reliable. That is, since integrating system data across business units to generate a report is time-consuming, and since executive needs shift frequently, it is difficult for executive-level reports to keep up with demand. DWs eliminate a level of complexity by moving the job of system integration from the individual reports to the databases. Now select data is pulled from business unit databases and stored in a central database, the data warehouse. It is from this consolidated system that enterprise-level reports can run.

## Analytics and Business Intelligence

Centralizing data from disparate systems isn't as easy as it looks, especially if data quality is lacking in divisional systems. As a result, programs tend to be written that check and clean data before it is allowed into the DW. According to Tony Politano, author of "Chief Performance Officer," deciding what not to consolidate is just as important as deciding what to consolidate. These processes of cleansing, integrating, reconciling, and filtering data should all be done while keeping the unexpected needs of the executives in mind. The art of DW management comes into play when initially designing the data model to most efficiently accommodate all future (and unknown) needs. In essence, complete, core-level designs of performance management systems may end up going through the same (i.e., redundant) exercise that risk managers go through when conducting scenario and options analysis of future possibilities.

This process of designing the DW to accommodate future system installations is a small part of the data-analysis equation. The bulk of activity comes when the stored data is presented in a format that better accommodates the varying scenarios and options of risk analysis. Rather than listing all customer orders for a month, averages and trends are presented by geography. Then, if forecasts and recommendations are calculated from historical data, the company is leveraging an advanced form of analytics known as business intelligence. According to Amazon chief executive officer (CEO) Jeff Bezos, decisions made based on such data analysis "are the best kinds of decisions. They're fact-based decisions" [14].

Harrah's casinos refers to a successful BI implementation as "closed loop." For example, it found through data analysis that its customers prefer certain rewards programs over others. After making changes and comparing before-and-after data, Harrah's was able to map revenue to BI output. Such successful mapping required meticulous monitoring of how projects, processes, and their associated metrics were delivered. That is, by first applying analytics to project and process metrics, Harrah's was able to indirectly close the loop by linking these metrics to the bottom line [15].

### Latency

Another way to understand the need for IT systems to support EPM is to first understand the effects of information latency on business performance. Besides data quality, the effectiveness of decisions Amazon and Harrah's make based on BI are dependent upon anther variable: time. Once a business event occurs, the value-add of reacting to that event decreases over time. Therefore, it would be in a business's best interest to reduce the time between business events and decisions made about them, even if the decision results in not taking any action. This is the premise behind Richard Hackathorn's analysis of business efficiency [16]. He has postulated that this time gap is made up of three components: data latency, analysis latency, and decision latency (Figure 4.13).

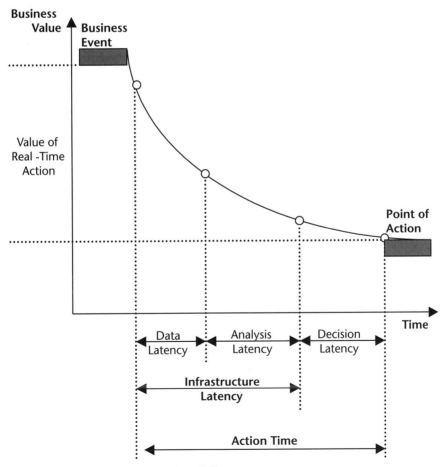

**Figure 4.13**   Value of reducing action time [16].

- *Data latency:* As fast as computers may be, the process of extracting, cleansing, consolidating, and analyzing data from many independent databases is measured in hours. Since this feeding process into DWs takes so long and can slow down operational systems, the process is usually done in batches during off hours (i.e., at night and on weekends). This means that if a business event occurred at 8 a.m., systems-provided data wouldn't be available to decision makers until the next morning (e.g., for 24 hours). While DW tuning can reduce such delays, a quicker (but incomplete) source of information can come from the EAI system. That is, the strengths of both data sources can be leveraged by generating reports that depend on the integration of EAI and DW systems. For example, customer order rates can be fed by an EAI system, while the order demographics can be fed by the DW.

- *Analysis latency:* In the early days of EIS, data analysis was "hard coded" to the needs of the executives. Latency came into play when those needs shifted frequently and executives had to wait for manually "tuned" reports to be delivered. To allow for more flexible and responsive data analysis, standard middleware languages and complex analytic packages have been developed to improve data-analysis options. This new technology allows for raw operational data that is stored in a DW to be quickly formatted and filtered with equations, graphs, and charts.

- *Decision latency:* Once analyzed data (now called "information") is presented to a decision maker, decisions should be made. This is where automation becomes less integral to timeliness. Nonetheless, there is a new type of software called business activity monitoring (BAM) that aims at reducing decision latency. By linking pager alarms, on-screen stoplight indicators, and trigger-forwards (automated delegation of standard-operating-procedure alerts) to business events through analytics, executives can automate their decisions. The thresholds for contacting them have been programmed, the criteria for grading a metric as critical have been set, and intersystem notifications have been predetermined.

## Real-Time Performance Tracking

### Automation/Technology

Automating business processes can be a tricky business. Most executives have the battle scars from failed IT initiatives that promised such things as paperless offices and instant communications with any employee. In this section, we will introduce a type of automation that, while many have failed to implement it successfully, some have demonstrated clear value-add. DW, EAI, BPA, and BAM are all categories of systems that can improve a company's performance management. DWs and their associated reports cause a company to spend its time looking backward at past performance. EAI, BPA, and BAM help reduce how far back the company looks, thus reducing data latency and improving reaction times.

### EAI and BPA

EAI provides a platform that translates, coordinates, and tracks messages between different business systems. Message translation is necessary because when companies merge or when managers don't align their technical purchases, companies tend to acquire systems that just can't talk to each other. Message coordination helps improve the speed and timing of message delivery between systems. Message tracking acts as another source of information that can help with business analytics and system tuning. Figure 4.14 shows three example systems that EAI can support: an enterprise resource planning (ERP) system, a customer resource management (CRM) system and a sales force automation (SFA) system. Each of these has an operational data store (a database) that feeds a data warehouse in batches during off hours. During business hours, these systems need to communicate with each other. For example, when a salesman makes a sale, he needs to update his SFA system with the status of the lead. As a result, a message with customer information is sent to the CRM system via the EAI "highway." Also, a message with purchase order information is sent to the ERP system. This allows managers to see customer growth by demographics (e.g., campaign results through the CRM system) and by revenue (through the ERP system) within seconds of a salesman's entering the information. The only data latency in this case is the time it takes the salesman to enter the sale.

Figure 4.14 also shows how translators (T) are added to each system during EAI installation (1). These translators convert the messages sent by the systems into a common language (2). With the BPA tool feeding process information to the EAI system (3), EAI can manage multiple process stage or gates. For example, the EAI system can hold on sending sales information to the ERP system until the CRM system confirms that the customer data has been accepted for that sale. Also, for reconciliation purposes, timers can be put into place to alert IT of a failure after a set amount of time if the CRM system doesn't respond. Thus, the EAI system can manage the order and timing of message delivery according to workflow definitions

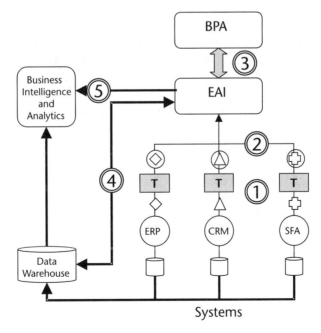

**Figure 4.14**   EAI and BPA integration.

passed to it by the BPA tool. Not only can the EAI system spit out rapid reports or display real-time activity in a GUI (such GUIs are also known as dashboards and digital scorecards), but it can also access the DW to show real-time forecast-to-reality reports (4). Finally, since EAI is aware of the timing of all automated business activity, such information can be fed to the BI or analytics engine to support reports (5).

### BAM

The acronyms we've presented in this chapter so far have been created by research companies to more easily group vendor technology offerings. For example, Gartner has BAM, BPM, and EAI vendor reports that position competing vendors into a "Magic Quadrant" graphic. Such graphics allow potential buyers of technologies in these areas to compare the relative strengths of the competing vendors. While such scoring is subjective, it helps buyers shorten their request-for-proposals process by creating a "short list" more quickly. Things can get tricky when innovative vendors take different approaches to solving similar problems. BAM, for example, is a newer acronym coined by Gartner to explain one of the ways EPM can be applied. While EPM covers all the processes, systems, metrics, and methodologies needed to manage the overall performance of a company, BAM refers to a way to use systems to get metric results to reviewers quickly.

According to Nesamoney Diaz, BAM is "a process by which key operational business events are monitored for changes or trends indicating opportunities or problems" [17]. Such a system bridges business events to the opportunities and threats analysis typical of strategic design sessions. That is, BAM incorporates some of the analytics capabilities of a business intelligence system. "Pure-play" BAM tends to be very real-time by eliminating access to the DW and embedding rules and summarized historical data directly among all the business events. Examples of such events could be retail radio-frequency identification (RFID) scans (as pioneered by Wal-Mart) and casinos' RFID-based chip trackers. To design a complete BAM solution, a company needs to ensure that their entire systems architecture is focused on intersystem communication. Figures 4.14 and 4.15(a) show how an EAI system adds translators (T) to each IT system so that messages are speaking the same language as they pass over the network. With BAM, all system components speak the same language [i.e., no translators are needed, as in Figure 4.15(b)]. While Wal-Mart can pick and choose its vendors based on RFID compliance, companies can choose their IT systems based on another BAM-supporting standard called Service Oriented Architecture (SOA). A system that supports SOA will allow IT staff to configure outgoing messages to speak a company-defined language understood by other systems. This in turn reduces the need for an EAI system.

### EPM and Processes

Figure 4.12 showed what F. Melchert, M. Klesse, and R. Winter refer to as "execution with BI," one of three legs that EPM aims to support [3]. The other two legs, strategy formulation and process design, are shown in Figure 4.16. We'll link EPM to strategy in the following section on scorecards, so let's look at the EPM process

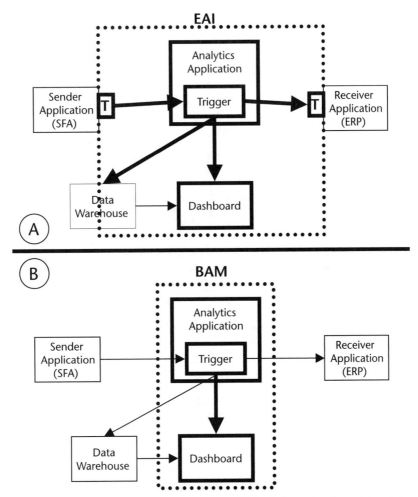

**Figure 4.15** While enterprise application integration (EAI) platforms implement translators to allow disparate applications to communicate (a) business activity monitoring (BAM) platforms leverage common application architectures to avoid the need for translators (b).

link. There are two components to process design: business process modeling and process performance management. The former provides a way to document business processes, and the latter acts as a feedback loop to improve processes. BPM is supported by a suite of technologies and methodologies that help businesses more efficiently abstract, or model, their processes or work flows. PPM takes data from BI systems and compares to-be processes with as-is processes to better understand how new implementations will affect the organization. Basically, PPM can be seen as a type of simulation activity. Combined, this process design leg is primarily influenced by the enterprise strategy (referred to here as top-down strategic design). However, process design is also influenced to a lesser degree by how the company is currently executing. Such execution tends to have a momentum behind it that ultimately influences how the enterprise strategy is formed (referred to here as bottom-up strategic design).

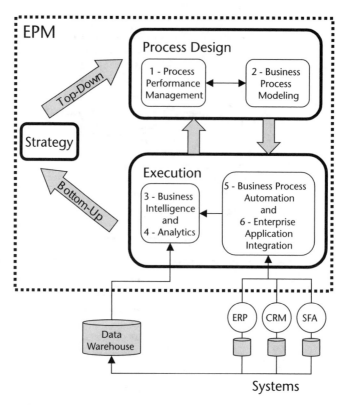

**Figure 4.16** Detailed view of the three legs of enterprise performance management and the six subcategories of IT that support these legs.

The six subcomponents that make up EPM as shown in Figure 4.16 also map to trends in IT products. Such trends, in turn, will end up simplifying a company's efforts to integrate strategic systems, strategic designs, and strategic business processes [3]. Figure 4.16 also shows the relationships with strategy formulation: enterprise strategies influence process designs, and BI execution influences enterprise strategies.

## Enterprise Performance Management Control

### Scorecards and Dashboards

Business process analysis (BPA) is a way to generate information, the data warehouse (DW)is a way to gather information, enterprise application integration (EAI) and business activity monitoring (BAM) are ways to pass and track information, and business intelligence (BI) is a way to analyze information. Now let's go over how to best present information to support enterprise performance management. Responding to the dissatisfaction of users tired of "hunting and gathering" for information in BI systems, IT departments started implementing dashboards or strategic scorecards [18]. The major advances from newer dashboard or scorecard systems were their flexibility, their integration with DWs, and their integration with EAI systems. Though this introduces integration issues such as preventing "dueling data," it also allows dashboards or scorecards to "predict rather than just report on status"

[19]. Both dashboards and strategic scorecards tend to display and update real-time KPIs on a screen; however, they have different historical roots.

- *Dashboards* tended to be associated with detailed operational data such as plant performance, store inventory levels, or fleet usage numbers. These systems were referred to as performance measurement systems. They tended to result from strategic drives to either reduce costs or improve process performance (e.g., through Six Sigma, TQM tools, or statistical process control [SPC] methods). In short, dashboards were used to help management *do things right*.
- *Strategic scorecards*, on the other hand, supplied highly summarized data for executives. Strategic scorecards were born as EIS displays and then became more sophisticated as new models were introduced. With a more strategic focus, strategic scorecards helped executives direct managers to *do the right things*. In the last few years, however, the recent rise of SOAs, EAIs, and BI has led to a merging of these two concepts. "The new mantra for performance management reflects the best of both worlds—*doing the right things right*" [20]. While dashboards focused more on performance measurement, strategic scorecards became known as "performance management systems" [20].

The lowest level dashboard that serves the needs of the line employee "should be limited to the two to five things an employee has control over in their job that they can readily calibrate to enhance their performance" [9]. Then, as these dashboards summarize themselves up to the executive-level scorecard, the final KPIs will be linked to controllable, lower-level values. Again, we see the checks-and-balances benefits of a combined bottom-up and top-down approach to EPM.

## Customized versus Noncustomized Scorecards

There have been two major pushes in the implementation of strategic scorecards: customized and noncustomized. At Verizon, for example, Chief Information Officer Chaygan Kheradpir broadcasts a set of KPIs to hundreds of PCs around the organization. His team worked with businesses to come up with a set of standard metrics (also referred to as KPIs) and then displayed each grouping of the KPIs in 15 second increments [14]. This is an example of a strategic scorecard that is not customized to the needs of particular business units. In contrast to this, Booz Allen Hamilton developed a "performance scorecard strategy" for an investment bank's IT organization [19]. This strategy designed different strategic scorecard presentations for different audiences. The infrastructure, customer service, and applications groups each had a display that showed KPIs relevant to their particular operations. Pinnacol Assurance of Denver, Colorado, also developed custom strategic scorecards for each of its business units. In this case, the dashboards were customized to each of the profit-center business units. Depending on the technical budget, the business needs, and the maturity or complexity of the organization, some combination of custom and standard dashboards can be deployed.

Both custom and noncustom solutions have their benefits and drawbacks. Custom solutions cater to the specific needs of different viewers but also support further divergence, or siloing, of the business away from a common set of goals. However, as long as a subset of metrics common across the dashboards is used, such siloing can be controlled. There are other challenges to offering custom solutions: they require a lot of work (1) to document and support the KPIs needed to satisfy all the custom interfaces and (2) to integrate and summarize KPIs for an executive-level scorecard. In such a scenario, different levels of scorecards would need to be reviewed periodically for relevancy. If changes needed to be made on either side, integration efforts to link the two systems should be timely. According to Software Spectrum's director of business process and loyalty, Roy Chavez, information integration is the toughest part going forward with a dashboard system [21].

### Scorecards and the Project Portfolio Management Office

When implementing a performance management architecture, most companies just have employees fill in spreadsheet dashboards with metrics, by hand. As the audience for these dashboards progresses up the food chain, the dashboards get more summarized. So far, we've shown how complex it can get if a company tries to automate such a labor-intensive task. This complexity goes down, however, if a strict architectural alignment review is enforced for all new technical purchases for IT-based projects. For example, if a company wants to implement BAM, it can require all new systems to adhere to an SOA. This can be done by ensuring that the project portfolio management office (PMO) approves those projects that are aligned with an architecture that supports performance management.

Typically, executives will want to monitor the health of projects that require a relatively large capital expenditure and put the company's survival at greater risk compared to other financed projects. Such monitoring tends to occur in parallel to their stream of corporate performance reports. For example, at a major U.S. electrical utility, any project that costs over $20 million requires sign off from the CEO and will receive special attention in the form of project performance metrics that are passed up for periodic executive review. A PMO can consolidate the risk, cost, and health of smaller projects and present the status as a portfolio-level report to executives. But why should all of this be separate from a central strategic scorecard? Consolidation of project portfolio status with process performance metrics (Figure 4.6, feed 5) allows executives to see everything at once.

### Key Performance Indicators

### Strategic KPIs

Before any strategic scorecard or dashboard is created, a sound business strategy and architecture should be developed. Then, "dashboards and scorecards [can] translate the organization's strategy into objectives, metrics, initiatives and tasks" [21]. Too often, IT departments have worked with business units to develop KPIs that don't show information critical to moving the company in the desired direction. In the case of the EIS systems of the early 1990s, there was a KPI implementation latency and inflexibility; not only did chosen KPIs represent the needs of the business from six months before, but they couldn't be changed easily in resulting strategic scorecards. The result was that either managers falsely believed they knew what was going on in their units, or they just ignored their fancy EIS systems and had staff update and cross-check metrics by hand. With today's performance management systems, KPI metric criteria can be easily updated to reflect changing strategies. Such flexibility of performance management systems puts the ball back in the executive court. Executives are now more visibly accountable to keep the strategy and project portfolio aligned with their market demands. This approach of building the dashboards after first aligning the business's process and project portfolios is critical. Then, once dashboards are in place, metric changes shouldn't be made without first understanding the effects on business processes. Usually, a formal project would need to be implemented to realize a metric change or addition to the scorecard. Booz Allen Hamilton takes this to heart by making sure that a change in dashboard needs doesn't change business processes [19]. But if a project is launched to accommodate new metrics, there can be some collateral effects on processes once the project (or metric change) is delivered. With a strategy in place, the initiators of such projects can prove to a PMO (before project financing) that affected processes will maintain their alignment.

When a large local government I worked for implemented its performance management system, it created graphical information system (GIS)-based reports to satisfy ad hoc requests from its mayor's office. Hundreds of specialized maps were created that showed everything from how many wing nuts were collected to how many city vehicles broke down. Most of these layered map reports led to no action because no one knew what to do with this information. That is, dashboard reports were created before a strategy was developed. Just as critically, these reports were generated with no thought given to how they would be actionable, or how the data would be used to improve city processes.

If a sound business strategy and process architecture is maintained, the metrics displayed in a dashboard or scorecard should be chosen based on "actionability." When choosing a metric, or KPI, the business unit should ask two questions:

1. How will that measure be used to keep performance within a given range?
2. If the KPI is out of range, what actions should be taken to get it back in acceptable range? [22]

While asking these questions to come up with KPIs, the performance management team should also make sure the business units aren't threatened by the adoption of new metrics. A plan should be developed to educate the users of dashboards on the benefits new metrics present to them and to the company [21]. Such an education plan will help set buy-in of metrics, but how does a company ensure staff is reporting accurately and consistently on these ever-changing numbers?

## Operational Metrics

We have referred to key performance indicators as a type of summary metric that should be included in strategic scorecards. Operational dashboards, on the other hand, tend to present more detailed indicators that aren't "key" to executives' understanding the general state of the company. Such nonkey indicators can be referred to simply as metrics. Metrics that do not allow for actionable responses or are strategically irrelevant; they "are a waste of time and money, and shouldn't have a home on your [executive-level] dashboard" [22]. However, many KPIs depend on an integration of metrics that are ineffective by themselves. It can be difficult to integrate disparate metrics to produce a good KPI that is key to successful metric design [1]. Lower-level metrics, or nonkey performance indicators, may be invaluable to lower-level managers, but once fed into a BI system, they can be combined through the analytics process to create metrics more relevant at the strategic level [3]. Figure 4.17 shows that when metrics are created, the current and anticipated needs of the executives (through strategic KPIs) and the customers (through service level agreements) should be considered. Designing actionable metrics for one stakeholder at the expense of another can lead to unnecessary process redesigns. Unfortunately, operational metrics may already exist that were created to support the performance goals of individual managers rather than the goals of the corporation. For this latter reason, it can be difficult to properly align operational metrics.

### Key Performance Indicators and Key Risk Indicators

Project metrics can compliment process metrics to provide a clear, balanced view of the activities down through the company. Another checks and balances can occur horizontally as well as vertically by including risks in the strategic scorecard as key risk indicators (KRIs). At a major electrical utility, executives look at certain critical metrics with the KPIs being earnings per share, power plant availability, customer satisfaction, and power outage duration; the key risk indicator is employee injury rates. Individually, each of the 12 executive decision makers is also responsible for other specialized metrics. Porter General Hospital is another organization that provides KRIs to its executives to compliment its performance indicators. Besides monitoring for fatalities or injuries like a utility does, Porter also includes the frequency of health record access, security violations, and postadmittance staph infections. To

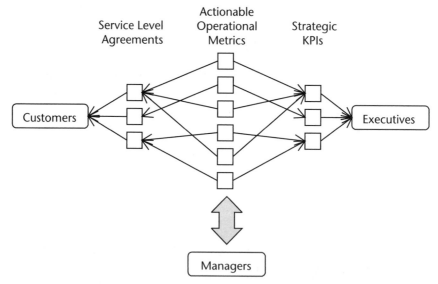

**Figure 4.17** Operational metrics are created to support customers, operational managers, and strategic KPIs. Unfortunately, these metrics tend to focus on manager support to the detriment of customers and executives.

provide well-balanced communications on the state of the organization, risk metrics should be included with performance metrics. If such integration doesn't exist, then performance reporting systems "will in the best case provide only limited value and in the worse case can misguide the organization's control efforts, possibly even obscuring more important strategically defined risks" [23].

KRIs tend to be measured with a different frequency than KPIs, however. For example, because forecasted risks change less frequently than daily operations, Porter Hospital updates its risk metrics monthly but monitors its performance metrics weekly. PePPR feed 6 (see Figure 4.6) is a critical component of performance measurement in that it provides the checks and balances that can help pull executives away from performance metric group-think.

### Industry-Specific KPIs

The source and definition of some KPIs should stay constant to show trends, but others should flex to most accurately represent the company. Since such constant updating will no doubt put added pressure on IT, "automated, process-oriented analytics will become increasingly necessary to keep up with metrics and KPIs" [18]. At Harrah's casinos, the IT department solves the problem of out-of-date metrics by providing management with a large number of metrics. Management can then mix and match these metrics to fit its goals. The key to this is in training the managers how to use the ad hoc (or custom) reporting tools. By passing some of the responsibility for metric management to the end users (management), IT can spend more time on developing KPI reports for Harrah's executives. Examples of such KPIs include the amount of game play at every location, food-and-beverage sales, "total rewards" metrics, and retail statistics. Once problems are identified from these KPIs, resources can be assigned to create more detailed metric reports or to implement any needed marketing, staffing, or operational changes. The detailed metric reports can drill into such measures as "slot and table play, player behavior, hotel occupancy, marketing and promotional campaigns, restaurants, events, and retail sales" [15]. Some examples of other industry-specific KPIs include:

- *Pharmaceutical/health sciences:*
  - Clinical performance measurement;
  - Health demographic trends;
  - Product portfolio management;
- *Financial services:*
  - Mortgage banking metrics;
  - Insurance risk claims reporting;
  - Operational risk mitigation (e.g., Basel II);
- *Manufacturing:*
  - Supply chain planning;
  - Process performance reporting (e.g., SPC Six Sigma);
  - Equipment lifetime analysis;

- *Retail:*
  - Retail operational performance management;
  - Vendor performance management;
  - Inventory statistics;
- *Public sector:*
  - Police arrest and corrections metrics;
  - School regulatory act compliance rates;
  - Citizen complaint levels [2].

## Extended EPM

As the leaders and generals of history gauged the performance of their allies, as well as of their own armies, so business leaders today monitor their extended organization, including distributors and suppliers. EPM can go beyond just measuring and controlling the single company; it can look at the entire supply chain as one virtual enterprise. Two major components of EPM have two contrasting approaches when looking at enterprises in this way. While control of intercompany processes is usually done through negotiation and relationship building, performance measurement is done more through continuous sharing of information. When companies breakdown communication walls, build trust, and integrate systems, they provide for ongoing and accurate intercompany reports. In fact, some feel that one of the biggest challenges to successful EPM implementation is providing easy access to other companies' data sources. At Nestle Waters, for example, cross-company EPM is implemented through a robust reporting architecture (Table 4.1). Here we see reports generated by both the business units and the distributors on a monthly, quarterly, and annual basis. Such communications help both sides improve their performance in serving each other. "Nestle Waters producers and distributors are forced to think strategically in terms of joint profitability as equal partners belonging to the same global organization" [24].

## Summary

Performance management, in its most basic form, has a long history. However, in the last couple of decades, two performance measurement steamrollers (performance measurement frameworks and event- or data-tracking software) have col-

**Table 4.1**    Nestle Waters Intercompany Report Architecture

|           | Distributors → Business Units | Business Units → Distributors |
|-----------|-------------------------------|-------------------------------|
| Monthly   | Actual sales statistics, specific comments on trends regarding international brands | General global comments on sales performance of international brands, specific comments on international brands |
| Quarterly | P&L outlook by brand | End-to-end P&L by brand and market |
| Annually  | Actual P&L by format and brand, monthly sales budget by format, P&L budget by brand and format | Actual end-to-end P&L by brand, format, and market |

*Source:* [24]

lided to create the elusive enterprise performance management speed car desired by many organizations. We started by combining several definitions of EPM to understand that it involves planning, measurement (metrics), processes, systems, and reporting (e.g., score-carding and dashboards). We then looked to a long string of performance measurement frameworks that have tried to guide companies in how to best plan, measure, and report on performance. In short, a company shouldn't be pigeonholed into adopting all components of a single model. Rather, a performance measurement approach should draw strengths from different models that best fit the company's maturity, industry, and strategy and that allow for the adaptability necessary in today's dynamic market spaces. From balanced versus process-based versus stakeholder-based versus custom frameworks, we went to data warehouses, business activity management, and enterprise activity integration. The framework options provided the foundation for technical and nontechnical process and project tracking; the technical options provided the foundation for quick and accurate results. It is then up to executive support, management tenacity, and staff excitement to make sure that the metrics reported are accurate, actionable, and aligned with customer and executive needs. With frameworks and support driven from the top, technology and hard work delivered from the middle, and accuracy and enthusiasm provided from the bottom, clear corporate performance visibility can result.

# References

[1] Politano, Tony, "Chief Performance Officer," Business Intelligence, http://businessintelligence.com/ex/asp/id.5/page.1/xe/biextractdetail.htm (last accessed on February 17, 2006).

[2] "The Evolution of the CPM System," Cognos Corporation, 2006, www.cognos.com/pdfs/whitepapers/evolution_of_cpm_system.pdf (last accessed on June 2, 2007).

[3] Melchert, F., M. Klesse, and R. Winter, "Aligning Process Automation and Business Intelligence to Support Corporate Performance Management," Proc. 10th Americans Conference on Information Systems, New York, August 1, 2004, www.unisg.ch/org/iwi/iwi_pub.nsf/ wwwPublAuthorGer/ 6233B5B0A53A2580C12570 C400647676/$file/2004%20-%20Melchert,%20Winter,%20Klesse%20-%20Aligning %20Process%20Automation%20and%20Business%20Intelligence%20to%20support %20CPM.pdf (last accessed on February 17, 2006).

[4] Leahy, Tad, "The Business Performance Management Commitment," *Business Finance Magazine*, January 1, 2003, www.businessfinancemag.com/magazine/archives/article.html?articleID=13931 (last accessed on February 17, 2006).

[5] Sink, D. S., *Productivity Management: Planning, Measurement and Evaluation, Control, and Improvement*, New York, NY, Wiley, 1985.

[6] Sink, D. S., and T. C. Tuttle, *Planning and Measurement in Your Organization of the Future*, Norcross, GA, Industrial Engineering and Management Press, 1989.

[7] Lynch, R. L., and K. F. Cross, *Measure Up! Yardsticks for Continuous Improvements*, Cambridge, MA: Blackwell, 1991.

[8] Kaplan, Robert S., and David P. Norton, "The Balanced Scorecard: Measures That Drive Performance," *Harvard Business Review*, 1992.

[9] Wood, Michael R., "BPI and Scorecards: Perfect Partners," Gantthead.com, February 14, 2006, www.gantthead.com/articles/articlesPrint.cfm?ID=229791 (last accessed on February 17, 2006).

[10]  Mosng, B., and H. Bredrup, "A Methodology for Industrial Studies of Productivity Perfor-
       mance," *Production Planning and Control*, Vol. 4, No. 3, 1993, pp. 198–206.

[11]  Neely, A., C. Adams, and M. Kennerley, "The Performance Prism: The Scorecard for Mea-
       suring and Managing Business Success," London: Financial Times–Prentice Hall, 2002.

[12]  Rolstadas, Asbjorn, "Enterprise Performance Measurement," *International Journal of
       Operations and Production Management*, Vol. 18, No. 9/10, 1998, pp. 989–999.

[13]  Taylor, Greg, "The Value of Enterprise Performance Management," DMReview.com,
       May   1,   2005,   www.dmreview.com/editorial/dmreview/print_action.cfm?articleId=
       1026062 (last accessed on February 17, 2006).

[14]  Davenport, Thomas, "Competing on Analytics," *Optimize*, February 1, 2006, pp. 41–46.

[15]  Stanley, Tim, "High Stakes Analytics," *Optimize*, February 1, 2006, pp. 28–37.

[16]  Hackathorn, Richard, "Minimizing Action Distance," *Data Administration Newsletter*,
       February 1, 2004, www.tdan.com/i025fe04.htm (last accessed on March 29, 2006).

[17]  Nesamoney, Diaz, "BAM: Event-Driven Business Intelligence for the Real-Time Enter-
       prise," DMReview.com, March 1, 2004, www.dmreview.com/editorial/dmreview/
       print_action.cfm?articleId=8177 (last accessed on February 17, 2006).

[18]  Schwartz, Susana, "Google's Foray into Web Analytics: Does Low Cost Mean Low End?"
       *Intelligent Enterprise*, Vol. 9, No. 2, February 1, 2006, p. 15.

[19]  Tillman, G., D. Prosko, and K. DeNatale, "IT Performance Scorecards," Booz Allen
       Hamilton, November 2004, www2.cio.com/consultant/report3072.html (last accessed on
       February 17, 2006).

[20]  Bauer, Kent, "The Power of Metrics: The CPM Dashboard: The Profile," DMReview.com,
       March   1,   2004,   www.dmreview.com/article_sub.cfm?articleId=8192   (last accessed on
       February 17, 2006).

[21]  Eckerson, Wayne W., "See It Coming," *Intelligent Enterprise*, Vol. 9, No. 2, February 1,
       2006, pp. 25–29.

[22]  Schiff, Craig, "Maximize Business Performance: Industry Dashboards to the Rescue,"
       DMReview.com, August 1, 2004, www.dmreview.com/editorial/dmreview/ print_ action.
       cfm?articleId=1007643 (last accessed on February 17, 2006).

[23]  Lawrie, G. J. G., D. C. Kaiff, and H. V. Andersen, "Integrating Risk Management with
       Existing Methods of Strategic Control: Avoiding Duplication within the Corporate Gover-
       nance Agenda," 2GC Limited, August 1, 2003, www.2gc.co.uk/pdf/2GC-CP0803.pdf (last
       accessed on April 15, 2006).

[24]  Busco, C. et al., "Integrating Global Organizations Through Performance Measurement
       Systems," *Strategic Finance*, January 1, 2006, http://www.allbusiness.cond/buying-exit-
       ing-businesses/mergers-acquisitions/872975-1.html (last accessed on February 17, 2006).

## CHAPTER 5

# Process Management

In the previous chapters, we showed how, during strategy development, frameworks and models can be used to get a better handle on dynamic internal and external environments. To mitigate risks and improve performance, investments can be made that follow the chosen framework. In this chapter, we will look at enterprise-level frameworks that not only aim to improve individual operational subprocesses but also hope to improve the combined portfolio of enterprise-level processes so that the organization marches forward, in step and in alignment.

Unfortunately, many implementations of these frameworks are applied locally for the benefit of one division at the expense of another division or even the whole enterprise. Departments may find better ways to manufacture products, market services, or collect receivables, but for a company to improve its capabilities across departments, it needs an enterprise approach. Before looking at these frameworks, we will look first at what processes are and then how PePPR management helps avoid a siloed framework implementation.

## Business Processes

Adam Smith documented the idea of a business process as early as 1776 with his famous pin factory in *The Wealth of Nations*. Over a century later, Frederick Winslow Taylor applied such scientific principles as measurement and controls to processes [1]. Eventually, more in-depth statistical analysis was applied, and the concept of quality control was embraced in the 1920s and 1930s. Frank Gilbreth introduced process charting in 1921 [2], Walter Shewhart expanded this with Shewhart charting in the late 1920s [3], Allan H. Mogensen began training business people in the concepts of industrial engineering in the early 1930s [4], and then Edward Deming developed quality control frameworks for the Japanese in the 1950s. The birth and evolution of business process identification, analysis, and improvement were long processes until the introduction of information technology (IT) in the 1980s and 1990s. At that point, business process analysis took on additional importance in companies.

Many felt that IT would automate processes, thus reducing the need for process analysis. In fact, while much automation did occur, processes didn't necessarily disappear; they just got more complex. Problems really started to pop up when legacy systems and humans were unable or unwilling to change. The result was a booming set of industry specialties called organizational change, process reengineering, and systems integration specialists. These specialists relied heavily on their ability to sniff out and document "as-is" and "to-be" processes from the ground up proactively, before IT projects even started. They would then develop rollout plans and training bridges that would help organizations with their process and systems transitions.

But, before going on, what precisely do we mean by a business process? Alec Sharp and Patrick McDermott, authors of *Workflow Modeling*, define a process as "an event at one end, and at the other, the result and the customer expecting it" [5]. That is, after some initiating activity, multiple activities occur to ultimately produce a measurable output for a receiving entity, such as another process or resource (Figure 5.1). A process or capability, however, is nothing more than a thought if it isn't designed, understood, executed, supported, and measured. A machine operator may have a unique way to create a part that wasn't documented, but she thought it out in her head (designed the process), made sure the process was acceptable to her manager (support), established proper safety procedures (rules and regulations), implemented the process, ensured that all the components for the process were there (supported the process), and then confirmed that her approach was better or worse than others (measured the process). These six steps, referred to by Sharp as enablers, are critical to helping a process achieve its intended results (see Figure 5.1).

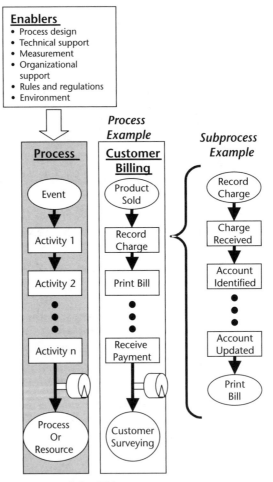

**Figure 5.1**  Process components. (*After* [5].)

A first step to making sure a process is mapped to measurable goals is to identify the process as a single, overarching activity. The alternative would be to have amorphous process definitions, such as "customer service," "supply chain management," or "product development." Better definitions would be "manage customer feedback," "transport raw materials to warehouses," and "design new products." While each of these could be processes that support the operations of one division, they could also support multiple divisions. Figure 5.1 illustrates how such scaling could work by embedding division-specific processes within enterprise-level processes. Sharp and McDermott refer to these as subprocesses, and they are the usual focus for workflow analysis and quality improvement efforts.

As was alluded to in the last chapter, many, if not most, end-to-end processes involve some technical components or IT systems. Either the process itself leverages or will leverage technology, or technology is used to help transition a process from one design to another. In fact Sharp and McDermott go so far as to say that "processes and information systems are inseparable" in corporate enterprises [5]. Since such systems were created to automate, or report on processes, it has become apparent that to successfully implement systems, a company should first identify and organize its processes. As more and more processes were automated with IT systems implementations, the complexity of business operations also increased. Transactions occurred much faster, activities became hidden in computer software and communication paths became less hierarchical. At about the time that the market for process analysis experts was growing, Michael Hammer published *Business Process Reengineering* (1993). He felt that too many companies were automating processes not because it would improve the efficiency of the enterprise but because it would improve the efficiency of some small set of activities. This was in tune with Michael Porter's declaration that companies silo too heavily into functions rather than focus on the cross-functional value chains that efficiently serve the customer [6].

Business process reengineering (BPR) required that companies remove those processes that didn't add value—that more than likely cropped up as a result of some siloed IT initiative—and strengthen those large cross-functional processes that supported the value chain. This is all fine and dandy until you start cutting perceived systems inefficiencies and laying people off. Chainsaw Al Dunlap was famous for this at Sunbeam, Lily, and Scott [7]. After some BPR debacles that resulted from an underemphasis on the human element, a stream of process and workflow analysis books entered the market with the hope of clearing up any confusion about how to properly identify and document processes. BPR was ultimately criticized by its own inventor [8] because it focused too heavily on the mechanisms of process to the detriment of human variability. Besides refocusing on human interactions, there was a push to separate actual activities from potential technical solutions. For example, Sharp and McDermott claim that when first identifying a business process, it is important to document the core activities, independently of technology. This helps avoid the problem of zeroing in on technology replacement at the expense of process improvement. We will show some methods in the next section that try to take a more well-rounded approach to identifying processes so that the problems associated with narrow-focused execution can be avoided.

## Strategic Activity Processes

Some of the more famous enterprisewide process improvement efforts involve quality frameworks such as Six Sigma and Kaizen. Nonetheless, there are several other efforts common across organizations that don't get the same headlines. The classic model of the 1980s and 1990s was Michael Porter's Value Chain, which framed a corporate strategy around its process portfolio. Then, as the IT revolution built momentum and corporate scandals ballooned in the late 1990s, more corporate processes were affected by risk, performance, and project portfolio initiatives that supported Porter's entire value chain model.

### Value Chain Processes

In 1979, Michael Porter introduced a model that allowed a company to frame its external environment around five "forces." These forces were grouped into threats of (1) substitute products, (2) established rivals, and (3) new entrants and into the bargaining powers of (4) suppliers and (5) customers. Porter's Five Forces model is a tool to use when researching the attractiveness of an industry or market. But this externally facing model isn't as valuable to the study of process management as is his internally facing value chain model. In this latter approach to strategic design, Porter claims that the elements of competitive advantage are the complete set of processes that make up a business. He devised a way to categorize these processes into two groups: primary processes and support processes. Table 5.1 lists some examples of these processes, and Figure 5.2 lays the processes out in Porter's value chain format.

When a company measures these two process groups and compares the results with those of other companies, an understanding of the firm's capabilities (or competencies) results [4]. Such a view not only helps clear up the dynamics, or activities of the company, but also how different parts of the company interact. Value chain analysis will help identify whether units are too decoupled to the detriment of product success, strategic achievement, or risk mitigation. For example, to better identify and classify the capabilities of the U.S. Federal Bureau of Investigation (FBI), the bureau's leadership created a value chain analysis. This helped it better understand

**Table 5.1**  Value Chain Processes

| *Primary Processes* | *Secondary Processes* |
|---|---|
| *Inbound logistics:* the receiving, warehousing and internal distribution of raw materials | *Firm infrastructure:* organizational structure, control systems, company culture, and so forth |
| *Operations:* the processes of transforming inputs into finished products and services | *Human resource management:* employee recruiting, hiring, training, development, and compensation |
| *Outbound logistics:* the warehousing and external distribution of finished goods | *Technology development:* technologies to support value-creating activities |
| *Marketing and sales:* the identification of customer needs and the generation of sales | *Procurement:* the purchase of inputs such as materials, supplies, and equipment |
| *Service:* the support of customers after the products and services are sold to them | |
| *Source:* [9]. | |

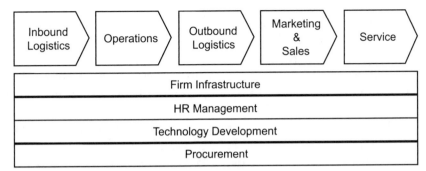

**Figure 5.2**  Value chain analysis. (*After* [6].)

the links between its core processes (law enforcement and counterterrorism) and its supporting and noncore processes (see Figure 5.3).

We should be careful here, however, in assuming that the value chain diagram represents a strategic process map. It is a common mistake for companies with the foresight to develop such a map to attempt to improve the functional areas of the value chain to the detriment of the whole. The value chain approach is a framework to help identify the components of your organization that are strong or weak and how those components support the overall, or cross-functional, goals of the com-

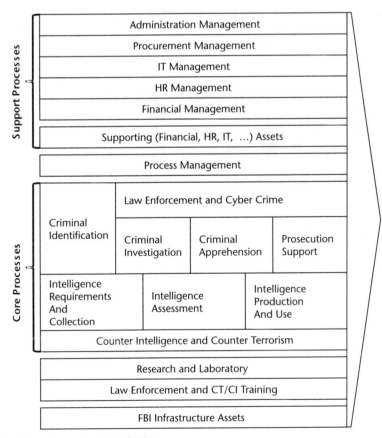

**Figure 5.3**   FBI value chain. (*After* [10].)

pany. When prioritizing process improvement initiatives in your project portfolios, the higher ratings should go to those that focus on collaborating interfunctional processes for the benefit of the customer. "A value chain is all the processes, taken together, that deliver value and pleasure to customers and assure that they will come back for more. To focus on anything less is to risk achieving efficiency at the expense of overall effectiveness" [11].

When the value chain of an organization is extended beyond its boundaries to include such external entities as its customers, suppliers, regulatory agencies, business partners, and trade groups, Porter refers to this as a value system or a cross-enterprise value chain (Figure 5.4). This approach helps extend the value chain method of strategic analysis from focusing internally to one that also considers external forces. In today's world of partnerships, consortiums, and alliances, a firm's value chain can be heavily influenced by another firm's values. This can be seen in the rapid rise in the importance and increased number of software solutions developed for supply chain management.

Figure 5.5 splits a value system into a demand chain and a supply chain. Here, the customer is the source of value, and value flows from the customer in the form of demand and to the supplier in the form of cash flow [12]. In the opposite direction, we have the typical flow of a Porter's value system: from supplier to customer. "In common parlance, a supply chain and a value chain [system] are complementary views of an extended enterprise with integrated business processes enabling the flows of products and services" [13]. So, value can be thought to flow in both directions, "with suppliers accruing value from the financial resources, payment terms, stability, and future order cover that their customers provide, while customers derive value from the delivered products and services" [13].

Michael Porter split processes into core and support in 1980 (through value chain analysis), and Michael Hammer split processes into necessary and expendable in the 1990s (through business process reengineering). In general, Porter focused on identifying and developing value-adding processes, while Hammer focused on iden-

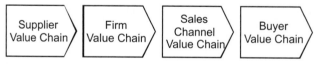

**Figure 5.4**  Value chain system analysis.

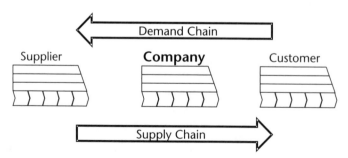

**Figure 5.5**  Value chains.

tifying and eliminating non-value-adding processes. Both approaches strived to reduce the risks associated with a poor process portfolio and to improve corporate performance. Integrated PePPR management helps ensure that continuous consideration of all activity dimensions are made when developing and executing a strategy. The value chain and BPR approaches are just two of the many frameworks that help highlight the need for an integrated, rather than a siloed, framework set.

### Risk-Based Processes

In project management verbiage, risks are undesirable events that could occur with some probability and issues are undesirable events that have occurred with complete certainty. Companies that strive to minimize the occurrence of issues do so by mitigating risks. One central area in which risks sprout is the organization's process portfolio (see Figure 5.6). Oftentimes, a major part of this portfolio can be changed to support some organized, enterprisewide risk mitigation activity. Examples include purchasing another company to avoid problems in a current industry, instituting policies to comply with new regulations, and expanding security procedures to cover increased information security threats. Of these three, only regulatory compliance is mandatory. In the following examples, one company created two separate organizations to handle the extreme number of process risks it faced, another created layers of backup processes just to mitigate risks, and two companies integrated project portfolio processes with risk management processes.

At the major electric utility we referenced earlier, regulatory-based processes became so critical that a separate internal organization was created. Before the late 1990s, regulators controlled the prices, return on investment (ROI), and risks of utilities. Then, according to David Shimko, president of Risk Capital Management in New York, "with deregulation, everyone got excited about lower prices and fancy contracting services, but they didn't realize that they also needed to manage risks in a completely new way. The industry became awash with people needing help managing risks without implicit governmental support" [14]. Since this company is a strongly regulated utility, it established both a regulatory department and a risk management office. The regulatory lead is an senior vice-president–level manager who reports to the utility system president. This organization, in turn, monitors and reports on how the company's processes mitigate compliance-based risks.

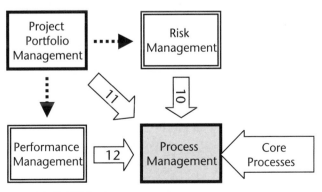

**Figure 5.6** Processscentric PePPR feeds.

The risk management office, on the other hand, monitors issues related to market risk, safety, and equipment lifetime. This is not unusual in this industry because, according to a survey by the Conference Board of Canada, Tillinghast Towers Perrin, and the University of Georgia, 40% of America's chief risk officers work for utilities and energy companies [14].

A primary operational risk at nLight Corporation, on the other hand, is with safety and environmental regulations at both the state and federal levels. Employees at nLight work in a high-hazard environment where toxic chemicals such as arsine and phosphine are used. As a result, simply documenting processes isn't enough; the company has to strive for perfect execution while also developing backup processes to ensure safety and environmental compliance. For example, its gas tanks are stored in secondary containers and monitored for leak detection to allow for immediate triggering of audible alarms and shutdown of gas lines. These complex, automated processes in turn have manual backup processes in place to guarantee compliance. In this case, the company has implemented a system of tracking, stocking, and maintaining personal protective equipment, including eyewear, gas masks, heavy aprons, and gloves. Also, nLight has a comprehensive emergency response team process to address promptly and thoroughly any incidents that may arise to mitigate their severity. Many layered processes have to be established and tested that could ultimately lead to expensive production shutdowns and evacuation of the fabrication plant. The culture of risk mitigation at nLight can be seen in these layered approaches. Besides being subjected to a regular stream of inspections by government regulators, nLight goes beyond basic regulations to avoid risk realization by formalizing and testing its processes. Put another way, through the implementation of operational process controls (standards, frameworks, accountabilities, audits), it has achieved better risk control.

At Porter General, since regulatory compliance is such a critical part of doing business, risk reviews are a required part of the hospital's change-control process. That is, all process changes and project proposals are subjected to a formal risk analysis. Porter, then, has effectively integrated project portfolio prioritization with risk management as a standard process. Finally, Western Gas Resources, a full-stream solutions company recently purchased by Anadarko Petroleum Company, started to appreciate the risks that emanated from the federal government after regulators shut down its entire Wyoming operations for two months. Eventually, according to former vice president of engineering David Keanini, the company realized that it was subject to particularly harsh scrutiny due to its focus on drilling in the Rocky Mountains. As a result, it created a government-affairs group, which included increased lobbying efforts at the state and federal levels and reviewed all new proposed initiatives for regulatory risk before they were financed. While it streamlined or eliminated many groups within Western after the purchase, Anadarko actually added to and enhanced this government-affairs/lobbying group after learning more about the regulatory issues. This expanded project portfolio review process linked strategic risk management directly to strategic goal implementation. Like the public utility company we referenced, an internal organization was created just to manage the new processes realized from a risk mitigation initiative.

At our electric utility, nLight, Porter General, and Western, comprehensive risk management strategies propagated through the value chain to ensure the satisfaction of a non-revenue-generating customer: the government. Ultimately, with such processes and structures integrated into their cultures, these organizations had positioned themselves to proactively mitigate nonregulatory risks as well.

## Performance-Based Processes

In addition to risk-initiated process creation, there is performance-initiated process creation. With the exploding capabilities in performance measurement provided by ever-improving technology, business intelligence (BI) projects are becoming commonplace. In a few years, the buzzword may change, but the concept of consolidating, refining, and aligning performance metrics will continue. As a result, new ways of doing business (new processes) will develop to more efficiently support the new technologies and the constant need to measure a company's performance. At the turn of the millennium, McKesson Pharmaceutical, a $71 billion business unit of the San Francisco–based McKesson Corporation, "began an extensive business-intelligence implementation. Executive management had identified opportunities where BI could provide gains in productivity, close off profit leaks, and improve business processes" [15]. This resulted in over 30 process-based analytic solutions that focused on "several critical areas: finance/profitability; sales and marketing; procurement; customer and supplier contract management; and distribution-center operations" [15]. In this example, a company leveraged a need for improved performance management as a reason to undergo a major business process reengineering (an old buzzword but an ongoing practice). This activity ultimately provided an opportunity for improved alignment through a strategy- to-performance-to-process improvement cycle.

To help other companies that strive to achieve similar breakthroughs, M. Goold and A. Campbell created a framework for strategy formulation that merges process management with performance management [16]. The approach focuses on finding those processes that are most broken and have the greatest effect on key performance metrics, or critical success factors (CSFs). The first step is to identify these CSFs (listed horizontally in Table 5.2 as A, B, C, D, and E). Chapter 4 went into more detail on this, but the basic premise is to look at both operational process metrics and project health metrics. J. Rockart, the original author of CSFs, claims that you should have about five CSFs [17], "but most organizations have between seven and fifteen" [5]. Next, identify your key strategic processes (listed vertically in Table 5.2 as 1, 2, 3, 4, and 5). Whether you are developing a departmental or a corporate-level strategy, there shouldn't be more than about five such processes for your level. Once your CSFs and major processes are listed, build a matrix of the two that then allows you to grade the impact a process has on a CSF (e.g., 1 = little impact, 5 = high impact). Then, to prioritize which processes to fix first, assess the "brokenness" of each process. In this way, you are able to invest resources in improving those processes that appear most problematic and are most visible (through key metrics or CSFs). This in turn can act as a tool used by the project portfolio office to prioritize process improvement proposals.

As performance management becomes embedded in a culture, more processes are introduced that include all members of the company. At the electric utility, company employees are provided with opportunities to suggest improvements in the

**Table 5.2**   Strategic Analysis Using Processes, Performance Metrics, and Risk Scoring

| Processes | Brokenness | CSFs A | B | C | D | E | Score | Priority |
|-----------|-----------|--------|---|---|---|---|-------|----------|
| 1 | 2 | 3 | 2 | 5 | 3 | 4 | 34 | 2 |
| 2 | 4 | 3 | 1 | 2 | 1 | 2 | 36 | 1 |
| 3 | 3 | 4 | 1 | 3 | 3 | 1 | 36 | 1 |
| 4 | 1 | 5 | 4 | 2 | 4 | 1 | 16 | 4 |
| 5 | 2 | 5 | 1 | 1 | 1 | 3 | 22 | 3 |

way the company monitors its performance through quarterly goal-update and strategy sessions. This process allows business unit leaders to pass suggestions directly from the line up to the executive committee (Figure 5.6, feed 12). That is, the company has integrated the improvement of its performance management into its strategic analysis and design processes.

By linking strategic-level metrics to operational metrics, nLight has simplified processes that support performance management improvement. The company tracks two central metrics of customer complaint levels and income (specifically earnings before interest, tax, depreciation, and amortization (EBITDA) to help indicate if subordinate metrics are either poorly updated or metric thresholds are poorly chosen. Such layered, or prioritized, monitoring of metrics has the collateral benefit of propagating strategic key performance indicators (KPIs) down through operations. That is, lower-level metrics aren't just developed as a result of a new strategy; they are also developed to help reevaluate and define higher-level KPIs and target thresholds (sometimes referred to as critical success factors, or CSFs). This is easier to do at smaller companies with less expansive operations and, thus, a smaller jungle of detailed metrics to align.

Dr. Diane McCallister of Porter General is trying to supplement the hospital's strong risk culture with a performance-focused culture by introducing an industry standard performance measurement methodology by Quint Studer. Combined with the rollout of their computer information system to track performance and risk metrics, Porter is taking a strong top-down approach to building such an integrated culture. But this performance culture can't stop with just Porter's internal staff; it needs to propagate out to its partners to maintain Porter's complete reputation for service and compliance. Therefore, Porter General Hospital is applying process changes to support needs for risk and performance management across its value system.

## Project Portfolio–Based Processes

Several industries have managed their project portfolios like financial portfolios since the publication of Harry Markowitz's Nobel Prize–winning book on financial portfolio management. Manufacturers started in the 1950s, followed by more complex organizations, such as defense, space, and biotech companies [18]. Only recently, with the boom in IT, has the project portfolio gained new steam in the support and control of IT-based projects. Unfortunately, the processes and structures put in place by companies tend to follow a roller coaster of executive commitment.

When projects are failing, investments are made in project management offices (PMOs). After projects are doing better and PMOs have failed to benchmark, thus prove value, their financing is yanked. Only the more mature organizations—and, again, maturity is not indicative of size—have been able to institutionalize PMO processes that weather executive churn and support.

If it is decided that a process change or addition is needed, then a project is financed to implement the change or addition. One important criterion for such projects, according to Sharp and McDermott, is that they address the whole process. Sure, the project may be as simple as changing the format of your invoices in an invoicing process, but the project should review how such change may affect other areas of the process. Otherwise, problems associated with local optimization could result (i.e., the proverbial horse blinders). For example, will a new invoice format accommodate potential new account number lengths, or will billing system designs need to be changed to accommodate the new format? Will it include data customers are familiar with, or will it delay payments because of increased confusion? The initiative review process of a project portfolio office should evaluate process improvement projects for such criteria to help reduce the risk of collateral damage to other processes. Many times, before a process change idea even becomes an initiative proposal, it goes through a process change review board. I know, more bureaucracy to slow innovation. But with larger, more complex processes, such scrutiny (or risk assessment) can help avoid bigger "collateral" costs. This flow is represented as the reverse of feed 11 in Figure 5.6. The direction that feed 11 indicates is how the existence of a project portfolio effort adds to or changes the corporate process portfolio.

At the electric utility, a well-established set of processes continues to maintain a dependable project portfolio. To more easily compare and prioritize project submissions, the company requires the project sponsors to fill out a standard template if the project is to cost more than $50,000. Since the company is so big, there is no way to centrally monitor every one of these "over-fifty" projects. So, the company has local business unit personnel perform reviews of all projects and has set up a centralized planning and budgeting group to coordinate the business units in reporting on high-priority projects. All major strategic projects are periodically reviewed by the executive committee, which comprises the most senior employees, including the chief executive officer (CEO). Classic project portfolio tasks such as risk balancing, strategic alignment, return maximization, and resource balancing occur primarily upon project approval. While ongoing status reporting, ROI validation, and project support activities may occur for projects in each business unit, centralization of such PPM tasks is reserved only for the larger projects and handled by the CEO's office.

At nLight, proposed business initiatives, such as new facilities, IT projects, or product changes, use a business case template that includes key aspects of a detailed business plan. According to Steve Norgaard, vice president of operations, "We started this formal process about a year ago to avoid the mistakes we made in our first six years." The template must be used if the investment is over $5,000. If the investment is over $25,000, then the template requires more detailed ROI calculations. "While not all projects go through this quite yet (currently, 75% of investments adhere to this scrutiny), we are improving on it."

## Process Frameworks

Changing a business process in any way, including making an improvement, can grow in difficulty as the number of other processes and humans affected by the change increases. Such difficulty can explode if there is a drive to systematically alter a wide swath of processes across an enterprise. For example, when a machine operator comes up with a new and better way to machine a tool, she is improving the quality of the process. When executives feel that their methods for doing business are out of date, they may initiate a process reengineering program across the enterprise. Kaizen, Lean, and Six Sigma all provide structured ways to do this across all processes in a company. At the strategic level, executives focus on high-level, cross-organizational activities supported by many lower-level processes. Where the machine operator alters processes from the bottom up, executives can alter whole sets of processes from the top down. Unfortunately, with this latter action, executives can be unaware of the depths of complexity they are throwing their companies into.

When the machine operator makes a change, there is a sense of pride and ownership. When executives dictate change, there can be resulting organizational backlash. Change is tough when processes define technical systems, habitual behaviors, and compensation metrics. But it is less tough if a company has been conditioned to flex to changing market needs. When engaged in a major process engineering exercise, established companies will usually have to alter, or even dismantle, current processes in order for newer, innovative processes to be developed. Newer companies, on the other hand, have the less complex but equally challenging task of establishing initial processes from scratch with less room for error. David Teece refers to a company, either established or new, that is able to efficiently build, integrate, alter, and eliminate processes (at the core level or not) as highly "dynamic capable" [19]. As was shown in earlier chapters, such flexibility is needed to better mitigate the risks of market change. Here, we will review four types of process "change" frameworks: one type that is forced with new systems implementations, another that is applied enterprisewide, a third that is applied to a specific strategic process, and a fourth that is applied to a support function in the value chain.

### Systems-Based Processes

The large systems implementations of the late 1990s (e.g., customer relationship management [CRM], enterprise resource planning [ERP], sales force automation [SFA]) were well known for their disruptive force on organizations. In order for such commercial-off-the-shelf (COTS) applications to fit and be effective within an organization, business processes had to be modified. Though such three-letter-acronym, or "TLA," projects became expensive when companies were unwilling to modify their behaviors to fit the new software, the long-term effects were that companies were eventually forced to become more flexible.

Many process modeling standards can be leveraged before making process changes (for the purpose of systems implementation or not). As will also be shown, such models can be dictated by enterprise-level systems installations. Executives are well known for declaring that such systems will be implemented "out of the box" to avoid the crippling nature of customizing COTS software. To customize a COTS software package and then expect support from the vendor is akin to rebuilding a car and then calling Fiat, Honda, or General Motors to honor a warranty. According to executives, the lesser of two evils between large-scale organizational change with uncustomized systems (a stock car) versus less organizational change with highly customized changes (a rebuilt car) is the former. That is, they tend to look at the dependability of long-term systems vendor support as less costly than the effects of greater organizational change to fit the processes of the new system. This could be due to those who experienced the death spiral associated with such customization efforts in a major systems installation project. For them, process reengineering became the unspoken necessity before such projects began. But because BPR had acquired such a bad reputation, it was reborn as business process management (BPM) from its days of failure to reemerge as a necessary component of IT systems success.

Supply chain management (SCM), ERP, CRM, and SFA systems are installed with their out-of-the-box processes and workflows. The real pain with such systems installations has to do with the change not only in the sponsoring department that is initially installing the system but in all other departments that must interface with the sponsoring department. Figure 5.7 attempts to first show a high-level value chain along the bottom that flows from idea and suppliers to customers. Then, the functional silos are shown above the value chain. The graphs are meant to show that these different functional silos receive different levels of value for each "enterprise" system that is installed. Configuration management software that tracks products from design through to customer delivery and back serves the needs of the product manufacturing or engineering teams the most. ERP systems that handle all finances for all departments serve the needs of the finance division the most. Also, CRM systems that support customer inquiries and demographics serve the needs of the marketing and sales divisions the most. Nonetheless, each of these systems tends to require input from divisions that receive less value in order for the systems to be successful. Such distribution of value-add, coupled with the massive process changes, add to the challenges of enterprise system installations.

### Enterprise Quality: Kaizen and Six Sigma

In the early-1940s, a component of the U.S. War Manpower Commission established the Training within Industry (TWI) organization to help American companies maximize industrial productivity during World War II. Later, TWI was introduced to Japan by U.S. occupying forces as a tool to help rebuild Japanese industries. After executives were hired, supply chains restored, equipment purchased and installed, and employees found, the leader of this effort, Homer Sarasohn, recommended the famous quality expert Edward Deming to teach his concepts on statistical quality control (SQC). SQC brought the concept of production quality to a new level by applying a more analytical approach than was previously used. As a result, throughout the 1950s, Pareto charts, histograms, and cause-effect diagrams were introduced throughout Japan with wide success. Specifically, in 1954, with Dr. Joseph M. Juran's introduction of Total Quality Control, systematic business-level improvements could be designed. That is, process

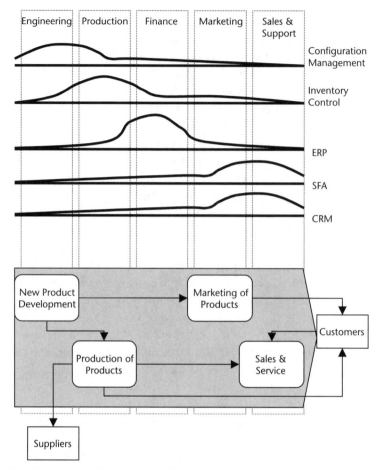

**Figure 5.7**   Relative value-add of enterprisewide process automation systems.

quality was "elevated from the factory floor to the total organization." Ultimately, the Japanese industrial machine was reborn and quickly became an economic force [3].

During this effort, Taiichi Ohno, the father of the Toyota Production System (also known as the Lean System), became a certified TWI trainer. While the Toyota Production System didn't gain steam until the 1980s and the Lean System of process improvement wasn't formalized until 1986, other methods became well known, Kaizen being one of them. Later, in parallel to Toyota's development of it production system, Six Sigma was developed throughout the 1980s and then trademarked by Motorola in 1993 [3]. Today, Kaizen, Six Sigma, and Lean are some of the more popular frameworks for process improvement to ensure high-quality production.

### Kaizen

In Japanese, *kaizen* means continuous improvement. In business, it is a framework used to improve the competitive advantage of an entire organization. According to Masaaki Imai, author of *Gemba Kaizen*, "The Japanese view of management boils down to one precept: maintain and improve standards" [20]. Within the activities associated with improvement, there is innovation and *kaizen* (Figure 5.8). Examples of some of the tools used in Kaizen include quality circles, automation, suggestion systems, just-in-time delivery, Kanban, and 5-S. The Kaizen framework acts an umbrella for these tools that can be used to improve processes at all levels of the organization.

According to Raphael L. Vitalo, PhD, Kaizen can be grouped into the following categories:

- Individual versus teamed;
- Day-to-day versus special event;
- Process level versus subprocess level [3].

Most forms of Kaizen involve teamed efforts to identify and improve problematic processes. However, Kaizen Teian, or personal *kaizen*, is the only form that relies on an individual's submitting what Masaaki Imai refers to as "proposals" (as realized more often in Japan) rather than simple suggestions (as indicative of Western organizations and as the direct translation of *teian* suggests) [21]. Also, the more common form of Kaizen is a one-off event, referred to as Gemba Kaizen. These events result from the identification of a problem and the resulting team formation to resolve it. The less common form is the quality circles approach to Kaizen that involves weekly proactive searching for problems as a team. Where Gemba is reactive, quality circles are proactive. Finally, Kaizen is mostly used to improve the quality of an organization's subprocesses. This is analogous to the systems-based process frameworks that try to improve such lower-level processes as customer bill distribution, online bill payment, and employee payroll completion. While enterprise-level processes such as cash flow tend to be at too high a level to apply such frameworks, the intent is for the accumulation of subprocess improvement to ultimately improve higher-level processes. Nonetheless, Flow Kaizen and Kaikaku Kaizen exist to "seek radical improvements at the value stream or business level" [3].

Kaizen is fairly all-encompassing. It provides processes to proactively mitigate risks through quality circles, leads to projects that resolve performance problems, and can be applied strategically across division or operationally within teams. At the strategic level, its "plan, do, change, act" (PDCA) can launch from the strategy

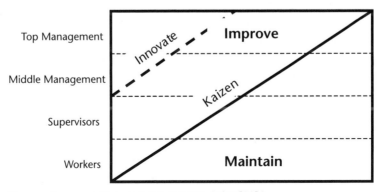

**Figure 5.8**   The one Japanese management precept. (*After* [20].)

as a project portfolio review process that aims to change the direction of a company. However, as well used as it is at the operational level, it is criticized for its lack of analytical diligence.

## Six Sigma

The Greek letter sigma is used in statistics to signify variability and can be measured as number of defects. In business, six sigma is the phrase used to represent 3.4 defects per million opportunities (DPMO). To help identify processes that produce more defects than this, the Six Sigma framework has its own philosophy: define, measure, analyze, improve, control (DMAIC). Similar to the Kaizen PDCA, Six Sigma's DMAIC places an emphasis on the analytical nature of its output. Such a statistical approach can be applied to both quantitative outputs, such as gauge and meter readings, and qualitative outputs, such as customer satisfaction surveys [22]. Combined with its hierarchical green belt/black belt certification process, Six Sigma provides just the strict controls many chaotic companies need.

A large manufacturer of building and roofing products needed such structure as it emerged from bankruptcy in the late 1990s. This organization became so adept at implementing Six Sigma that it went beyond just process improvement and found ways to integrate Six Sigma into its risk and project management cultures. To reduce project failure rate, management decided to enforce the assignment of one Six Sigma expert to any project with a capital budget greater than or equal to $1 million. The expert would ensure that where any processes were affected or created by the project, such processes would undergo a failure mode and effect analysis (FMEA). FMEA is a derivative of Six Sigma that adds structure to a risk analysis [23]. In the case of one project, the assigned Six Sigma expert would form a project subteam to review the ways affected processes could fail (failure modes) and what effect such failures would have on the project and on operations (effects) [24]. This process acted as a proactive risk analysis to help improve project success rates. Because the company has been able to leverage a sound risk management process from the Six Sigma methodology, its risk culture grows with its process improvement culture project by project.

Many organizations, however, have become quite efficient at establishing and adhering to process standards. But these same organizations tend to stifle innovation at the expense of standardization. For example, Wharton management professor Mary J. Brenner and Harvard Business School professor Michael Tushman recommend that Six Sigma process improvement initiatives be applied selectively and not completely. Within a business unit, managers should be able to "specialize in either more process-oriented functions with the benefits of Six Sigma efficiency or more innovation-oriented activities without Six Sigma constraints" [25]. They reached these conclusions through a study they conducted of both the paint and photography industries. They found that "as process management activities increased, exploitation increases at the expense of exploratory innovations" [25]. Most notably, the number of International Standards Organization (ISO) certifications a photography company had was found to be inversely proportional to the number of patents based entirely on new knowledge contributed to that same company.

Kaizen and Six Sigma are two powerful tools that have been proven to help companies of all sizes for decades. Since they have the same historical roots, they overlap each other. They diverge, however, in the set of tools each has to offer. It is up to each organization to then pick and choose tools from several such process improvement frameworks to apply to its unique environment and situation. Besides improving the performance of a company's process portfolio, these frameworks can also be used (as was shown at the building products manufacturer) to support more tightly controlled project portfolios and to further the goals of a risk management plan. In essence, process improvement frameworks act to better integrate the elements of PePPR management. But with custom selection of these frameworks should come custom application of their associated controls so as not to restrict innovation or the flexibility needed in today's enterprises. As will be shown in Chapter 7 on risk management, a risk profile should be created that is part of, or links to, the business strategy. This same philosophy can be applied to how strict process frameworks should be adhered to when applied differently across different functional areas. For example, strict ISO9000 or Six Sigma processes may be applied to the manufacturing floor, but less framework scrutiny may exist for such creative-intensive organizations as R&D and marketing (i.e., different process control profiles).

## Supply Chain Management: Global Supply Chain Forum and Supply Chain Operations References

When a consumer visits a jewelry store, he or she may notice the glass case that contains the high-margin engagement rings. Before these rings sit in their final resting place, hopefully on the ring finger of a happy bride, they will have gone through a long string of events. Miners chopped away on dirt in caves, the dirt was sifted for diamonds, the diamonds were sent to cutters, the cutters sent the diamonds for independent grading, the middlemen brokered the cut diamonds to ring makers, the ring makers sold them to retail stores, and the retail stores sold them to future grooms. This path from dirt to finger is an example of the supply chain of engagement rings. Along this chain, inventory, transportation, financing, marketing, and communications steps are taken by each of the players in this supply chain. To shorten this chain, some companies will take responsibility for two or more of the steps outlined above in the delivery of diamond rings. Therefore, the supply chain can be implemented by integrating business functions both across companies and within companies.

Supply chain process frameworks can be interesting due to their heavy reliance on relationship building. While some view supply chain management from the perspective of measurable logistical, procurement, and operational transactions, others view it as the process of building and maintaining relationships between supply chain members [26].

This is a similar concept to the value chain/system, where coordination between functions or companies, or both, was a key element of successful implementation. However, while supply and value chains can both be a part of the strategic plan, they differ as to which strategic measures they seek to improve. "While supply chains focus primarily on reducing costs and attaining operational excellence, value chains focus more on innovation in product development and marketing" [27]. Fortunately, two frameworks similar to the Value Chain method, but specific to supply chains, have been developed. The Global Supply Chain Forum (GSCF) framework is a companywide methodology that requires senior executive support, cross-departmental organizational change, and profit maximization; the Supply Chain Operations References (SCOR) framework is a logistics- and procurement-focused methodology that puts more weight on automation, transaction processing, and cost cutting. While these two frameworks have different views on how to improve supply chain processes, they cover similar ground. They each basically provide a set of process templates, explain how to execute these processes, and define control mechanisms to help monitor and improve the processes.

## GSCF

Created in 1996, the GSCF framework claims that SCM is implemented through three elements:

1. The supply chain business processes;
2. The management components (control mechanisms and execution steps);
3. The supply chain network structure (or control mechanisms).

The supply chain business processes are split into eight categories. Of these eight, GSCF puts greater importance on ensuring proper implementation of customer-facing processes. These are listed primarily as the first two in the list below, but they are also referenced in some of the other process categories.

1. *Customer relationship management:* Develops and maintains customer relationships;
2. *Customer service management:* Implements product and service agreements consistently;
3. *Demand management:* Balances customer requirements with supply chain capabilities;
4. *Order fulfillment:* Delivers to customer expectations while minimizing costs;
5. *Manufacturing flow management:* Maintains manufacturing flexibility and plant throughput;
6. *Supplier relationship management:* Develops and maintains supplier relationships;
7. *Product development and commercialization:* Develops products jointly with customers and suppliers;
8. *Returns management:* Manages returns, risks, and stage or gates.

GSCF continues with the human interaction theme by explaining that the processes listed above are implemented most effectively through persistent cross-functional teams. That is, teams that aren't just flashes in the pan but, instead, exist indefinitely can build legitimacy if there is continual executive support and if they draw from multiple divisions. This same approach will be seen in Chapter 8 when we propose how integrated PePPR management offices should be supported. Then, to ensure controlled execution, GSCF has defined nine control mechanisms. These mechanisms can in turn be categorized into "human-related" and "other" control processes.

- *Human interaction processes:*
  - Work structure;
  - Organization structure;
  - Management methods;
  - Power and leadership structure;
  - Culture and attitude;
- *Other processes:*
  - Planning and control;
  - Product flow facility structure;
  - Information flow;
  - Risk and reward structure.

## SCOR

SCOR is more of a mechanical approach. If we were to compare it to Value Chain, SCOR looks more at support processes. These are split into a smaller set of five categories that sound vaguely similar to Kaizen's PDCA and to Six Sigma's DMAIC.

1. *Plan:* This balances aggregate demand and supply to develop a course of action that best meets sourcing, production, and delivery requirements.
2. *Source:* This includes activities related to procuring goods and services to meet planned and actual demand.
3. *Make:* Here finished goods and services are developed using the procured supplies.
4. *Deliver:* This provides finished goods and services to meet planned or actual demand, typically including order management, transportation management, and distribution management.
5. *Return:* This deals with returning or receiving returned products for any reason and extends into postdelivery customer support.

Again, SCOR doesn't look at how to structure the tiger teams to help execute the framework processes like GSCF. Instead, the framework focuses on a maturity model concept so that companies can determine if they are executing effectively. These processes are then implemented in four levels of detail:

- *Level 1:* The number of supply chain metrics are known.
- *Level 2:* Planning and execution occur.
- *Level 3:* Transactional element flows are determined.
- *Level 4:* Implementation details are documented and refined.

SCOR's control mechanisms follow traditional process improvement approaches. The processes are also implemented around three components:

1. *Business process reengineering:* Perform enterprisewide "as-is" and "to-be" analysis.
2. *Benchmarking:* Determine target values.
3. *Best practices analysis:* Identify management practices and software solutions successfully implemented by other companies in similar industries.

### GSCF and SCOR Compared

Douglas M. Lambert, author of "An Evaluation of Process-Oriented Supply Chain Management Frameworks," developed a review method that rated these two frameworks around four criteria: strategic alignment/scope, intracompany connectedness, intercompany connectedness, and drivers of value creation [26]. Table 5.3 summarizes the results of his analysis.

SCOR focuses on purchasing, logistics, and manufacturing processes, while GSCF includes all functional areas. "This might make SCOR easier to implement since in many firms these activities are more likely to be somewhat integrated within the corporate structure. The trade-off is that one is attempting to manage the supply chain without critical input from marketing, finance and research and development" [26]. The point to be made here is that while both frameworks are based on the experiences of many, they each diverge sufficiently to raise the question, which one will work best for my company?

The standard answer to this question is that a company shouldn't pigeonhole itself into any single framework. As with the varying systems-based models sprinkled throughout the organization, and as with validity of applying Kaizen quality circles to administrative staff and Six Sigma certifications to manufacturing staff so a combination of frameworks should be chosen for any particular strategic process such as supply chain management. This is directly analogous to how varying degrees of PePPR management are integrated and implemented in an organization. Integrated PePPR management promotes best-of-breed frameworks that don't work in

**Table 5.3**   GSCF and SCOR Supply Chain Management Frameworks Comparison

| Framework Criteria | GSCF | SCOR |
|---|---|---|
| Strategic Alignment/ Scope | Each of the GSCF processes is linked to the corporate strategy. | SCOR processes are developed based on the operations strategy. |
| Intracompany Connectedness | This focuses on integration across all corporate platforms. | This focuses on interaction among a few key functions. |
| Intercompany Connectedness | This focuses on managing relationships in the supply chain. | This focuses on the achievement of transactional efficiency. |
| Drivers of Value Creation | GSCF links to other supply chain members through the customer-supplier relationship and process activities. It is centered on the firm's earned value analysis and profitability reports for customers and suppliers. | SCOR links to other supply chain members through the "source," "deliver," and "returns" process activities. It is centered on cost reductions and improvements in asset utilization. Managers with less efficient processes may find a bigger return from SCOR implementation. |

isolation. A risk management framework should be chosen that provides links to performance and project portfolio management. A project portfolio management framework should be chosen that integrates with performance and process improvement management. All of these should then be implemented to some degree in any organization. The industry, market, culture, and capabilities should then dictate to what relative degree each framework set should be executed.

## Information Technology: Information Technology Infrastructure Library and Control Objectives for Information and Related Technology/Val IT

The systems-based, enterprise-quality-based, and core-process based frameworks we've presented so far address the primary value chain processes. Here, we introduce a process framework type that addresses one of the support process groups of the value chain. In the IT field, several frameworks have evolved that try to guide organizations on how to provide IT-based services, implement governance, and maintain security. The Information Technology Infrastructure Library (ITIL) provides guidance to IT organizations on how to better support an enterprise. The Control Objectives for Information and Related Technology (COBIT) covers service support and delivery, but also it covers governance, introduces a maturity model, and is addressed primarily to business managers. Val IT then expands on COBIT by covering the complex issue of IT project portfolio management control. As with the quality improvement frameworks, the best implementers will mix the ideal components of each into a custom solution for different organizations. Here, we briefly review ITIL and COBIT/Val IT, then show their fit with PePPR management.

### ITIL

Developed in the late 1980s by the British Office of Government Commerce (OGC), this framework provides a structure and set of processes that address IT service management. Specifically, the core processes of ITIL are split into two publications:

- *Service support processes:* Incident management, problem management, configuration management, change management, release management, and service desk function;
- *Service delivery processes:* Capacity management, availability management, financial management for IT services, service-level management, and IT service continuity management.

Combined, both service support and delivery provide a well-rounded set of process frameworks that allow IT organizations to track best practice implementations. Without such a framework, critical activities such as configuration management or capacity management could get ignored. The result would be incompatible document types within the organization or unprepared systems overloads, respectively.

ITIL was recently upgraded to a version 3 and released in June 2007. While the process subcategories remain essentially intact, they have been reorganized into a new set of publications. Whereas before these publications were organized by IT delivery sectors, they are now organized around more of a life cycle approach. The framework reorders and updates the process templates from the earlier version to support the management of IT services within this service life cycle. While version 3 also focuses less on IT and business alignment and more on the creation of business value and ROI, it is still written primarily for IT management. Below are the five new publications:

1. *Service strategy:* Starting with the needs of internal and external customers, a strategy is developed to help identify markets. Key parts of this volume are service portfolio management and financial management.
2. *Service design:* From the strategy, processes are designed to support the proposed services. Key parts of this volume are availability management, capacity management, continuity management, and security management.
3. *Service transition:* With a design in hand, this volume explains how to build a production-level service that maintains and improves its quality. Key parts of this volume are change management, release management, configuration management, and service knowledge management.
4. *Service operation:* Once a production-level service is in place, this volume explains how to keep it running as defined in the service-level agreements. Key parts of this volume are incident management, problem management, and request fulfillment.
5. *Continual service improvement:* Here ITIL provides the tools to help apply process quality improvement concepts to the services provided. Key parts of this volume are service reporting, service measurement, and service-level management [28].

Whereas Six Sigma and Kaizen aim to identify the most critical processes across an enterprise and then meticulously improve them, ITIL zeros in on a particular subset of processes. So, if a chief information officer (CIO) were to integrate ITIL with an enterprise quality improvement framework such as Six Sigma, he or she would first frame the approach around ITIL. Then, to squeeze the last defects (i.e., defects per million opportunities, or DPMO) out of problematic processes, the CIO would leverage Six Sigma tools. ITIL provides a framework specific to IT that helps managers avoid forgetting to address all areas of IT service delivery. In its latest release, it also provides a link to process quality improvement frameworks such as Six Sigma and Kaizen in the continual service improvement publication.

## COBIT/Val IT

COBIT is an IT management framework created by the Information Systems Audit and Control Association (ISACA) and the IT Governance Institute. The first edition of COBIT was published in 1996, followed in 1998 by the second edition, the third edition in 2000, and the fourth edition in 2005 [29]. COBIT provides managers and auditors with a governance model and a set of metrics, thresholds, and processes to help maximize the benefits derived through the use of information technology. COBIT has 36 high-level processes that cover 210 control objectives categorized in four domains: planning and organization, acquisition and implementation, delivery and support (as in the earlier version of ITIL), and monitoring.

COBIT is a process-centric framework that propagates from the concept of IT governance. That is, it is the desire of COBIT to provide top-down control of processes rather than a bottom-up, or operationally derived, control. This is evident in what COBIT refers to as the IT governance focus areas. Here the framework parallels PePPR management to a great degree by integrating such strategic activity management areas as risk and performance management. The other three focus areas are strategic alignment, value delivery, and resource management.

- Strategic alignment focuses on ensuring the linkage of business and IT plans; defining, maintaining, and validating the IT value proposition; and aligning IT operations with enterprise operations.
- Value delivery is about executing the value proposition throughout the delivery cycle, ensuring that IT delivers the promised benefits against the strategy, concentrating on optimizing costs, and proving the intrinsic value of IT.
- Resource management is about the optimal investment in, and the proper management of, critical IT resources: applications, information, infrastructure, and people. Key issues relate to the optimization of knowledge and infrastructure.
- Risk management requires risk awareness by senior corporate officers, a clear understanding of the enterprise's appetite for risk and of compliance requirements, transparency about the significant risks to the enterprise, and the embedding of risk management responsibilities into the organization.
- Performance measurement tracks and monitors strategy implementation, project completion, resource usage, process performance, and service delivery, using, for example, balanced scorecards that translate strategy into action to achieve goals measurable beyond conventional accounting [30].

COBIT provides explanations of the various processes that would be needed to help a company achieve success with each of these governance focus areas. The writers of COBIT (ISACA) feel that such a structure for IT-based processes is necessary to support the quick and successful decision making required in "today's complex environments" [31]. COBIT also provides a maturity model that helps an IT organization know how well it is implementing the processes within a healthy governance framework. Figure 5.9 shows a three-dimensional space that has control (e.g., risk management), capability (e.g., strategy), and coverage (e.g., performance management) as its axes. Processes are then plotted to show the balance of maturity among all IT-based processes. This can act as a quick way to prioritize the processes that need improvement. Where Goold and Campbell's prioritization process looks primarily at the effect processes have on performance management, COBIT's prioritization process looks also at strategic alignment and risk management. Since only IT-based processes can be plotted in this model, however, ISACA came up with a new model to address IT-based initiatives or projects.

Val IT introduces the concept of project portfolio management by focusing on investments, ROI, and strategic alignment. Where COBIT focuses on the execution (are we doing them the right way, and are we getting them done well?), Val IT focuses on the investment decision (are we doing the right things?) and the realization of benefits (are we getting the benefits?) [33]. Figure 5.10 shows where the lines

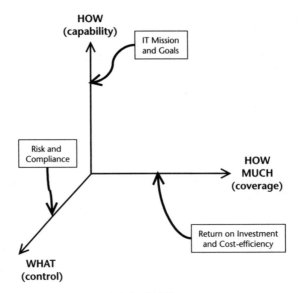

**Figure 5.9**   COBIT process maturity grid. (*After* [32].)

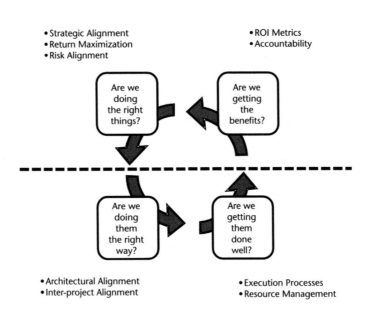

**Figure 5.10**   The Four Are's of COBIT and Val IT. (*After* [33].)

are drawn between Val IT and COBIT using these "Four Are's." In the lower half,
COBIT is seen as providing the means to the Val IT end. The figure also shows how
the processes of operational improvement and project portfolio management feed

each other in a cyclical integration. This diagram can be confusing if you don't change your process hat to a project hat as you go across the dotted line. For example, when looking at "Are we doing them the right way," you need to be referring to processes. A side consideration when taking such a perspective is to make sure new projects are architecturally aligned, do not adversely affect other projects, and support the furtherance of the processes in question. Also, when looking at "Are we getting the benefits," you need to be referring to projects. From this perspective, the question can be reworded as "Are the projected ROIs as specified in the business plans being realized?" The side consideration then would be "Which processes should we be measuring to validate a project's ROI metrics?" If your company's process improvement teams work independently of your project portfolio management teams, then such integration will be less apparent and more difficult. The result will be feet-stepping, frustration, turf wars, and, ultimately, heightened risk and lowered performance.

Val IT also introduces a large set of processes that are grouped into three major categories: value governance, portfolio management, and investment management. Combined, these three categories focus more on controlling the project portfolio through singular portfolio management offices, prioritization approaches, and project auditing. As will be seen in Chapter 6, this is a narrower view of the much broader concept of project portfolio management. Though Val IT doesn't cover such contemporary subjects as project portfolio architectures, portfolio-level support, or strategic activity management integration, it does provide a good set of controlling processes that support PePPR feed 11 (Figure 5.6).

## Enterprise Architectures

While this book focuses primarily on activity management, Chapter 8 will introduce how organizations can be structured to support these rapid dynamics found in today's organizations. Nonetheless, we will briefly cover here a growing process/structure integration school of thought. The thinking goes that a strategically aligned combination of events, processes, and structure can make what many are now calling a business architecture. Such a view of the internal components of a business was born from the evolutionary need to automate these components [34]. That is, the idea of a business architecture was conceived to support the development of a corresponding IT architecture. By slicing and dicing the company into events, processes, and structures, IT implementers can more clearly see where efficiency can be introduced and redundancies eliminated. This then allows them to more accurately align their technical implementations with the needs of the company rather than with the offerings of IT vendors and the fascinations of individual users or managers.

Once such an architecture is developed, it can (1) be combined with performance analysis to get a better understanding of the firm's capabilities, and (2) be linked to a technical architecture to get a better understanding of the firm's IT alignment. This order of implementation is important because as David Genovese puts it, an enterprise architecture is "a business/operational thing first and foremost—the technical architecture follows the operational architecture" [35].

Hans-Erik Eriksson expands on this brief definition by including the goals of the company. "Business architecture is the basis for describing and understanding an enterprise: it lists the required parts of a business, how the parts are structured and interact, and how the architecture should evolve" [36], Then, based on work done at the Software Engineering Institute, Rick Kazman and Hong-Mei Chen, authors of "Aligning Business Models, Business Architectures and IT Architectures," narrow this definition by splitting the business architecture into two components: the business model and the business architecture.

1. *Business model*: drivers, strategies, revenue streams, investments, environment, constraints, regulations.
2. *Business architecture*: business processes, workflow, data flow, applications, knowledge, employee skills, organization.
3. *IT architecture*: hardware, software, networks, COTS/components, interfaces, standards, platforms. [37]

Ralph Whittle and Conrad Myrick, authors of *Enterprise Business Architecture: The Formal Link between Strategy and Results,* support this latter definition by explaining that strategic planning results in the business model, while enterprise architecture planning results in all the components of an architecture [38]. The two architectures listed are broken down further into what some refer to as models [39] and others refer to as architectures [40].

1. *Business model*: Products/services. This defines the near-term and strategic requirements of the organization.
2. *Information model:* Data definition/organization and business processes. This reviews the business model goals and outputs and determines what data, process entities, and integration need to be defined to optimally achieve them. It typically shows the lack of data integration.
3. *Operational model:* Organization and resource alignment. This defines the business structure (e.g., the organization chart) and allocates the resources (e.g., people, materials) to that structure so as to optimally work the model defined in layer 2.
4. *Organizational model: Humans, Systems, Environment.*These entities are integrated in a fashion that is both cost-effective and functional. Integration takes place in two forms:
    a. Physical integration is organizationally based.
    b. Logical integration is information based.
5. *Architecture model:* Overall IT design. This examines the outputs from layers 2 and 3 and defines an optimal IT topology.
6. *Infrastructure:* Tools, products, and IT processes. This defines those IT components that are in place, such as hardware and networking.

Some of these concepts are covered in the more expansive COBIT and ITIL models; some are not. The point is that process frameworks, in general, don't stop with processes. They include explanations of process enablers, one of which is the structure of the organization. Also, a common theme is a realization that since every enterprise is different, a key to success is customizing standard frameworks or architectural approaches to your specific enterprise. A wide swath of models and frameworks exists, and each is based on the experiences of many. But they also tend to be developed by democratic committees that choose those least-common denominators that will allow passage by vote. If you can find a single model that fits your company like a glove, great! But the odds are that your organization will actually need parts from several frameworks to achieve your strategic objectives while also minimizing the pain and inefficiencies of organizational change. For example, a bottom-up drive for IT operational process improvement could use ITIL, while a top-down drive to implement IT project portfolio management could us Val IT.

## Summary

Process analysis, implementation, and improvement have been studied for centuries. In the last few decades, however, some notable advancements have been made by such contributors as Edward Deming and his quality control frameworks, Michael Porter and his Value Chain, and Michael Hammer and his business process reengineering. From these sprouted Value Systems, Kaizen, business process management, Supply Chains, Six Sigma, and ITIL. It could even be argued that performance management had its beginnings in process measurement and improvement. All of these process improvement models, in turn, have led to industry, systems, and functional-specific implementations. Process specialization can't be more clearly shown than in the various strategic activity management frameworks that exist. Enterprise risk management, strategic performance management, and project portfolio management frameworks all tend to be processcentric. Integration of these comes into play when organizations realize the value of establishing reporting processes that include both risk and performance metrics, implementing project management processes that are consistent between projects, and enforcing project-portfolio-level procedures that report project health alongside process health in performance dashboards. Many of the classic, as well as the newer, enterprise process improvement models support some level of such integration. The sooner enterprise-level process improvement champions understand and embrace this, the sooner companies will realize more efficient (i.e., less conflicting) strategic design sessions and more effective strategic execution.

## References

[1]   Taylor, Frederick, The *Principles of Scientific Management*, New York: Harper & Row, 1911.

[2]   Gilbreth, Frank B., "Process Charts—First Steps in Finding the One Best Way to do Work," presented at the Annual Meeting of the American Society of Mechanical Engineers, New York, 1921.

[3]   Vitalo, Raphael L., "Six Sigma and Kaizen Compared: Part 1," Vital Enterprises, March 2005, www.vitalentusa.com/learn/6-sigma_vs_kaizen_1.php (last accessed on November 12, 2007).

[4]   Grant, Robert M., *Contemporary Strategy Analysis: Concepts, Technologies, Applications*, 4th ed., Malden, MA: Blackwell Publishers, 2002.

[5]   Sharp, Alec, and Patrick McDermott, *Workflow Modeling: Tools for Process Improvement and Application Development*, Norwood, MA: Artech House, 2001.

[6]   Porter, Michael, *Competitive Advantage: Creating and Sustaining Superior Performance*, New York, NY, Free Press, 1980.

[7]   Byrne, John A. *Chainsaw: The Notorious Career of Al Dunlap in the Era of Profit-at-Any-Price*, New York: HarperCollins, 2003.

[8]   White, J. B., "Re-engineering Gurus Take Steps to Remodel Their Stalling Vehicles," *Wall Street Journal*, November 26, 1996, pp. A1, A13..

[9]   "Porter's Generic Value Chain," NetMBA.com, www.netmba.com/strategy/value-chain (last accessed on January 25, 2007).

[10]  "A Review of the FBI's Trilogy Information Technology Modernization Program (2004)," National Academy of Sciences, Computer Science and Telecommunications Board, Washington: The National Academies Press, 2004.

[11]  Harmon, Paul, "Value Chains vs. Process Silos," Business Process Trends, January 31, 2006, www.bptrends.com/publicationfiles/bptadvisor2006Jan31.pdf (last accessed on November 17, 2007).

[12]  Walters, D., and M. Rainbird, "The Demand Chain as an Integral Component of the Value Chain," *Journal of Consumer Marketing*, Vol. 21, 2004, pp. 465.

[13]  Ramsay, J. "The Real Meaning of Value in Trading Relationships," *International Journal of Operations and Production Management*, Vol. 25, 2005, pp. 549.

[14]  Burr, Michael T., "Energy Risk Management: Rise of the Chief Risk Officer," *Fortnightly Magazine*, October 1, 2002.

[15]  Stanley, Tim, "High Stakes Analytics," *Optimize*, February 1, 2006, pp. 28–37.

[16]  Goold, M., and A. Campbell, "Many Best Ways to Make Strategy," *Harvard Business Review*, November–December 1987.

[17]  Rockart, J., "Chief Executives Define Their Own Data Needs," *Harvard Business Review*, March–April 1979.

[18]  Bonham, Stephen S., *IT Project Portfolio Management*, Norwood, MA: Artech House, 2005.

[19]  D. J. Teece, G. Pisano, and A. Shuen, "Dynamic Capabilities and Strategic Management," *Strategic Management Journal*, Vol. 18, 1997, pp. 509–533.

[20]  Imai, Masaaki, *Gemba Kaizen*, New York: McGraw-Hill, 1997.

[21]  Japan Human Relations Association, (ed.), *Kaizen Teian 1*, New York, NY, Productivity Press, 1997.

[22]  Breyfogle, Forrest W., III, *Implementing Six Sigma: Smarter Solutions Using Statistical Methods*, 2nd ed., New York, NY, Wiley, 2003.

[23]  Smith, Deborah L., "FMEA: Preventing a Failure before Any Harm Is Done," iSixSigma LLC, 2007, http://healthcare.isixsigma.com/library/content/c040317a.asp (last accessed on November 15, 2007).

[24]  Mohr, R. R., "Failure Modes and Effects Analysis," FMEAInfoCentre.com, www.fmeainfocentre.com/handbooks/fmeamanual.pdf (last accessed on November 15, 2007).

[25]  "TQM, ISO9000, Six Sigma: Do Process Management Programs Discourage Innovation?" Knowledge@Wharton, www.bettermanagement.com/library/library.aspx?pagetype=1&libraryid=13360 (last accessed on February 17, 2006).

[26]  Lambert, Douglas M., "An Evaluation of Process-Oriented Supply Chain Management Frameworks," *Journal of Business Logistics*, January 1, 2005.

[27]  Feller, A., D. Shunk, and T. Callarman, "Value Chains Versus Supply Chains," BPTrends, March 1, 2006.

[28] "The New ITIL (Version 3)," Office of Government Commerce, www.ogc.gov.uk/guidance_itil_4899.asp (last accessed on November 15, 2007).

[29] Information Systems Audit and Control Association (ISACA), www.isaca.org (last accessed on November 15, 2007).

[30] "COBIT 4.1, Executive Summary," IT Governance Institute, 2007, www.isaca.org/AMTemplate.cfm?Section=Downloads&Template=/ ContentManagement/ContentDisplay.cfm&ContentID=34172 (last accessed on November 7, 2007).

[31] "Aligning COBIT, ITIL and ISO 17799 for Business Benefit," IT Governance Institute and Office of Government Commerce, 2005.

[32] "COBIT 4.1 Excerpt," IT Governance Institute, 2007.

[33] "Enterprise Value: Governance of IT Investments: The Val IT Framework," IT Governance Institute, 2006.

[34] McDavid, D. W., "A Standard for Business Architecture Description," *IBM Systems Journal*, Vol. 38, No. 1, 1999, www.research.ibm.com/journal/sj/381/mcdavid.html (last accessed on November 17, 2007).

[35] Genovese, David, "CIO Q&A," *CIO Magazine*, November 19, 1999.

[36] Eriksson, Hans-Erik, "Business Modeling with UML," New York, NY, Wiley, 2000.

[37] Kazman, Rick, and Hong-Mei Chen, "Aligning Business Models, Business Architectures, and IT Architectures," *Software Engineering Institute*, Vol. 5, No. 2, 2nd Quarter, 2002.

[38] Whittle, Ralph, and Conrad Myrick, *Enterprise Business Architecture: The Formal Link between Strategy and Results*, Boca Raton, FL, CRC Press, 2004.

[39] Miner, Clyde, "IT Architecture—Where, What, Why?" EACommunity.

[40] Sims, David, "Enterprise Architecture: The Executive Advantage," EACommunity.

## CHAPTER 6

# Project Portfolio Management

On December 6, 2000, Armstrong World Industries, Inc. (a designer and manufacturer of floors, ceilings, and cabinets founded in 1891), filed for U.S. Chapter 11 bankruptcy to resolve its liability for asbestos personal injury claims [1]. The subsequent years centered on creating a lean, flexible business that would expand its market share footprint and reduce its costs. Then, in 2006, after much reorganization and business process redesign, it emerged from bankruptcy as a publicly traded company with $3.4 billion in annual revenue. As was mentioned in the chapter on maturity, however, while turnarounds can be a difficult task, so can sustaining success. Because Armstrong realized this, it was able to emerge from bankruptcy with a new strategy and a rearchitected set of business processes. A key component of this strategy was speed to market of new and innovative products. Armstrong felt that combining such an adaptive approach with a sprawling structure of 30 plus project teams, 42 plants, and multiple business units could lead to chaos quickly if controls weren't implemented well. In fact, the company found it "challenging to set priorities, share information, facilitate collaboration and balance resources company-wide" [1]. Its various product development projects relied on processes siloed in different organizations. The resulting inefficiencies with information flow "increased the risk of overbooked resources, missed customer deadlines and opportunities lost" [1].

To address these problems, Armstrong realized that it had to establish and enforce standards. It facilitated this organizational change effort by implementing a project portfolio management (PPM) system that would allow the company to better manage its resources, effectively balance the needs of its entire portfolio of new product development (NPD) projects, and reliably meet its customer demand. Eventually, combining its cultural change efforts with its new process automation system, Armstrong was able to cut new product project life cycles in half. The company's vision in 2005 was to cut this cycle in half again and to provide complete "visibility across every business unit in the organization" [1].

## Core Project Portfolio Management

PPM is an approach used to manage everything from NPD to construction to information technology (IT) projects. It was first implemented in the 1960s by manufacturers who found value in Harry Markowitz's 1959 Nobel Prize–winning approach to managing many financial investments [2]. Markowitz's Modern Portfolio Theory (MPT) was written for the management of financial investments and recommends a four-point approach: avoid high correlation, reduce uncertainty, align with the strategy, and maximize for return. If the first three are not adhered to, then the portfolio is at risk of not achieving the fourth. To apply financial-based MPT to projects, some modifications need to be made. First of all, a fifth point needs to be added that addresses the issue of managing project resources. Sure, the performance of investments is influenced by resource activity, but investors only have the ability to manage those resources when they invest in their own companies or in one where they control the resources. With projects, on the other hand, managing equipment, facilities, humans, and vendors is a constant effort. Through strong management of such resources, time, budget, scope, and risk can be optimized.

Another alteration to MPT is with how risks are handled. While a balance of high- and low-risk projects should still be a goal (as it is with financial investments when avoiding correlation), projects can be managed to reduce or mitigate their individual risks. With financial investments, on the other hand, the only way to mitigate investment risk is through increased research, thus through knowledge. Again, the minority exception is when investments are made in self-controlling interests.

Figure 6.1 lists the four key criteria of MPT on the left. To achieve these criteria, the tasks listed in the boxes under financial portfolio management are fairly common. With the investment proposals task, investments are normally researched, proposed, and purchased. For the individual investor, or even for large brokerages with automated systems, these steps (within the investment proposals task) may take place in a few seconds. When more research is desired or when a new portfolio-wide strategy is proposed, this first task can take longer. With a project portfolio, this task is realized as the initiative review task (or process). In basic PPM, business cases are researched, written, and proposed; resources and risks are identified; projects are prioritized; funding is allocated; and start dates are assigned. Then, in the investment monitoring task, where investments are monitored for their fluctuations against their target values, projects are audited for fluctuations against their business cases and any midstream scope shifts. Finally, in the portfolio valuation task, just as with a financial portfolio, projects are rated for their consolidated value-add to the strategic goals of the organization. We end up with the resulting criteria necessary to manage a portfolio of projects: return maximization (e.g., in productivity,

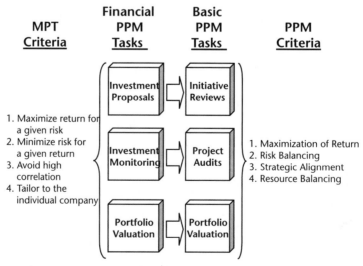

**Figure 6.1** Translating MPT to PPM. (*After* [3].)

growth, or cost savings), risk balancing (e.g., between divisions and projects), strategic alignment, and resource balancing (between projects).

While financial portfolio management quickly became popular after the 1959 publication of MPT, project management took a little longer to mature. In the 1950s, Critical Path Management (CPM) and the Program Evaluation and Review Technique (PERT) were introduced and well used in projects. Some larger projects, such as those run by the U.S. Air Force (USAF) and the Trans-Mountain Oil Pipeline in Canada, helped popularize these concepts [4]. In the 1960s, as CPM and PERT became more popular and project cost management was introduced, the primary industries that still implemented project management concepts were the construction, aerospace, and defense industries. In addition, project management societies were formed (e.g., the International Project Management Association in 1965 and the Project Management Institute [PMI] in 1969). In the 1970s, other concepts, such as work breakdown structures, earned value analysis (i.e., project performance), and conflict management techniques, were developed and adopted by other industries. With the evolving contract laws and higher interest rates of the 1970s, greater attention to time, cost, design, and documentation issues became the norm. In the 1980s, risk management and value–return on investment (ROI) analysis were used on more projects. Along with the publication of the PMI's PMBOK, project management techniques were seen more in the development of products (as was popular at Armstrong). In the 1990s and on, incorporation of process improvement approaches (e.g., Six Sigma, TQM, International Standards Organization [ISO]), implementation of program management, and reporting tools, and refinement of program and portfolio management was seen (see Table 6.1) [5]. Widespread integration of project management and MPT didn't really become popular until the late 1990s.

In short, integrated within the history of project and then portfolio management are the strategic activity management concepts of risk, process, and performance. This is all substantiated by tools, standards, and trade organizations that saw the value of such integration (see the later section in this chapter called "Standards and Frameworks"). But while the evolution of project portfolio management integrated the elements of activity management, organizations continued to silo them with process improvement initiatives, risk management organizations, and performance management dashboards. Though the high-risk, capital-intensive projects that supported each of these siloed activity management efforts were typically tracked at the

**Table 6.1** Overlapping Definitions of Project, Program, and Project Portfolio Management as Presented by the British Office of Government Commerce (OGC)

| Projects | Programs | Portfolios |
|---|---|---|
| Focus on outputs or deliverables; finite start and end date; delivery of product, service, and output; accrual of benefits once the project is complete | Focus on outcomes; vision of an "end state"; coordinated organization; direction, and implementation of a portfolio of projects that together achieve outcomes and realize benefits; benefits realized during the program and afterwards; change brought to and within the organizational culture | A set of projects and programs selected to be aligned with the corporate strategy, balanced for risk and resource usage, and maximized for benefits realization |

executive level, the status of the consolidated portfolio of remaining projects tended to be excluded. Fortunately, organizations have recently learned the strategic value-add of keeping an executive pulse on the portfolio.

### Strategic Alignment

Projects shouldn't be created simply as ends in themselves; they should act as the mechanism that helps organizations achieve their strategic objectives [6]. In Chapters 4 and 5 on performance and process and in Chapter 7 on risk, we touch on the importance of strategically aligning the metrics, frameworks, and risk profiles with the core goals of the organization. This is especially true for projects since these are the activities that actually guide the company, government, or nonprofit in a particular direction. If investments are made in projects that don't fit the needs of the company like a glove, then the company will end up at the mercy of whatever the project deliverables are. A poorly designed product can lead to less market share, a hastened systems installation can lead to unproductive processes, or an ill-conceived community project can lead to an undesirable reputation. These are all examples of what can happen to a company when driven by bad project investment choices.

### Enterprise Portfolio Management Office

With project portfolios, alignment can occur through the aid of an enterprise portfolio management office (PMO). Such organizations are able to provide early business case review and guidance to those who hope to improve the organization. Such presubmittal reviews, in turn, can reduce the number of unaligned projects that are then reviewed by an executive committee. During the executive review process, the enterprise PMO can provide such support as bubble charting (for balancing), real options analysis, resource availability reviews, cross-project synergy, architectural reviews, organizational readiness assessments, and alignment verifications. All of these activities will then help the decision makers finance those projects that most efficiently advance the goals of the organization. Then, once projects go "active," the PMO can audit their compliance with each individual business case. Audit frequency can align with project deliverable dates, quarterly performance reports, or status risk flags. If scope changes, PMO representatives can verify that such scope shift continues to align with the corporate strategy.

### Prioritization

From my experience, the most common reason for managing a company's set of projects as a financial portfolio is to get a better handle on projects by prioritizing them by risk (or health). The more a project deviates from strategic alignment, projected cost, timeline, and functionality, the greater its risk of failure. Then, if a company is forced to change it strategic direction or to reduce costs associated with project investments, it would rather cut those projects that are at greater risk and that provide less value-add to the organization than those at lower risk with greater value-add. The only way for a company to have the visibility required for such an exercise is to understand the current state of all projects in its portfolio. According to a survey conducted in 1993 of companies that rated product development projects for financing, 78.3% used strategic fit as the primary metric for prioritization, followed by payoff. About 50% of surveyed companies rated product proposals by their probability of success. Figure 6.2 shows that these metrics were all part of their first prioritization rounds. A typical round-two prioritization process included other metrics and had about 40% of respondents either evaluate for the first time or reevaluate risk and the probability of success. But even more striking is the fact that every one of these criteria evaluations is a risk assessment: what is the risk that the project won't be a strategic fit, won't provide an acceptable payoff, or won't be technically possible? While this survey applied to new product development, it foreshadowed the value of rating project investments for risk during the growth of PMOs through the 1990s.

Coty, the $2.9 billion fragrance company based in New York City, has linked project prioritization to its performance measurement program. Coty provides managers with the enterprise's five strategic "imperatives" over the next two years and the amount the company has for capital expenditures. This lays the ground rules for how executive-level prioritization will occur and how managers can better align their proposals with the needs of the company. It also allows them to "have budgets in line with strategy and planning, and systems that can measure performance of strategy and plans going forward" [8].

But can ongoing projects also be prioritized with new proposals? While cancelling a project that is underway has associated costs not found in unfinanced proposals, it is important to also prioritize new initiatives against ongoing projects. In many cases, the value-add of a new project can outweigh the costs associated with shutting down an obsolete or unwanted project.

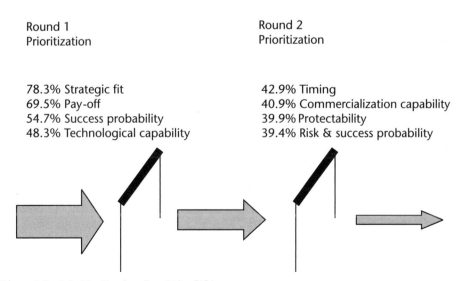

Round 1
Prioritization

Round 2
Prioritization

78.3% Strategic fit
69.5% Pay-off
54.7% Success probability
48.3% Technological capability

42.9% Timing
40.9% Commercialization capability
39.9% Protectability
39.4% Risk & success probability

**Figure 6.2**   Prioritization hurdles. (*After* [7].)

## Balance

Financial portfolios are balanced for risk and projected return. Project portfolios are balanced for risk, projected return, resource usage, organizational acceptance, and architectural alignment, among other things. While balancing doesn't result in a prioritization list, it can affect a project's placement on such a list. If a project would have been dropped during belt-tightening exercises due to its risk-return ratings, financing may continue if it maintains a balance that reduces portfolio-wide risk and or provides for downstream ROI options not evident with its first deliverable. Figure 6.3 shows some examples of how balancing can occur for an individual project and for several projects. The upper part of the figure shows a spider diagram that can be used to rate the coverage of key prioritization metrics for a project. Then, if such a spider diagram is held up against other project spider diagrams, a multidimensional view of balance can be seen. A more consolidated view can be represented by the bottom two "bubble" charts. These represent more dimensions than the basic $x$- and $y$-axes by coloring, sizing, shaping, and labeling the bubbles. Examples of variables that can influence the geometry of these bubbles could include risk, cost,

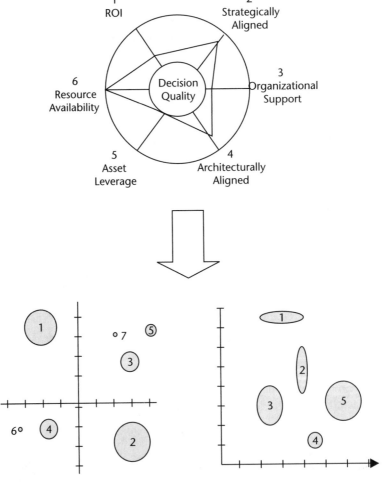

**Figure 6.3**   Sample portfolio balancing process.

timeline, resource needs, overall health, and complexity. While balancing can be a rather subjective exercise, it does a good job of letting reviewers see where strategic gaps exist (e.g., are investments not following the corporate risk profile or is too much money going to one division that has shown a relatively better ability to sell itself).

## The Project Pipeline

The corporate strategy guides the risk profile, the resource levels, and the performance objectives (Figure 6.4, no. 1). All of these in turn affect the decisions made on which projects to invest in. The project pipeline is made up of initiative proposals (2) that get fed into a funnel (3), where these strategic guidelines are applied (4) so that a set of financed projects is spit out the other end (5). Based on resource availability, project start times are set and then the PMO auditing machine takes over. The much narrower funnel (6) of running projects undergoes a different kind of scrutiny—project methodologies, rather than strategic guidelines, are used to monitor the health of projects. Finally, when projects come out the far end of the project funnel (7), risks, resources, and updates objectives are fed back (8) into the strategic management bowl for use in the next strategy design sessions. Figure 6.4 illustrates this set of funnels, or project pipeline, that necessitates the oversight of a project portfolio management office. The next sections will address how such a PMO can provide both control and support of processes to reduce risk and improve performance of the project pipeline.

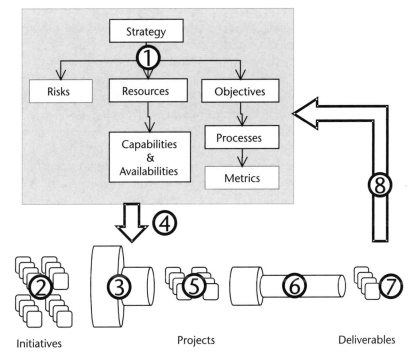

**Figure 6.4**   The project pipeline.

## Portfolio Control

As noted earlier, the application of modern financial portfolio theory to projects is a concept that has been around for a while. But since such an approach was used sporadically only by the largest companies, little was published on their effects. Once the information age had reached full steam in the early 1990s, PPM principles became much more popular because business units had increased their financing for IT-based projects or business-sponsored projects (e.g., a building, a product, or a process) with strong IT components (e.g., computer-aided design, manufacturing automation, or a cross-divisional system). As a result, because of the increased complexity and volume of such IT-based projects, programs, and portfolios, it was realized that more robust methods needed to be used to manage them. As a result, many times the seeds of corporate PMOs will sprout from the IT department.

One example of such a PMO evolution is that of Molson-Coors (soon to be renamed the Miller-Coors Corporation). Its implementation of project portfolio management was widespread and was applied to product development, construction, and IT-based projects—both business sponsored and IT sponsored. Its PPM infrastructure started in the PMO successes of its new product and packages (NPP) and IT departments. The fact that the IT department alone was able to reduce project failure rates by 30% was enough to ultimately cause other interests in the company to implement PPM processes. Executive management was also sufficiently impressed to create a central executive vice president position that reported directly to the chief executive officer (CEO). This office of the strategic PMO was responsible for making sure that best practices were distributed between all the divisional PMOs, such as the business unit–specific NPP and IT PMOs. This was referred to as an operational portfolio architecture since it touched on so many components of the company's operations [9]. Large, capital-intensive projects were monitored by the office of the chief strategy officer but were also tracked and supported by the strategic PMO office (to be covered further in Chapter 8).

The executive involvement at Molson-Coors was crucial to long-term PPM success, and to maintain such involvement, the company's PMO had to constantly prove that the portfolio of projects was under control. In general, having solid communications in place that summarize project manager statuses into easy-to-read reports is a good start. Other valuable control mechanisms include prioritization metrics, business case templates, concept selection processes, project methodologies, and project auditing teams [3]. A PPM software deployment, using digital dashboards supported by these peripheral elements, provides a high level of transparency, control, and value-add to the executives. More precisely, PPM in your company would stand a better likelihood of success if the performance of the portfolio were frequently and accurately reported on in a performance management dashboard accessible by executives at any time.

Executive support can also be strengthened by the position in the organizational chart at which the PMO is created. If a PMO lead reports directly to a CEO, then any perception of bias in the selection of projects can be minimized. If a PMO lead reports to an executive with a department-level stake in which projects are selected, then the PMO can lose credibility, and organizational support can erode quickly. Also, the deeper in the organization a PMO resides, the less authority it will have to enforce policy when prioritizing projects. Executives will have less of an incentive to listen to the recommendations of the PMO, and project sponsors will revert to their own goals at the expense of the company as a whole. For less mature companies that haven't implemented a graduated PMO architecture, an argument may be made that more project support can be mustered by those PMOs that report to support departments such as IT or finance. For example, rather than getting in line behind other business unit requests for IT and finance support, projects would be able to skip to the front because these departments have a direct stake in project portfolio success. Figure 6.5 shows the results of a Meta Group survey of 219 IT professionals that put only 9% of PMOs as reporting directly to the CEO, 24% as reporting to another executive officer, 39% reporting to a lower-level chief information officer (CIO) (one who doesn't report directly to the CEO), and the rest as reporting to a mid-level manager.

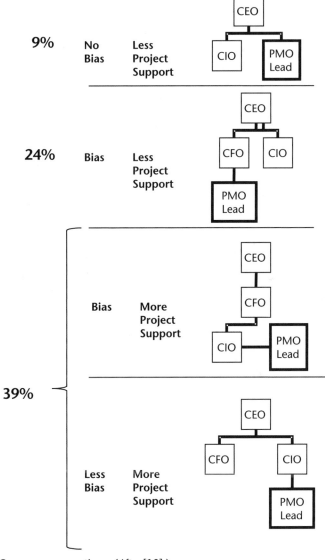

**Figure 6.5** PMO governance options. (*After* [10].)

## California PPM

Another way to establish credibility is by making sure that PPM oversight is truly independent. When large capital expenditures are proposed that involve some technical component, the U.S. federal government may require the project to fund an independent validation and verification (IV&V) consultant. The IV&V consultants would then follow such guidelines as provided by ISO's standard 1012-2004, PMI's PMBOK, or the Office of Government Commerce (OGC)'s Prince2 to determine how well a project deliverable meets the customer requirements (validation) and how well the project deliverable is actually built (verification).

At the state level, such controls may be put into place depending on the state's history of failures or the scrutiny of its constituents (the public or the press). The state of California is one example where strict policies and procedures are in place. For larger projects, the state not only requires an IV&V but also an independent process oversight consultant (IPOC). The IV&V maintains its independence by not reporting to the project manager but rather to the project sponsor. The IPOC, on the other hand, reports to a newly created and independent group run by the Department of Finance called the Office of Technology Review, Oversight, and Security (OTROS). Where the IV&V focuses more on project deliverables, the IPOC focuses more on how well the project is following sound processes.

To best determine the level of oversight a project will receive, OTROS has developed some criteria, or stage or gates. The four factors used are:

1. The project's estimated one-time costs (Table 6.2);
2. The project manager's experience (Table 6.3);
3. The team's experience (Table 6.4);
4. The project type (high technical complexity versus well-proven solution; Table 6.5) [11].

Once the project is rated according to these four criteria as shown in Tables 6.2 to 6.5, a score is computed where 3 is used for high, 2 for medium, and 1 for low. If the average rating is between 2.26 and 3.0, the project is rated has high; between

**Table 6.2**  OTROS Estimated On-Time Costs Project Rating Chart

| Estimated On-Time Costs | Rating |
|---|---|
| Greater than $10 million | High |
| $5 million to $10 million | Medium |
| Under $5 million | Low |

Source: [11]

**Table 6.3**  OTROS Project Manager Experience Project Rating Chart (after 11)

| Project Manager Experience | Rating |
|---|---|
| Has not completed a like project in a "key staff" role | High |
| Has completed one like project in a "key staff" role | Medium |
| Has completed two or more like projects in a "key staff" role | Low |

Source: [11]

**Table 6.4** OTROS-like Projects Completed Project Rating Chart

| Team Experience—Like Projects Completed by at Least 75% of Key Staff | Rating |
| --- | --- |
| None | High |
| One | Medium |
| Two or more | Low |

Source: [11]

**Table 6.5** OTROS Project Type Project Rating Chart

| Project Type—Criticality and Complexity | Rating |
| --- | --- |
| Core, critical path, high technical complexity | High |
| Noncore component, medium complexity | Medium |
| Noncore, simple component, low complexity | Low |

Source: [11]

1.51 and 2.26, the project is rated as medium, and between 1.0 and 1.5, the project is rated low. In all cases, the project is required to submit regular systems, risk, status, and methodology collateral. Only if the project is rated high is it required also to hire a full-time IPOC and IV&V. The catch is that all of these calculations are irrelevant if the department of finance feels that past project performance or unique risks warrant a higher score than that calculated. That is, though a formal process exists, it simply acts as a guide, not as an end-all for decision making. Since the risk of not being consistent in the application of a framework entails organizationwide perceptions of favoritism, such framework overrides should be applied rarely.

When such independent quality assurance, validation, and verification or process oversight resources are hired by an organization, a challenge to independence can occur. First of all, such auditors tend to be experts in their fields with a background in managing projects similar to the ones they are auditing. Second, the projects they are auditing will no doubt run into snags that could threaten the continuation of the paychecks that go to these auditors. This leads to an opportunity that many project managers take advantage of: allowing the auditors to act as advisors and, in some cases, contributors to the project. The auditor who simply monitors and reports is purely independent, but the auditor who lets the project team review recommendations, apply corrective actions, and then allow for more favorable reports is an auditor who is less independent but more supportive of project success. Of course, the project manager is ultimately responsible if the project acts on advice that proves disastrous.

California's implementation of OTROS is an example of a highly control-centric project portfolio management approach that screens initiatives, grades departments for maturity, deploys auditors, and adheres to strict standards. The costs are that the taxpayer now pays extra for auditors on each project, but the benefits are greater project successes (i.e., time, cost, and functionality) than in the past. The beneficial side effect has been the evolution of many smaller PMOs within each department that allow for less department of finance scrutiny over ever-larger projects. That is, a graduated PMO architecture naturally evolved from the scoring method used by OTROS.

## Death by Process

I recently worked with a different government client that had implemented a PMO and then shut it down. This was a large government agency that had established control processes to ensure that financed projects were spread out over a range of risks. Time and time again, however, executives would bypass these healthy processes to finance pet projects. The manager I worked with felt that when executives undermined the PPM processes that the rest of the organization was held accountable to, the PMO lost credibility as a value-add organization. After many months of reflection, this manager now looks at things differently. She now understands that her PMO had created so many processes that it took a rather long time first to get a project approved and then to have it meet preferred deadlines. Therefore, if executives could bypass lengthy review cycles to get projects running, they would. If project managers could prevent time-consuming audits by just rating their projects as healthy, they would. Such breakdown and the resulting credibility loss ultimately led to the closure of the PMO.

There is now talk of restarting the PMO based upon quick risk reviews. If an executive wants to fast-track a project, a small team from the PMO will conduct a quick technical, organizational, and financial assessment. They will then prioritize the project proposal in the list of existing projects. If the project is rated as high risk, then a larger assessment can be proposed. While the sponsoring executive can go either way, at least some level of review has been done. This approach will provide a graduated way to assess project proposals based upon their risk to the organization (and their less advertised political strength). If a project audit is to be conducted, a quick audit team will come in, review, and exit with minimal impact on the forward progress of the project. If it is then found that major problems exist or that the initial audit score doesn't match the health rating provided by the project manager, then a more intrusive audit can occur. By not holding all projects to the same scrutiny, the organization will be preventing the risk of death by process. Otherwise known as death by methodology, this concept is common in PMOs requiring that all projects use the same methodology and deliver the same project collateral (e.g., requirements, design, communication, test, budget, risk documents or plans).

If we scale this up to the PMO level, we see the results that our PMO manager saw: you can blame it on people for not following processes, but are your processes overly restrictive and thus rejection prone? In effect, process overkill can cripple corporate innovation and growth. "Companies may be tempted to apply process management approaches to ensure that they are 'improving' how they innovate or find new markets. But innovation may not lend itself to strict processes with measures" [12].

## Portfolio-Level Project Support

If PMO auditors become known as the "project Nazis" who slow projects, project managers can actively avoid audits and become hard to find. Besides avoiding PMO interaction, project managers can enter invalid data on status reports, ignore audit requests, avoid methodology requirements, and reject resource recommendations. Flexible or graduated enforcement of processes and methodologies is one way to eliminate such PPM breakdowns. Another way is to build a culture of project support at the portfolio level. For example, at Molson-Coors, several steps were taken to improve the success of its projects. Rather than just police for methodology compliance and status reporting, the PMO also offered support for project team members. Centralized training, project manager career paths, architectural reviews, asset reuse, and vendor relationship management were provided. By developing these and other support approaches, the project management staff can start to see more benefits returned than effort put into a PMO. Once this message is understood, cultural change will occur and PPM success will result.

### AARKV Management

In my first book, I referred to a concept called AARK management. This was an acronym for what I concluded to be the four key management activities that a PMO could administer to provide support for projects from a centralized portfolio level. Architecture, asset, resource, and knowledge management (KM) are concepts that can be applied both across an organization and within individual projects. Since then, I've added one more management activity known as vendor management—thus the *V* in AARKV. This addition identifies the value-add a PMO can provide to projects through preexisting vendor relationships, contracts, and agreements.

There are two sides to how these five management activities support the project portfolio:

1. *Up front:* Each should be applied during the business case writing and the initiative review process. Architectural reviews, asset reuse, resource access, lessons-learned leverage, and vendor expertise can all be used to support the project sponsor in getting approval for his or her proposal.
2. *At the back end:* These activities should also be applied while the projects are underway and, most commonly, after the projects are complete. While the direction of a project tends to stay on a particular course, drastic market shifts (or simple scope changes) can slightly alter its heading. Such shifts can in turn require new resources, assets, or vendor support that can alter architectures or designs. Midstream support needs for these scenarios are balanced by the additional need at the end of the project. Unused assets, architectural updates, freed resources, postmortem reviews, and vendor relationships can all contribute to future project successes if managed well at the beginning, middle, and end of each project.

*Architecture Management*    Businesses all have their own structures, processes, capabilities, and cultures. As pointed out in the "Enterprise Architectures" section of Chapter 5, the architecture of the business is roughly defined as the combination of these first two elements: structure and processes. In practice, the reason for viewing a business as an architecture is to ensure that (1) a systems implementation is aligned with a technical architecture, and (2) the technical architecture is aligned with the business architecture. In essence, architectural alignment is another way for technical folks to understand the concept of aligning the corporate strategy to an enterprisewide approach to technology. So, when architecture management is mentioned when referring to PMOs, one is usually referring to how the technical components of the project are aligned with the given technical environment of the company.

A common approach to architectural management is to have a review committee scrutinize the architectural fit and impacts of projects before approval, during execution, and after delivery. To help minimize misfits, some organizations disperse business analysts whose sole job is to ensure alignment of new ideas with existing or planned IT architectures. At Molson-Coors, the PMO team created a technology review board (TRB) with the IT architecture lead, security lead, and IT PMO lead as permanent members. The TRB would review a project's scope, timeline, and estimated costs prior to the completion of the business case and prior to project approval. Such an early review greatly improved the accuracy of the business case forecasts. The TRB reviews would also ensure that projects were aligned with the company's IT architecture. Such alignment helped reduce costs associated with vendor license violations, help desk training, hardware idle, and software redundancies.

*Asset Management*    I've run into more than one company that has had a problem monitoring the performance of its systems because it failed to institute dynamic asset management standards. Static asset management includes such one-off events as asset inventories and total cost of ownership evaluations, as well as such ongoing activities as automated tracking of fixed IT systems and Global Positioning System–enabled truck fleets. Dynamic asset management comes into play when PMOs alert such support organizations as procurement, IT, and fleet management of pending asset purchases due to project approvals. Standard identifiers such as radio frequency identification, Simple Network Management Protocol (SNMP), and vehicle identification codes are assigned along with other data so that trends can be developed on failure rates, depreciation objectives, and vendor quality. If a PMO is in place to enforce tracking standards for incoming assets, the assets can be more easily managed to support performance management needs. The operational performance metrics that result can then be linked to and thus support strategic-level key performance indicators (KPIs).

*Resource Management*    Managing resources between projects can be a highly complex task. As a result, this is the one component of PMOs that has led many companies to purchase advanced PMO software that can automate resource scheduling between projects. However, automation introduces its own complexities. Staff needs to be relied upon to enter its skill sets into a central repository and to update those skill sets whenever a new experience or training has been realized, project managers need to be relied upon to enter pending and actual availabilities of resources so other projects can be planned appropriately, and a PMO needs to be relied upon to make the proper association between skill available and skill needed. Larger consulting companies have achieved a level of success in this area. Their size prevents them from relying completely on word of mouth from upper management and forces them to use automated systems. Nonetheless, even the most advanced implementers of resource management software end up with untruthful staff members, resource-hoarding project managers, and disgruntled project assignees.

If your company is still teetering on the purchase of such a system or has backed away from using one, the PMO can still provide value with portfolio-level resource management. Human resource organizations are usually charged with providing training opportunities to staff, but a PMO better understands the needs of projects and project team members who have been "matrixed" away. That is, while corporate training programs are propagated through functional leaders by the central human resources group, staff members may find little immediate value because they have been temporarily assigned (or "matrixed") to a project with different needs. A PMO can foresee the needs of proposed projects and recommend training at different levels before the project needs the skills (see Figure 6.6). Such proactive training can subsidize or even be substituted for a strict resource management approach as found in automated systems at consulting companies.

*Knowledge Management*    To prove that a project proposal will mitigate a particular risk or improve a particular performance metric, business case writers usually research data available on the operations of their organization. If such data is kept in a central location and is easily accessible, business case writers can more quickly conduct research and validate their proposals before presenting them to executives. Such support can be managed by a central PMO to increase the number of new ideas and project proposals presented for financing. Recently, a new source of information, besides internal knowledge bases (KBs), has helped feed ideas for the innovative and adaptation-oriented company. The Internet provides an endless amount of data that can be searched and sorted by academic research sites, trade journals, trade groups, and such Web 2.0 tools as blogs.

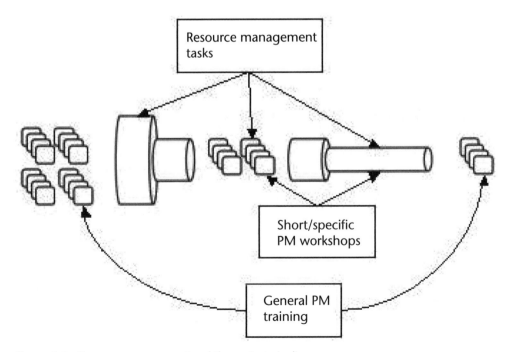

**Figure 6.6**   Resource management and the project pipeline.

A third source of information for the project sponsor is lessons learned and collateral from past projects within the company. Sure, experiences can be gathered from other companies via the Web, but many times such experiences don't fit the culture and standards of the company. As a result, project-specific KBs can be standardized so that when complete, a project can pass its documents and lessons to a central, portfolio-level knowledge base (see Figure 6.7). A common implementation of this is with document management tools that require the association of certain metadata tags with each data element to help with data searching. The PMO can provide for KM support through an internal team that manages the coordination of various project-specific knowledge bases with the central knowledge base. The KM team of the PMO can establish standards for the creation of project KBs and for how others access the central KB [3]. According to a 2003 survey of 303 companies by *CIO Magazine* and the PMI, 74% of companies that have implemented PMOs capture postmortems and lessons learned for use by other projects [13].

*Vendor Management*    An extension of asset management is to wrap the tasks of a typical procurement department with project-portfolio-specific needs. Vendor management for the project portfolio supports project managers by maintaining (1) vendor relationships, (2) support agreements, and (3) hard-won licensing contracts between projects. Such support can greatly reduce the task load for projects that are just starting. Different skill sets are required to establish an effective vendor management group for a project portfolio. For example, Figure 6.8 illustrates the need for legal expertise to create standard contract templates, financial expertise to confirm vendor-generated ROI projections, and technical expertise to validate vendor-proposed system functionality. With portfolio-level guidance, this can lead to better deals, contracts, and relationships with the company's portfolio of vendors.

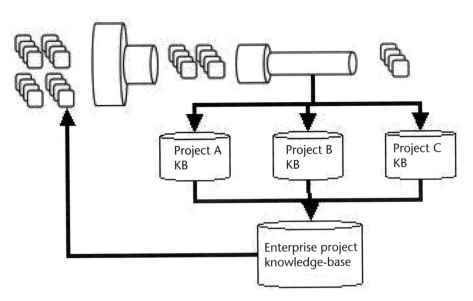

**Figure 6.7**    Knowledge management and the project pipeline. (*After* [3].)

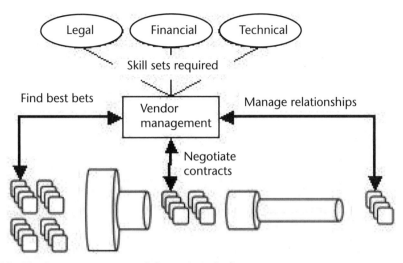

**Figure 6.8** Vendor management and the project pipeline.

### The Complete Project Pipeline

The higher you go, the more *control* oriented the mission. The lower you go, the more *support* oriented the mission. This is analogous to how NICE Systems, or the Performance Pyramid, implements a "balanced" performance measurement system. In these cases, the narrow focus on financials as a measure of success is more common at the top of the organizational chart. A broader, more well-rounded (supportive) view of the health of the organization is common lower on the organizational chart. This is no different when implementing PMOs across larger organizations. Reporting policies that feed consolidated portfolio metrics and auditing guidelines that dictate performance thresholds can be managed by a small component of a strategic activity management office (see Chapter 8). Lower-level PMOs can then implement not only more detailed control mechanisms but also more expansive support programs. The higher-level PMOs are interested in summary health metrics, while the lower-level PMOs are interested in individual program and project success. This leads to training programs, methodologies, career paths, resource sharing, asset reuse, knowledge management, architectural reviews, and vendor controls by these lower-level PMOs.

Before such a graduated hierarchy can be established, and before some wiz-bang software solution can be implemented, a culture of project, program, and portfolio management should exist. Staff should understand and adhere to the doctrine of project management, leverage the strengths it provides, and push for strategic success through portfolio management. Specific indicators that such a culture exists could include required project management certification for all projects, high project-methodology-adherence levels, business case references to PMO audits, and strict asset review processes. That is, a companywide culture should be in place before rolling out stress-inducing systems and organizational changes. Specifically, AMR Research conducted a survey in 2004 and found that a common theme among all survey respondents was that PPM processes need to be in place, as illustrated in Figure 6.9, before a PPM tool can be successfully implemented [14]. The PMO

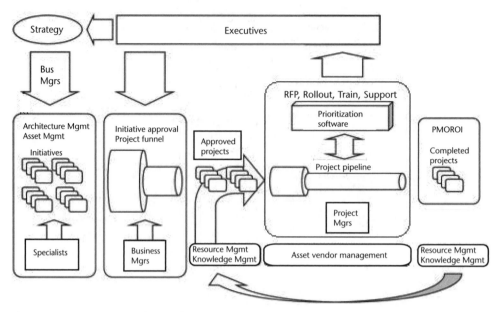

**Figure 6.9**   Components of a portfolio management culture.

touches on all areas of the corporate project pipeline. Along the top, you see how executives interface with the pipeline by creating a strategy and choosing which initiatives to finance. Concurrently, they receive periodic project portfolio health reports. The PMO also supports business unit managers, specialists, and project managers throughout the pipeline. Besides providing for executive support and AARKV management, the PMO also supports prioritization software, approval processes, and PMO ROI. As enablers are needed for processes to be realized, they are also needed for smooth operating project pipelines—pipelines that can then support PPM needs and reduce organizational disruption.

### Value-add

I once heard a client explain that several months after implementing a PMO, it presented its benchmark findings to its executive steering committee. The PMO team found that the project failure rate at the company was over 50%. Since the executives were under the impression that far fewer projects had failed prior to PMO rollout, they felt the PMO had contributed negatively to project success and promptly cancelled the PMO initiative. This client failed to impart to the executives, however, that no real benchmarking had ever been performed. Therefore, no prior understanding of actual failure rates could have been known.

Benchmarking is key to proving the value-add of a PMO initiative and must be done if PPM champions hope to institutionalize and culturalize the concept of project, program, and portfolio management in their organizations. But care must be taken to ensure benchmarks can stand up to statistical scrutiny. This is tricky since project successes, by their very nature, can be rather subjective. The first step would be to choose a model proposed by such project management standards bodies as the OGC and the PMI. Quantitative measures could then be applied to the classic project triad of time, cost, and functionality. Later evolutions of this triad have included such measurable elements as risk and perception (through surveys). Below is a list of possible benchmarks that could be taken when a PMO was kicked off and then periodically to show portfolio-level improvement.

- Projected versus actual ROIs;
- Project success rates (time, cost, functionality, return);
- Resource utilizations;
- Risk levels of portfolio;
- Balance of projects selected;
- Surveys of projects' stakeholders.

Project success rate is the easiest benchmark used to sell the value of the PMO. Within this benchmark, the easiest measures of the project triad are cost and time. If the project costs more or has continued longer than was projected in its business case, a clear and easy-to-raise red flag can be seen. However, more than one business manager I've met has failed to include delivery of expected functionality as a measure of success. If project stakeholders get less than they paid for, lost value should be quantitatively associated with this lost functionality. If an organization can prove that project delivery to cost, time, and functionality are improving by a certain percentage, they can then translate that improvement into real yens, euros, or dollars. Fortunately, over the last several years, many organizations have benchmarked their project failure rates both before and after realizing the benefits of a PMO. As a result, PMO implementation has snowballed into a standard way of doing business for companies worldwide. Below is a short list of companies, research firms, and governments that have been able to show the amount of improvement in project success rates (in percentages) after implementing their PMOs.

- 15%: Robbins Gioia survey of 232 companies (2001) [15];
- 70%: Hewlett-Packard (2003) [16];
- 30%: State of Iowa (2003) [17];
- 50%: Gartner analysis of PPM software vendors (2004) [18];
- 30%: Molson Coors (2006) [9];
- 34%: AG Edwards (2006) [19].

## PePPR PPM

The needs for new metrics, mitigated risks, and process improvements are all common reasons to start a project. Depending on the current focus of the organization, these project proposals can get prioritized differently. For example, if process improvement is a priority, business cases linked to Six Sigma, Control Objectives for Information and Related Technology (COBIT), or Supply Chain Operations References (SCOR) frameworks may prioritize higher than risk mitigation or metric improvement projects. But if a spread of projects can be linked to all three activity management silos, then a company can more easily adapt its execution and visibility strategy to market shifts. A company can also understand the evolving culture based upon where projects are coming from. For example, are more proposals based on desires to mitigate risks or to improve metrics? We will show how several companies address this issue when they've implemented this component of integrated PePPR management.

## Process-Based PPM

An enterprise process improvement initiative, such as Information Technology Infrastructure Library (ITIL), Six Sigma, or SCOR, ceases being a project when process improvement processes become culturalized. Once an organization reaches this state, process improvement efforts should lead to an endless stream of project proposals. The business cases for those process improvement projects that get proposed should identify the framework they are supporting. This then allows an initiative review committee to better prioritize proposals based on their furtherance of strategic process improvement goals (feed 7 in Figure 6.10). Executives can then also gauge the commitment of their organization to process improvement.

At Pinnacol Assurance of Colorado, process change initiatives can be the result of IT projects, regulatory requirements, market shifts, or customer needs. The launching pad for such initiatives derives from teams called strategic action committees (SACs). Pinnacol executives understood the need for custom processes for each sales group to better cater to its customers. However, some basic standards had to propagate across these departments to ensure consistent customer satisfaction and regulatory compliance. Rather than follow some industry standard process improvement framework, Pinnacol relied more on customer feedback and regulations to mold its own custom framework, one that acted as a feeder for process improvement projects.

While Pinnacol created its own process improvement framework around its SACs, Porter General Hospital and nLight turned to some popular standards for assistance. Porter General used Six Sigma to reduce and isolate the spread of bacteria by requiring hand washing before and after contact with any patient. This project included training, outreach collateral, timing, and constant follow-up to show ongoing value-add (i.e., statistically proven reduction in bacteria spread). At nLight,

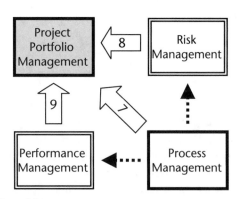

**Figure 6.10**   PePPR PPM model.

adopting the need to become ISO9000 certified did more than just lead to more projects; it was the impetus to start looking at such things as vision, mission, and several quality programs. This standard was adopted about four years into the company's life, after it had established itself as a viable business to its investors. Then through years five and six, as the quality management system became much more formalized (i.e., documented and followed), the company took on Six Sigma.

## Risk-Based PPM

At the Food and Drug Administration (FDA), an IT system was being installed that would dramatically affect how drug products were approved. So, while the project would result in improved processes, the central sales pitch for getting approval for the project was the fact that it would mitigate rising risks associated with drug-approval delays [20]. Efforts to mitigate risks can result in fairly large capital investments as illustrated by feed 8 in Figure 6.10. The reverse of this feed represents how the resulting projects can in turn act as a source of new risks. The FDA project was no exception. If not managed, such project-initiated risks can have a strong cumulative effect on an organization. Scott Berinato of *CIO Magazine* goes so far as to say that "risk analysis is as essential to real portfolio management as a processor is to a computer. Without it, portfolio management is simply a way to organize the view of projects that will almost certainly fail" [21]. We will cover this more in Chapter 7, but here we will focus on how risk mitigation goals feed the project portfolio pipeline.

Some feel that if an enterprise-level risk plan has been developed, an organization will be better prepared to track the success of risk-initiated projects [22]. Then, if a company maintains a set of risk management processes that change with a flexible strategy, then the prioritization criteria used to rate projects can change. This dynamism will lead to a project portfolio that is constantly aligned with the strategy through updated risk priorities, as well as flexible performance goals [23]. Examples of some major risks that led to mitigation projects at a major electric utility include power plant failure at peak usage times, electrical disruption due to storms, and power outages due to tree overgrowth. In fact, while monitoring the key performance metric, number of outages, the utility realized that the metric showed a problem: the company hadn't been sufficiently mitigating the tree overgrowth risk, and as a result, outages were getting very high and resulting in lower customer satisfaction. This led to a large-scale tree-trimming project to mitigate the unacceptable levels of outages.

While process improvement and risk mitigation needs can clearly feed projects to the project portfolio, each can also lead to the rollout of enterprise-level PPM structures and processes. At Western Gas Resources, risks not only led to a stream of projects but also altered how projects were approved. In Western's case, efforts to mitigate risks associated with Sarbanes-Oxley noncompliance resulted in a formal project submission process that overturned the traditional handshake approach the company used on projects as large as $10 million. In 2001, Lowe's implemented its enterprise portfolio management (EPM) program as a way to integrate its interproject resource management (a component of its PPM processes) with its risk management processes to determine which major capital investments were worth pursuing. This was, no doubt, a much larger effort than that undertaken by Western simply because of the relative sizes of the two companies. But, again, we see how enterprise-level risk can be the impetus to implement more complete strategic activity management approaches. In Lowe's case, CIO Steve Stone was able to deploy some software that not only accurately tracked when resources would become available due to project completion but could also time the execution of its strategy and thus more accurately set executive expectations. For example, risks associated with the company's planned expansion into Canada and its implementation of self-checkout counters were mitigated by better timing launch dates with resource availabilities, which was monitored by the EPM office [24].

## Performance-Based PPM

In Chapter 4 on performance management, we reviewed how the performance of the project portfolio was critical to understanding the complete health of an organization. Here, we show the other side of how performance and project portfolio management integrate. How does performance management feed the project portfolio? It can be by increasing corporate visibility, as was the case with the building products manufacturer through the implementation of a new performance management system, or it can be by improving corporate performance, as was the case with NICE Systems and Porter General Hospital in how they applied performance improvement criteria to the front end of their project approval processes.

At the building products manufacturer we referenced in Chapter 5, one of the key goals of its enterprise resource planning (ERP) projects was to implement a performance dashboard. Executives had gotten to a point at which they were losing the real-time pulse of the company and made such a dashboard a requirement to financing the project. But before a successful ERP implementation could result in an improved performance management system, executives realized that a complete business process realignment had to occur. So, in other words, the need for performance management led to two major projects: (1) an ERP system installation, and (2) a process reengineering effort.

Most of the time, however, performance management systems aren't the reason for new projects. Rather, identified performance improvements are elements of a business case that leads to project financing. At NICE Systems, before a project can get funded, sponsors need to prove the project's financial value to the company. For example, NICE's sales force realized that its current sales numbers weren't sustainable without some automation of its global processes and realized the need for a sales force automation tool that would take the company beyond its current quotas. To gain financing for this, it engaged the various regional leaders by showing how such a project would increase sales KPIs. The regional leaders were sufficiently impressed that all of them gave up a percentage of their budgets to help finance the project.

At Porter General, metric enhancement projects are also necessary to (1) better prove that the hospital is complying with regulations, and (2) validate ongoing funding for research. But before proposed metric changes can be approved for project financing by doctors and business partners, they need to be thoroughly marketed and reviewed for their value-add. Project sponsors must also prove that their proposed changes will integrated with, and be supported by, other existing processes and systems.

## Standards and Frameworks

As with performance and process management, PPM frameworks have been developed and standardized by independent trade organizations. While these frameworks were being created and deployed, organizations were coming up with their own custom approaches to PPM. In the late 1990s and early 2000s, many PPM maturity models were introduced. Most were developed by consulting companies to steer clients into purchasing more services, and a few were developed by standards bodies and academics. In my research, the following two models proved to be the most complete and the least proprietary:

1. Project, Program, and Portfolio Management Maturity Model (P3M3);
2. Organizational Project Management Maturity Model (OPM3).

### P3M3

P3M3 is a model that was developed by the Organization of Government Commerce (OGC—an agency of the British government) and derived from the Capability Maturity Model Integrated, or CMMI. Though originally developed by the Software Engineering Institute at Carnegie-Mellon University, this parent maturity model is the result of merging several models to create one that could be applied to any project type [5]. The British OGC has built a strong reputation throughout the world for such standards as the Prince2 methodology for project management and the ITIL framework for process improvement. In the history of PPM models, OGC's P3M3 was a relative latecomer with its release in early 2006.

A project may get initiated for several reasons. In this book, we have focused primarily on three PePPR sources: to mitigate one or more risks, to improve the ability to monitor performance, and to improve the performance of existing processes. Other sources of projects could include the desire to improve the capability of resources, to create new products, or to conduct a unique advertising campaign. With any of these, business cases should be developed. P3M3 places business case development at its Stage 2, after the organization has achieved an understanding of projects and programs. This means that the lower stages of PPM maturity support two stages of the inward PePPR feeds to PPM (i.e., the sources of projects; feeds 7, 8, and 9 in Figure 6.10).

P3M3 has five stages of maturity (initial, repeatable, defined, managed, and optimized), three project types (project, program, and portfolio), and six descriptive elements (goals, approach, deployment, review, perception, and performance). At Stage 3, processes are defined and integrated into normal operations (Figure 6.11, feed 11). For example, if someone with an idea wants to propose a project for funding, he or she would know exactly how to do so, whom to contact for help, and whether the idea aligned with the current strategy. Stage 3 also starts to address integrated management and reporting and intergroup coordination and support to

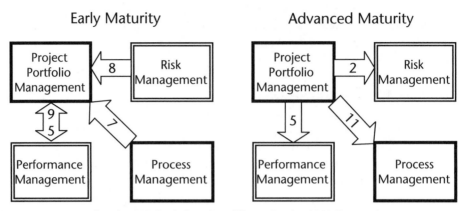

**Figure 6.11**   PPM-related PePPR feeds found at different levels of P3M3 maturity.

assist the early stages of such things as risk reports to a central risk management group (feed 2) and performance metrics to a central performance management group (early feed 5). Stage 4 PPM maturity is seen in companies that have full-fledged integration of performance management programs. This would include both metric frameworks (e.g., European Network for Advanced Performance Studies [ENAPS], Balanced Scorecard) and process improvement initiatives (e.g., Six Sigma and TQM) into PPM (feed 5 and back to feed 7, respectively). Stage 5 then follows the classic model of iterative and continuous improvement of the PPM processes.

## OPM3

OPM3 was one of the first models developed by an internationally recognized standards body. It was released by the PMI in 2003 to help explain how projects should be supported and controlled by an organizationwide structure and set of processes [25]. OPM3 is made up of three project management domains (project, program, and portfolio), four maturity stages (standardize, measure, control, and improve), and five process groups (initiating, planning executing, control, and closing). Like P3M3, the model can be represented as a three-dimensional cube. To determine where a company fits in this cube, an assessment is provided with a list of questions to ask. After determining the maturity of the organization, these questions help define what best practices should be applied to an organization to improve its maturity. Each best practice is made up of two or more capabilities that can in turn have several KPIs for measured outcomes (see Figure 6.12). After completing the assessment, the company applies the best practices and then conducts the assessment again until it has achieved the next stage of maturity [26].

At the portfolio level, OPM3 covers many process types, including risk management and performance reporting. One strength of OPM3 is its inclusion of such PPM support processes as training, standardized project methodology, knowledge management, and vendor or contract management. OPM3, like its sister framework, PMBOK, is light on technique but broad in coverage. That is, while it covers a lot of PPM ground, it doesn't provide the stepwise approaches, or techniques, to accomplish the proposed processes. Although this is typical of all the known PPM frameworks, some may provide slightly more detail (or depth) than others at the

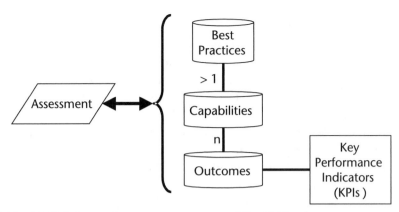

**Figure 6.12** OPM3 link to performance management. (*After* [26].)

possible expense of coverage (or breadth). Furthermore, while the primary applications of both OPM3 and P3M3 tend to be on IT-based projects, the sponsoring organizations (PMI and OGC, respectively) push for a broader application.

P3M3 is modeled in similar fashion to OPM3. While P3M3 focuses primarily on its descriptive elements, OPM3 goes beyond processes and goals by providing its assessment questionnaire, suggested key performance indicators (feed 5), and possible outcomes for the proposed PPM processes. In short, OPM3 provides more depth in the areas of process enablers and performance management through all maturity levels of its model. While OPM3 does address how performance metrics can be fed into a central repository in its level 1 (portfolio performance reporting) and level 2 (collect project, program, portfolio success metrics; provide central metrics repository), it doesn't really address outward integration with other strategic activity management silos, such as enterprise risk management and strategic process management (feeds 2 and 11). For example, all risk management activity is addressed through six process groups at OPM3 level 1 and focuses on mitigating risks within the PPM domain [risk management planning, risk identification, risk analysis (quantitative and qualitative), risk response planning, and risk monitoring and control]. Other areas of both PMBOK and OPM3 address the more basic PePPR feeds of where projects can sprout from (feeds 7, 8, and 9).

## Summary

Project portfolio management grew from concepts meant for the management of financial portfolios. By including consideration of resources and expanded risk management, however, projects can now also be managed as one would a financial portfolio in order to balance for risk, align with the company's goals, and maximize for return. In the late 1990s, PPM experienced a rapid adoption by businesses around the world due to the increasingly complex nature of managing large sets of IT projects. Today, PPM is so pervasive that it is difficult to find companies that haven't implemented some of its components. The benefits of PPM have been well documented to improve controlled visibility and provide strong support for an organization's investments. Because PPM is becoming a natural part of doing business in a technical world, integration with other strategic activity management efforts (i.e., PePPR) is also commonplace. The performance and risks of projects are now consolidated by PMOs and integrated with risk management offices and performance management teams. Besides the case studies, trade journals, professional organizations, and conferences, internationally recognized and competing PPM standards are available. This is the mechanical side to PPM; the soft side is the necessity for uninterrupted executive support, a control-versus-support balance by the PMO, and long-term organizationwide embracement. If the first two are achieved, the third will follow, and execution success rates will improve.

# References

[1] Young, Mark, "Case Study: Turning 'Ideas into Reality': At Armstrong World Industries Speeding Innovation Is a Top Priority," Chief Project Officer, October 1, 2005, www.chiefprojectofficer.com/article/144 (last accessed on November 29, 2007).

[2] Berinato, Scott, "Do the Math," CIO Magazine, October 1, 2001, http://comment.cio.com/comments/6183.html (last accessed on January 15, 2004).

[3] Bonham, Stephen S., IT Project Portfolio Management, Norwood, MA: Artech House, 2005.

[4] Kooyman, Brian R., "IT and Non-IT Project Management: Is There a Difference?" Presentation to Australian Computer Society, July 20, 2005.

[5] "Project, Program and Portfolio Management Maturity Model," Office of Government Commerce, February 1, 2006, www.ogc.gov.uk/documents/p3m3.pdf (last accessed on December 17, 2007).

[6] Kaplan, Robert S., and David P. Norton, The Strategy Focused Organization, Cambridge, MA: Harvard Business School Press.

[7] Cooper, R., and E. Kleinschmidt, "Stage Gate Systems for New Product Success," Marketing Management, Vol. 1, No. 4, 1993. pp. 20–29

[8] Banham, Russ, "Seeing the Big Picture: New Data Tools Are Enabling CEOs to Get a Better Handle on Performance across Their Organizations—Technology—Business Performance Management," Chief Executive Publishing, November 1, 2003, www.findarticles.com/p/articles/mi_m4070/is_193/ai_110811916/print (last accessed on February 17, 2006).

[9] Bonham, Stephen, et al., "The Molson-Coors Operational Portfolio Architecture," CAIS, December 2006.

[10] Metamorphosis Conference Survey, The META Group, January 2003.

[11] "Information Technology Project Oversight Framework," California Department of Finance, February 2004.

[12] "TQM, ISO9000, Six Sigma: Do Process Management Programs Discourage Innovation?" Knowledge@Wharton, www.bettermanagement.com/library/library.aspx?pagetype=1&libraryid=13360 (last accessed on February 17, 2006).

[13] Santosus, Megan, "Why You Need a Project Management Office (PMO)" CIO Magazine, July 1, 2003.

[14] Gaughan, Dennis, and Carline Durocher, "AMR Research Report—IT Portfolio Management Software: Clear Benefits, Converging Marketplace," AMR Research, Boston, MA, June 1, 2004.

[15] Robbins-Gioia, "ERP Survey Results Point to Need for Higher Implementation Success; Robbins-Gioia LLC identifies Lack of Focused Management Surrounding ERP Implementations," Business Wire, January 28, 2002.

[16]   Graham, Peter J., *Creating an Environment for Successful Projects: The Quest to Manage Project Management*, San Francisco, CA: Jossey-Bass Publishers, 1997.

[17]   National Association of State Chief Information Officers, "State of Iowa Return on Investment Program Nomination Form for State IT Initiatives Award," as referenced by Susan Combs in "GG19, Ensure Returns on Investments in Information Technology," eTexas, January 2003, www.cpa.state.tx.us/etexas2003/gg19.html (last accessed on May 5, 2006).

[18]   Light, M., and D Stang, "Magic Quadrant for Project and Portfolio Management, 2004," Gartner, Inc., Stamford, CT, February 7, 2004.

[19]   Levinson, Meridith, "Project Management—When Failure Is Not an Option," *CIO Magazine*, June 2006, www.cio.com/article/21413/Project_Management_When_Failure_Is_Not_an_Option (last accessed on December 17, 2007).

[20]   Holmes, Allan, "Rx for Risk," *CIO Magazine*, March 15, 2006, pp. 56–62.

[21]   Berinato, Scott, "Playing with Fire," *CIO Magazine*, July 1, 2003, www.cio.com/archive/070103/fire.html (last accessed on April 30, 2006).

[22]   Minsky, Steven, "Developing Risk Plans," EBizQ, June 24, 2005, www.ebizq.net/topics/bpm/features/6021.html?&pp=1 (last accessed on April 30, 2006).

[23]   Lawrie, G. J. G., D. C. Kaiff, and H. V. Andersen, "Integrating Risk Management with Existing Methods of Strategic Control: Avoiding Duplication within the Corporate Governance Agenda," 2GC Limited, August 1, 2003, www.2gc.co.uk/pdf/2GC-CP0803.pdf (last accessed on April 15, 2006).

[24]   Waxer, Cindy, "Portfolio Management: How Lowe's Grows," *CIO Magazine*, December 1, 2005.

[25]   Schlichter, John, Ralf Friedrich, and Bill Haeck, "The History of OPM3," adapted from a paper written for PMI's Global Congress Europe 2003 in Den Haag, the Netherlands, March 8, 2003, www.pmforum.org/library/papers/2003/historyofopm3.pdf (last accessed on December 17, 2007).

[26]   "Organizational Project Management Maturity Model (OPM3) Knowledge Foundation," Project Management Institute, Stamford, CT, December 31, 2003.

## CHAPTER 7

# Risk Management

## Operational Risk

If you've ever studied quantum mechanics, you know that absolute certainty cannot be applied to any one event; there will always be some level of uncertainty that an event will occur as expected. That is, at the most basic level of human understanding (and the known laws of the universe), nothing can be done without some probability that it won't happen. Various physics instructors famously illustrate this when they first explain that electrons can pass through an atom with some probability and then follow up with the notion that we can all also pass through a wall with some (albeit much lower) probability. Fortunately for business enterprises, the laws of the universe are aligned with the basic goals of a company: improbability (or uncertainty) is the basis of risk, and risk is one of the driving forces of growth.

The simple definition according to the dictionary is that "risk" is the possibility of loss, injury, or harm [1, 2]. If we were to fit this definition to the world of business, then risk would be the combination of two variables: the probability that an adverse event will occur and the impact it will have on the goals of the business. For example, a harbor master would consider a hurricane to be a highly adverse event that would have an extremely negative impact on business. A roofing company, on the other hand, might consider the same event as a highly opportunistic event that would have an extremely positive impact on business. While a roofing business wouldn't wish for a hurricane in its strategic plan, the harbor master might mention one as a risk and a reason for investing in certain mitigation steps. How a company rates adversity and impact can be very subjective. However, if all risks are rated according to probability and the same adversity/impact scale, then they can be prioritized relative to each other to create a custom "risk profile." But before diving into how companies profile their risk portfolios, let's get a longer definition of operational risk by looking at how it has been categorized, typed, and framed over the years by risk experts.

While nuclear physics frames improbability in terms of the four forces of nature, Phil Rosenzweig, author of "The Halo Effect, and Other Managerial Delusions," frames corporate risk in terms of four sources of uncertainty [3].

1. *External environment:* Companies should first recognize the fundamental uncertainty of the business world: will markets continue to provide a demand, will innovation cause industries to become obsolete, or will supply chains dry up?
2. *Customers:* Companies should look specifically at the uncertainty that involves customers: will customers embrace or reject a new product, will

they act as a strong or weak reference, or will they engage in predatory litigation?

3. *Technology:* A third source of uncertainty comes from technological change. Digital music disrupted the music industry, the Internet demolished the travel agent industry, and enterprise resource planning (ERP) rollouts have brought a multitude of companies to their knees.

4. *Internal environment:* A final source of uncertainty concerns internal capabilities, or operations: are the right projects being selected, are processes improving at a rapid pace, and is staff capable of flexing to new market shifts?

The risks that then generate from these four sources of uncertainty can then be categorized into three well-known corporate risk types: credit risks, market risks, and operational risks. Credit risk applies to how lending and rating companies view a company's health and ability to pay debt. With banks, credit risk has two dimensions: how dependably the bank can borrow from other lending institutions and how dependably its borrowers can pay the bank back. Market risk applies to how stable customer demands and supplier flows are. If a company sells its product or service to a volatile customer base or has an undependable supplier portfolio, then its market risk is greater.

Credit and market risks are the subject of numerous studies, regulations, and frameworks that have been adopted by companies and governments for decades. While all risks are commonly based upon the uncertainty a company has with certain business elements, credit and market risks have their own, different forms of mitigation. With credit risks; company history, maturity, and industry can be tracked by analysts to more accurately grade a company, and research approaches abound on how to mitigate risks associated with a company's market. While there will continue to be risks unique to each of these categories, many frameworks exist to better understand and mitigate their uncertainties.

Operational risk, on the other hand, applies to how dependably management has implemented internal organizational structure, culture, processes, and investments. In 1999, the Bank of International Settlements' Basel committee defined operational risk as "the risk of loss resulting from inadequate or failed internal processes, people and systems or from external events" [4]. With banks across Europe forced to mitigate such risks via their compliance with the Basel II accord, this definition is becoming well accepted and the source of many companies' operational risk management (RM) frameworks. So, let's review each component.

- *Process:* Chapter 5 defines business processes and strategic process portfolios. Examples of common business processes that can have some level of risk include payment and settlement, product and raw material delivery, sales, contract settlements, product pricing, and performance reporting. The risk that a process is slower than a competitor's, incurs avoidable costs, or erodes corporate culture can be very tangible and should be addressed.

- *People:* While we have addressed individuals' influence on projects, processes, and performance in other chapters, we will not look at risks associated with the individual. Examples of such risks that we won't cover include employee fraud, unauthorized or illegal activities, employee churn, and employment law.

- *Systems:* Since information technology (IT) permeates just about every part of a company's operations, an IT-specific set of risks tends to be identified. IT departments are known for spearheading such risk management efforts. Examples of risks these departments are addressing can include new system investment, user access, network and data capacity, system failures, and information security.

- *External:* Risks can come from outside the walls of the company. Later in this chapter, we will introduce business continuity management (BCM). BCM can be considered a part of risk management, or it can be considered an independent activity all together. Either way, it is useful in mitigating such external risks as legal problems, criminal activities, outsourcing issues, supplier bottlenecks, disasters, and regulatory compliance [4].

With the recent rise in need for regulatory compliance, business continuity, and information security, a school of thought on corporate risk management has developed called enterprise risk management (ERM). Its purpose is to promote the consolidation and prioritization of all the risk types into a single collective. It is believed that if a coordinated risk message is delivered to staff, there is a better chance that a culture of risk will blossom. By combining credit, market, and operational risk management under one roof, consistency rather than confusion will also feed the strategic design process; the same risk profile, or level of risk, will be applied consistently across the enterprise. Finally, establishing and maintaining ERM procedures is also a proactive approach to guide departments in managing their risks consistently. This can in turn help reduce bureaucracy and minimize the problems caused by complex blindsides. It is believed that risk management should be a part of every business planning decision [5], not a temporary, narrowly focused effort on regulations. Nevertheless, according to Michael A. Bailey and Edward T. Hida, authors of Deloitte Development, LLC's 2004 Global Risk Management Survey, since "ERM continues to be an elusive concept that varies widely in definition and implementation," it can take many years for a company to see value-add from an ERM roll out [6]. Understanding how ERM is linked to and supports the other components of PePPR management can help clarify the benefits.

Jeff Tetric, chief financial officer (CFO) of Pinnacol Assurance of Denver, Colorado, has taken such a step by integrating risk identification into that company's enterprise-level strategic action committees (SACs). Pinnacol's SACs are distributed across the organization to focus primarily on process consistency in its sales units. Since the company is a well-regulated agency, it has to follow documented processes when selling or servicing workman's compensation policies. While its SACs help ensure internal compliance with the documented processes, executives also saw the opportunity to have these units help with bottom-up risk identification. Thus, Pinnacol was able to formalize PePPR feed 1 (see Figure 7.1) with committees that help "pull" process risks from the organization on a regular basis. This eliminated the need for separate risk management units to support the risk identification process.

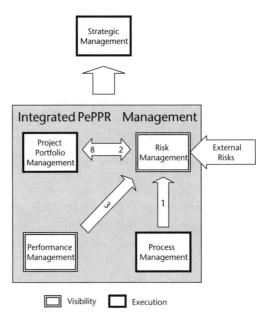

**Figure 7.1**  Risk-based integrated PePPR feeds.

Whether you have a small or a large company, the risks you take are unique to your situations. For this reason, when establishing a risk management policy (either formally or informally), it is important to create one customized to your organization. Sure, it is a good idea to research market, industry, and academic risk frameworks as a foundation, but be sure to modify such frameworks to accommodate your culture and business environment [7]. Integrating risk management into the processes of your organization is the first step; relentless executive support will then smooth it into the culture. According to the Treasury Board of Canada's Secretariat, "Effective risk management cannot be practiced in isolation, but needs to be built into existing decision-making structures and processes" [8]. The next section consolidates several frameworks to create a best practices approach that can be used for complete ERM.

## An Enterprise Risk Management Methodology

When individuals decide to buy insurance, they usually go through a decision-making process. They identify a risk (e.g., car theft, hurricane, injury), assess its impact on their lives (e.g., no transportation, no house, no health), and decide to mitigate the risk through an insurance purchase. While these three steps make up the core components of most risk management methodologies, there are other peripheral activities on either end (see Figure 7.2). Before risks are identified, individuals have developed a level of risk aversion or acceptance. That is, based on age, personality, and experience, they have determined which risks they'll take and which they'll avoid; they've created a mental risk strategy (or a personal risk profile). After risks are mitigated (e.g., through an insurance purchase), individuals experience a level of customer service from their insurance company (Figure 7.2, item 1), hear about alternative policies from competing companies (Figure 7.2, item 1), and reevaluate their level of risk aversion (Figure 7.2, item 2). In short, they improve their approach to mitigating their risks (or how they purchase their insurance (Figure 7.2, item 3).

In some cases, individuals' aversion to risk is forced on them by government regulations. This can force them to purchase insurance to mitigate those risks that can affect others. For example, in some countries, automobile insurance is required before a license is issued. Such laws are meant to reduce the number of car accident victims who must rely on free hospital care. Besides the obvious benefit to the insurance industry, this also helps protect the hospital industry. Where insurance purchases could be considered a form of risk management out-sourcing, leveraging one's own resources could be considered a form of risk management in-sourcing. In other words, when insurance is not required or desired, people tend to mitigate risks in their own way. Security alarms can be added to cars, houses can be built on stilts, and hazardous jobs can be avoided. Companies approach risk mitigation in similar ways: quantitatively through the purchase of insurance or qualitatively through the implementation of cross-functional teams [9]. Either approach follows the same process of risk strategy, identification, assessment, and mitigation.

### Risk Strategy

According to Hewitt Roberts, author of "Enterprise Risk Management: A Long-Term Solution for Compliance, Governance, and Sustained Growth in Share-

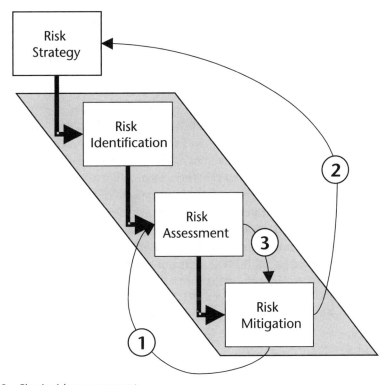

**Figure 7.2** Classic risk management.

holder Value," "The most compelling reason for implementing an enterprise risk management system is that it is undeniably the most efficient, effective and proactive approach to increasing shareholder value" [10]. Since a company's exposure to or willingness to accept risk is ultimately decided by its strategy, some reference to risk management should exist in the strategy [11]. Such references could focus on whether a risk management organization will be created, who the leader of such an organization will report to, which regulations the company must adhere to, and examples of business- and industry-specific disasters the company will avoid (i.e., basic scenario analysis). Then, when the strategy is distributed, company staff will better understand how risk management supports the corporate strategy and where lines are drawn between unacceptable and tolerable risks. Unfortunately, it takes more than simply e-mailing out a strategy document to set the cultural mood on risk. Actions need to be taken by executives and seen by employees on a continual basis. Over time, a culture and evolving strategy will set a foundation for improved approaches to risk management [5, 9]. The perception of risks will then not be confined to such operational specifics as task completion time, inventory levels, or attendance records. Rather, the understanding of risks will be linked to such strategic goals as cost reduction, profit improvement, and customer service. That is, where employees originally looked at risks as threats to the success of their jobs, they will now also look at risks as threats to the success of the entire company. While Rosenzweig frames risk types around four sources of uncertainty, Bill Sharon, author of "The Elusive 'Risk Culture'," presents four items that can be identified through strategic (or enterprise-level) risk management. Strategic ERM helps identify:

1. Risks that can limit business continuity (business continuity management);
2. Risks associated with new investments (project portfolios);
3. Risks associated with business efficiency (process architectures);
4. Opportunities that derive from risk mitigation plans (project portfolios) [12].

The first element refers to high-risk items, or hazards; the second two refer to standard risks, or uncertainties; and the last element refers to opportunities, a side effect of good risk management. According to Martyn E. Jones and Gillian Sutherland of the Center for Business Performance, risk management includes the management of opportunities. That is, decision makers begin to see risk as "not only 'bad things happening,' but also 'good things not happening'" [13]. They discover not only threats but also opportunities for the organization. These four elements make up what Sharon refers to as a "hazard/uncertainty/opportunity risk continuum." Such a continuum that links operations with new investments positions the risk manager as the coordinator of information between business and operational managers and the corporate strategy. Risk management then "becomes a communications vehicle for furthering the strategy and a source for innovative ideas" [12].

This risk continuum is precisely what can be seen in the PePPR model as feeds 1, 2, and 8 in Figure 7.1. New investments create their own risks, which are managed using project management principles (feed 2). At the same time, risk mitigation activities can be realized as financed projects (feed 8). Also, an ongoing stream of risks flow from everyday business processes. Even though processes exist primarily because they have proven stability, the ground they sit on may be changing. A standard way of machining a tool may change due to innovations in metallurgy, a standard way of distributing meals on a flight may change due to new industry-pricing models, and a standard way of collecting overdue bills may change due to new government regulations. Traditional process-centric risk management mitigates the problems introduced by such changes through proactive scenario and options analysis. Incorporating project portfolio management into this traditional process-centric approach to risk management helps round out the continuum.

The final component of the risk side of integrated PePPR management has to do with performance metrics. A major electric utility has established a popular process for reviewing performance metrics to reduce the risk that executives are monitoring the wrong information (feed 3). The company's executive committee periodically reviews its core performance metrics for applicability to the strategy. The board is also given the opportunity to weigh in on metrics at the annual strategic session. Thus, by enforcing risk reviews at the highest levels, the company helps keep strategic goals constantly aligned with implementation performance. Porter General Hospital doesn't just regularly validate performance metrics for internal process and projects; it also validates metrics for external entities, such as the performance of an oncology practice of which it owns 50%. Regular performance metric validation gives companies an opportunity to reduce the risk of executives' looking the wrong direction as market speedballs or capability land mines come their way.

## Risk Identification

Once a risk strategy is outlined and linked to the corporate strategy, risks can be identified. To better identify risks, we'll introduce a framework that will help categorize them. Figure 7.3 shows a matrix with internal and external risks along the horizontal access and strategic and nonstrategic risks along the vertical axis. This risk profile shows risks that have been categorized for demonstration purposes only, and it is understood that different corporate strategies can lead to different risk profiles. For example, for some companies "customer churn" might be a central strategic issue; here we show it as an internal, nonstrategic risk type.

Along the bottom of this figure, we show how a company can implement its risk profile in phases. The first phase implements the process explained in the previous section. Namely, external, strategic risks can be identified by executives as they develop the corporate and enterprise risk management strategies. The second phase focuses more on internal, strategic risks such as those that are operational, financial, or IT related. But this second phase also wraps up coverage of such external risks as reputation, as well as details of the market, such as price pressures and brand effects. Also, being the phase that establishes a central risk management organization, phase 2 redundantly reviews the other risk areas. The third phase involves identifying long-term and nontraditional risks, such as those that are cultural, employee-growth oriented, and customer-satisfaction related [13]. As a company progresses through these phases, it starts to develop the culture required of long-term ERM, culminating in a companywide awareness of what levels of risk to take within each profile.

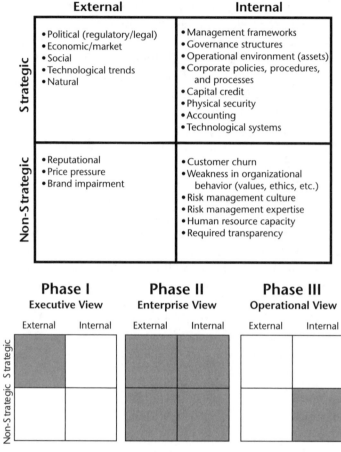

**Figure 7.3**  Phasing risk identification [8, 13–15].

Figure 7.4 shows how a company can roll out its formal risk process. Traditionally, "phases" refer to steps that follow each other, and it is no different here. However, our risk implementation phases occur iteratively. In the first iteration, the three risk implementation phases do occur in order, but in later iterations, they will overlap. The first activities come from phase 1, external strategic risk identification. As external threats are identified, phase 2 ERM reviews should ramp up. These can include identifying internal strategic risks that are associated with capital-intensive projects, core process, and performance metrics. Other phase 2 activities, such as operational risk identification, should occur at regular intervals both preceding and following strategic-level intervals. This helps provide grounding for the ERM team to both guide executives in their identification of risks and for the ERM team to be influenced by the output from the executive sessions. Phase 3 activities should start after the initial phase 2 process and require less effort due to the groundwork laid by the ERM team in phase 2. Frontline workers will review all their work processes and identify possible risks. Then, as time progresses, they can be trained about how to continuously be on the lookout for risks in their work environment. Such an ongoing approach should establish a culture of risk illustrated not by periodic efforts but by the curve shown in Figure 7.4.

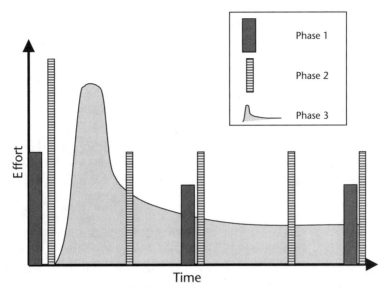

**Figure 7.4** Risk identification phased rollout.

### Phase 1: Executive View

Besides developing a strategy and establishing a risk management organization, executives also have an opportunity to identify strategic-level risks. Examples can include risks associated with mergers and acquisitions, product-line changes, or major market shifts. Details about how to assess and mitigate the risks may or may not be included in a distributed plan depending on their sensitivity. Even though risk mitigation strategies may be kept private, simply including the primary strategic risks in the corporate strategy can spearhead the risk awareness of the company. Making executive commitment to risk management visible to the rest of the organization will gain more than just the attention of the staff; risk management accountability will start to trickle downward.

In this phase, you will want to first tackle external risks with an industrial or market analysis. Internal risk assessments can be folded into phase 2. If no formal process exists to help identify risks, either use the process developed by the ERM team to identify phase 2 risks, leverage the process used by the board-level audit team, or create a process from scratch that will be used by some future ERM team. If you are creating a process from scratch, then you should first consider the different dimensions from which you would like to approach it. You can look at both short-term and long-term risks (time oriented), project and process risks (growth and continuity oriented), or regulatory and legal risks. Then, after establishing this structure for categorizing your risks, you need to figure out how to introduce it to the company. The section on risk mitigation will split this out into board-level versus executive-level risk management.

### Phase 2: Enterprise View

Once external strategic risks have been identified, a risk management approach has been defined, and the strategy has been broadcast, the formal companywide and strategically aligned ERM process can begin. The primary focus of a phase 2 ERM is on internal, strategic and external, nonstrategic risks. But since ERM groups act as the heart of all risk management in a company, overlap with the other risk categories in our framework will exist. For example, the ERM team can train and guide both executives and frontline workers in how to identify risks. The ERM team can also schedule risk reviews and help propose mitigation approaches for external, strategic and internal, operational risks (Figure 7.5).

In short, phase 2 roll out of risk management in a company is considered the central rollout component; all four quadrants of Figure 7.3 are covered. Phase 2's extensive coverage allows us to present a perspective on identifying risks by looking at a company's processes, assets, and projects.

*Processes*    When the ERM team first helps executives with the strategic risk reviews, one approach would be to first identify key business processes, or "critical path" processes [9]. Then, as the ERM team moves on to work with the various business units to identify risks, more expansive reviews of business processes can take place. Conducting business process reviews to help identify risks is a good approach at all levels of the company because processes touch areas that aren't usually investigated; they cross both external and internal organizational boundaries. Supply chain, customer delivery, accounts receivable, and marketing processes are all examples of the sources of risk. Since such coverage is so expensive, phase 2 guidance should iterate with phase 3 identification of operational risks.

*Assets*    Another more static approach would be to identify the risks associated with the various corporate assets [16]. For example, what would happen to an airline company if its hangars burned up, what would happen to a software company if its backups were lost, and what would happen to a biotechnology company if its patents were prematurely rejected? A company should combine corporate dynamics (processes) with corporate statics (assets) to provide for a more multidimensional view of risks. This approach also rounds out the strong activity theme of integrated PePPR management. With ERM, statics (temporary and

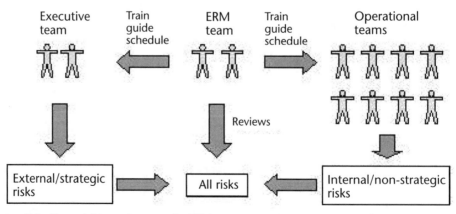

**Figure 7.5**  Flow of risks and support by ERM team.

permanent) are now part of the equation. We will address these sorts of asset-loss-related risks below in the section on business continuity risk.

*Projects*    Each project that a company invests in should have its own risk management activity. Whether the project is to build a bridge, develop a new drug, run a charity event, or roll out a new technology, it will have its own list of risks that could lead to project failure. So, how does the ERM team get involved with project-level risk management? In two ways: first, the team sets guidelines on risks to be propagated by the project portfolio management office; second, the overall risk levels of the highest-priority projects get included with ERM executive reports. If the project portfolio management office (PMO) is in tune with the ever-changing corporate strategy (and thus with the risk profile of the organization), the ERM team's job is that much easier. Such strategic alignment will allow the ERM team to create a more detailed set of guidelines, which can be leveraged by the PMO and project managers. As organizations grow, not only do risks from key projects get passed to central risk managers but a consolidated report of all operational risks can be passed up—like the report sent on project portfolio health [17]. ORM goes so far as to define risk management as the process of assessing "both quantitatively and qualitatively the opportunity for success of business initiatives" [17]. This definition drops consideration of processes, people, and systems in favor of financed projects as the driving force behind risk management.

### Phase 3: Operational View

Once a program is in place to identify, assess, and report on risks for the executive dashboard, the ERM team can then validate the risk review processes used at the operational level. Many would consider this a chicken-or-egg scenario in which it might be better to create a risk culture first and then start reporting results to the executives.

But, as in the dynamic execution environments of the racing sailboat or the hospital emergency room, someone needs to man the rudder or make final life or death decisions. A direction needs to be set before synergy can be realized; otherwise, different risk profiles and approaches can propagate. One department may decide to invest more in bleeding-edge IT systems, while another may chose to stay with dependable legacy systems—one chooses improvement, growth, and high risk, the other stagnation, inefficiency, and dependability. A company that first sets risk policy at the strategic level benefits from an organization that can react quickly to sudden market-level demands. Otherwise, the cowboy departments will continue riding broncos during a realignment, and the stagnant departments will continue looking out office windows during a rapid growth phase.

Those operational risks that carry enough cost weight to get executive attention can be either associated with a large outlay, such as an enterprise-level project, or a core asset, such as a patent. But smaller operational risks can also reach the executive desk if they are consolidated into a portfolio report, as would be done by a project portfolio management office, a departmental risk management office, or a process improvement team. Many failed small projects may indicate a need for enterprisewide project management training, improved project selection guidelines, or a revamped resource hiring approach. Quality gaffes with multiple products may indicate a need for enterprisewide process improvement initiatives, updated asset lifetime calculations, or employee culture renewal. Smaller risks are invaluable to operational managers but act as noise and distraction to the executive manager. Small-risk consolidation and large-risk prioritization through a strategic activity management office (see Chapter 8) can add credibility to those risks that feed executive dashboards from the depths of the company.

## Risk Assessment

Once you've identified risks, it's time to compare them against each other to determine which ones deserve greater attention. This comparison activity should in turn be a well-understood and -implemented process to ensure a consistent assessment of the risks. A very common first step is to grade each risk for impact and likelihood of occurrence. This subjective type of review relies on the grader's expertise for accuracy, but more importantly, it relies on the grader's consistent objectivity in his or her review. Also referred to as risk profiling, this activity starts with the identification approaches we discussed earlier and culminates in the graphing of each graded risk on a matrix split into four, nine, or more sections [13]. The more common, less complex approach would be to split an impact/likelihood graph into four sections. In such a diagram (see Figure 7.6), the actual scores would be less apparent than the relative scores (or how the scores are compared against each other). To ensure consistency in this form of risk grading, the optimal approach would be for the risks to be graded by one person. Unfortunately, the person most qualified to grade any particular risk may change over a group of risks. In that scenario, where multiple risk graders are used to improve accuracy and reduce subjectivity, the side effect would be to also reduce consistency. Consistency between risk raters can be improved, however, if a complete risk grading process is documented, communicated, and audited. "The process," says Raytheon's CIO, Rebecca Rhoads, "is so much more important than the math rigor. Mature, consistent processes—you need that first" [18].

Figure 7.6 shows a four-by-four matrix where scored risks can be placed. Once you've plotted the risks on such a matrix and then multiplied the likelihood by the impact values (Table 7.1), you can clearly see how to prioritize them. The chart gives a view of the risks and how they are positioned against all other risks. If too many risks show the same overall risk scores, then assessors can reduce this by setting weights to either impact or likelihood, based upon which is more important.

While impact/likelihood analysis is very common, there are other ways a set of risks can be assessed. Two of these are Monte Carlo analysis and real options analysis.

- *Monte Carlo analysis:* In science and engineering, many unknowns are functions of a set of variables. To quantify these unknowns, equations are designed that propose how the variables depend on each other. If these variables are based on random uncertainty, then a technique known as Monte Carlo simulation can be used. For example, one of the variables in such an equation can be based on an either-or situation, like a coin flip, and another variable can

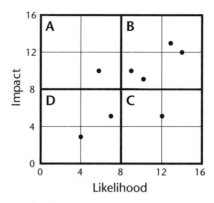

**Figure 7.6** Impact/likelihood graph.

**Table 7.1** Risk Impact/Likelihood Profiling and Prioritization

| Risk | Impact | Likelihood | Impact × Likelihood |
|------|--------|------------|---------------------|
| Project A: turnover | 13 | 13 | 169 |
| Debt declared due | 12 | 14 | 168 |
| Competing product introduced | 9 | 10 | 90 |
| Supply chain affected by union strike | 10 | 9 | 90 |
| Project B: cost overruns | 10 | 6 | 60 |
| Corporate merger delayed | 5 | 12 | 60 |
| Project C: natural disaster | 5 | 7 | 35 |
| Board turnover | 3 | 4 | 12 |

have one of six outcomes, like the roll of a die. A Monte Carlo simulator (or software program) flips the make-believe coin and rolls the make-believe die hundreds of times, then applies the outcomes to the equation for each instance. Afterward, an outcome distribution can be viewed for the equation. Monte Carlo excels most "when many risks are in play at once (such as launching an ERP project)" [18]. This approach works wonderfully if you are able to translate a process or risk into an equation or even an assumption into a variable. Many times, however, this is not the case in business.

- *Real options analysis:* Another approach to introducing probability is through the use of a decision tree. A decision tree proves most useful "at mapping either-or situations and the sequential risks that follow each decision (for example, either I build a new factory or retrofit an old one)" [18]. Probability is attached to each branch, which leads to compounded probability numbers at the "leaves" of the tree. A more advanced version of this approach is known as real options analysis, where net present value forecasts are also applied to each branch. Since this latter form of decision tree analysis can get rather complex, I have seen many apply this method only when presenting larger, more capital-intensive projects. That is, smaller projects may be flirting with an analysis-paralysis disaster if they use real options analysis. Also, since this form of analysis more clearly shows the dirty laundry of "what if it fails," many shy away in order to better sell their proposals.

### Risk Mitigation

While visionary leaps and innovative investments are keys to corporate growth, delusional expectations and blind faith are keys to corporate demise. Well-thought-out and -implemented risk mitigation approaches can help industry risk takers fall on the growth side of the fence. How aggressively these approaches are implemented depends primarily on the direction of the strategy: if executives are optimistic, less rigor is applied; if executives are pessimistic, robust risk management approaches are applied companywide. By including at least a simple risk management process at the strategic level, executives will be forced to look at the negative as well as the positive components of the business. This will help to reduce what Dan P. Lovallo, author of "Distortions and Deceptions in Strategic Decisions," considers a problem with strategic decision makers: over optimism [19]. One way to keep executives in tune with the actual capabilities of the organization is to have access to past risk mitigation results. But since such results are only available if they've been tracked and logged, steps should be defined to thoroughly document the risk identification and assessment results before implementing any mitigation steps. Such risk management tracking will support forecasts that "reward realism, and frown on over-optimism" [19].

### The Board

Risk management is a critical component of board-level governance. If risks are mitigated at this level, the company will have one more catalyst for healthy strategy maintenance by the executives. As an example, imagine a company that decides to expand into a foreign market. A boardroom that supports a company by just reacting to metric shifts (e.g., financial ratios, stock prices) will miss opportunities to protect the best interests of the company. However, a board made up of directors who have experience in this area and are aware that overoptimism can be dangerous will take action [13]. Control versus support is a theme we continue to focus on throughout this book. With board-level risk management usually undertaken by an audit committee and a board-hired independent auditor, opportunities can exist where board members can support mitigation tasks, as well as control risk through audits.

### Executives

The actions taken by the board can have a strong influence on how the executives manage not only risks but the entire company. If too much weight is placed on just monitoring near-term financial metrics, executives and operating managers will tend to "optimize short-term performance at the expense of long-term corporate health" [19]. Thus, a key risk to mitigate at the board level (or at the level of owner representatives) is how well executive incentives are aligned with the core goals of the owners. When the incentives of employees are misaligned with the goals of company owners, a phenomenon known as the principal-agent problem can result. We saw many publicized and criminalized examples of such an approach to management at the turn of the century (e.g., WorldCom, Enron, and Adelphia). In contrast, if incentives are aligned with the goals of company owners, executives will adhere to, as well as be accountable for, the success of their strategy. With board-level risk management processes in place, executives will be guided by example, and a culture of risk leadership can propagate. Continuous and consistent risk leadership can then lead to aligned risk profiles, improved resource usage, and, ultimately, better cost management.

## Operations

Determining what controls to put into place to mitigate risks at the board and executive levels can be complex. As risk mitigation efforts are applied at lower levels of the organization, such mitigation controls can be just as complex. In general, however, there are three categories of risk controls: preventive, detective, and reactive. By mitigating risks in all three categories, the company is able to mitigate risks with some level of structured redundancy. This approach is used widely to mitigate corporate security threats. To prevent facility intruders and software viruses, security check-in stations and e-mail filters are installed; to detect intruders and viruses that have breeched security layers, cameras and systems scanners are engaged; and to react to intrusions, security personnel and virus cleaners are deployed. A plan that accommodates these three layers of security provides a comprehensive view that in turn allows responses to be robust, fast, and anticipated [16].

## Iterative Mitigation

In the section on risk assessment, we showed how risks can be charted to compare the likelihood of their occurring with their impact. When mitigating risks, the scores from such an analysis need to be lined up against the available resources. Is there enough funding, staff, or both to mitigate the highest-priority risks? Are resources allocated correctly across the different risk mitigation efforts? Which risk mitigation efforts should be monitored more closely? G. J. G. Lawrie, D. C. Kaiff, and H. V. Andersen, authors of "Integrating Risk Management with Existing Methods of Strategic Control: Avoiding Duplication within the Corporate Governance Agenda," came up with a way to chart risks against business capabilities to better answer some of these questions. Figure 7.7 shows the cost of the risk (e.g., likelihood score multiplied by an impact score) along the $y$-axis and the ability of the company to control (or mitigate) the risk along the $x$-axis. This model shows precisely where enterprise risk mitigation links with project portfolio management (i.e., PePPR flow 8). Namely, when risks have a high cost and are difficult to resolve, investments are made and projects are launched to more aggressively attempt mitigation (upper left quadrant of Figure 7.7). The project portfolio acts as a way to then prioritize these types of projects against the swath of other projects that have been submitted for approval.

Because information-security needs can spread like ivy through so many parts of an organization, a midsized IT division I worked with recently decided to integrate security management with its project portfolio architecture. The lower half of Figure 7.8 shows the project pipeline split out into three major process areas: project selection, project control, and project evaluation. The chief information officer then represented these areas in a Venn diagram shown at the top of Figure 7.8. The overlap of these three areas helped define how the PMO was to be staffed. The

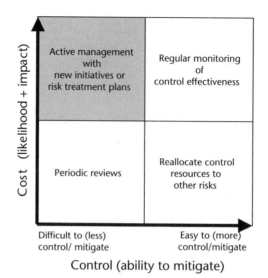

**Figure 7.7**   Risk mitigation scoring model. (*After* [5]).

enterprise architect would help select and control project technology, the portfolio manager would formalize the selection and return on investment (ROI) processes, and the director of portfolio security would audit projects for security compliance. This latter component clearly provides a vital link between enterprise risk management and enterprise project portfolio management. By creating this association, the organization made it clear that enterprise activity management silos can integrate with synergistic effect. No longer was the security manager made aware of security holes after systems were installed and running. Now the organization was able to ensure compliance before funding. "You don't build security into a system after it's [done]. You build it in on the front end. It's the same with enterprise risk management. You consider [risk] when deciding what systems to build and what business processes to automate" [20]. Activity management integration such as this brought the business representative and the technologist together with a key risk manager at the highest levels of strategic decision making.

So far, we have seen how subjective identifying and assessing risks can be. To remove some of the subjectivity, we introduced some approaches that can be used to more efficiently identify the risks, then more accurately and consistently assess them. After the initial assessment, more detailed analysis can occur to help design the mitigation approach. For example, a risk impact analysis can now include the resources needed and the cost to mitigate the risk. This, in turn, leads to an iterative process of mitigation and reassessment. Before an initial attempt at risk mitigation, impact analysis focuses on how the risk will affect the company in a worse-case scenario with no mitigation applied. After mitigation attempts, the impact analysis can focus on how the risk mitigation caused a reprioritization due to resource limitations. This iterative approach to risk analysis further helps address the objective nature of risk analysis and mitigation by zeroing in on the actual problem and reducing collateral damage. Keep in mind that the goal shouldn't be to eliminate all risks (since risk will always exist for those companies seeking growth). Rather, mitigation

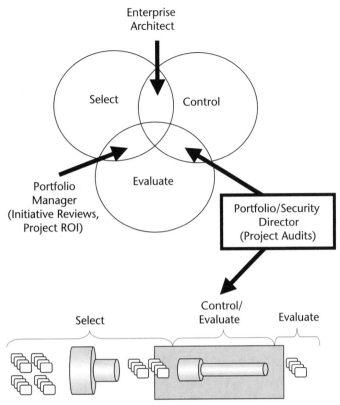

**Figure 7.8**   Inclusion of security risk management in a PMO governance model.

approaches should be implemented to bring risk analysis scores down to a level that aligns with the strategic risk profile of the company.

Figure 7.9 builds on Figure 7.1 by showing the need for iteration in the mitigation processes. The figure also shows some follow-on activities that should occur to round out the complete picture of enterprise risk management. The following list explains the steps in the figure:

1. Risk mitigation attempts need to be reassessed and validated for success. If the risk was not mitigated to a level that matches the risk aversion of the corporate strategy, then updated or new approaches may be needed.

2. Such controls can be consolidated and tracked for implementation, documentation, relevancy, and consistency [5]. A company can only improve upon its risk management process if it benchmarks, tracks, and constantly improves its risk control portfolio (i.e., its risk management processes). Risk control improvement should also be anticipated in any adaptive strategy; adding new controls or making changes to existing controls should be a regular process for the risk management team [14].

3. Part of each mitigation effort should include the placement of warning alarms to guard against risk reflash [13]. Such alarms can take the form of improved review frequencies. For example, unruly staff can have more

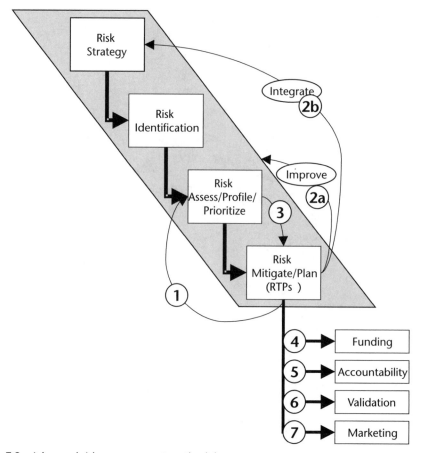

**Figure 7.9**  Advanced risk management methodology.

frequent performance reviews, older assets can have more frequent quality reviews, and treasury investments can have more frequent audits.

4. To help management understand its risk control landscape, it should track how it has funded mitigation steps. As we've shown, initiatives can be funded with an underlying goal of mitigating some risk [9]. Over time, perceptions may change, and the initiatives may be evaluated for their efficiency, improvement, or ROI achievements. By keeping track of those projects that have been funded to mitigate risks, the risk management portfolio can be more efficiently balanced.

5. Since risk management can be delegated to the various business units or departments, accountability needs to be tracked [13]. Those who received funding to mitigate an identified risk should periodically present the status of their initiative to some oversight organization (e.g., project sponsor, the executives, a PMO, or a risk management office).

6. Funded risk mitigation initiatives aren't the only elements of risk management that should be reviewed; proposed risk profiles should also be scrutinized. While the central profile sprouts from the corporate strategy, subprofiles can also appear as means to validate a mitigation effort. These

subprofiles should be reviewed horizontally by peers [9] and vertically by executives to provide contrasting views [13].

7. Progress toward risk control, like any activity management effort, needs to be constantly marketed for its value to the rest of the organization. Key risk indicators, like key performance indicators, should be benchmarked and tracked for improvement so that they can be used to prove the case for diligent activity management [13].

Many ERM methodologies and maturity models exist in academia and on the market. This book has chosen to present a hybrid of several such approaches to highlight how performance, project, and process management can integrate to better support dynamic organizations. Phased ERM rollout, iterative risk mitigation, integrated activity management, best practice leverage, and light but effective ERM teams are all ways to turn risk terror into bold and calculated action. The next section looks at two examples of how ERM is applied: regulatory compliance and business continuity.

## Applied Enterprise Risk Management

### Regulatory Risk

Enterprise risk management has hit the headlines so strongly in recent years in part due to laws passed by governments. The two most internationally pervasive of these are the Sarbanes-Oxley Act (SarbOx or SOX) and the Basel II Accord. While each of these has a core focus (corporate financial statements and bank risk, respectively), they also have something in common: they each require organizations to prove they have taken steps to mitigate operational risk. As a result, the affected companies were forced to create new processes that ensured they were complying with the regulations. Many companies that were already burdened by many industry-specific regulations (e.g., those that generate toxic waste, provide energy, save lives, or manage money) had regulatory compliance managers working side by side with their risk managers. Other companies had to invest new capital in projects that would create the structures and processes to support these new compliance activities. The downside of this was that organizations had to temporarily focus more on risk than on performance. The upside was that now enterprise risk management was becoming standard fare in public companies and banks where before it wasn't. With integrated PePPR management, the opportunity now exists to integrate the activities associated with both so as to provide a consolidated, simplified view of the health of the organization. Let's take a look at how some of these regulations led to the new awareness in enterprise risk.

In capitalist societies, a core goal is to provide as much freedom as possible to the elements of business so as to improve competition, thus innovation and consumer benefit. However, when given much freedom, businesses have been known to violate the freedom of others. For example, several laws went into place in the United States after the Great Depression to prevent companies themselves from restricting free competition (e.g., monopolies and trusts). Over the years, restrictive but needed laws were also passed to protect employees (e.g., child-labor and minimum-wage laws and work-hour restrictions). In the late 1990s, with the boom of the Internet, personal information became much more accessible. The United States passed the Gramm-Leach-Bliley (GLB) and Health Insurance Portability and Accountability (HIPAA) acts and the United Kingdom passed the Data Protection Act to lock down access to consumers' financial and health information. More recently, the governments of the European Union and the United States felt there was a need to further regulate public companies. Such reasoning is based on the fact that once a company becomes public, it has two core offerings: its service or product offering and its investment offering. Historically, the regulations that have been put in place to protect consumers from dangerous products and fraudulent services and to protect employees from harsh conditions ultimately affect a business's processes (or operations). But laws have also been put into place to protect investors from dishonest organizations (e.g., see Loi de la Sécurité Financière of France in Table 7.2).

One industry known for being the cause of many regulatory acts is the highly risk-aware financial industry. Financial institutions tend to be better known for how formal or structured they can get when managing risk. Moreover, since banks and investment brokerages act as one of the foundations of a thriving capitalist society, laws have been passed to help protect the public from corporate mismanagement of their money. Examples of such laws include the Federal Deposit Insurance Corporation Improvement Act (FDICIA) of 1991 in the United States and the 1999 Turnbull framework in Britain. The former is required for U.S. Securities and Exchange Commission (SEC)–registered U.S. banks, and the latter is required for London Stock Exchange–registered companies. While such regulations have traditionally

**Table 7.2** Various International and Local Regulations

| Risk Management Discipline | Regulation/ Standard/ Code of Conduct | Description | Jurisdiction |
|---|---|---|---|
| Enterprisewide risk management | SarbOx, Sections 404, 409 [21] | Mandates real-time issuer disclosures on a rapid and current basis of material changes in financial and nonfinancial risks to the financial position of a business | U.S. listed businesses |
| Enterprisewide risk management | Basel II [22] | Regulates the distribution of central capital to banking institutions based on the banks' proof of operational risk implementation | EU banks |
| Information security | Financial Modernization Act of 1999 [23] | Also known as the Gramm-Leach-Bliley Act or GLB Act, includes provisions to protect consumers' personal financial information | United States |
| Information security | Data Protection Act [24] | Regulates the processing of information relating to individuals, including the obtaining, holding, use, and disclosure of such information | United Kingdom |
| Information security | Health Insurance Portability and Accountability Act of 1996 [25] | Also known as HIPPA, regulates the protection of the privacy of personal health information | United States |
| Risk governance | Loi de la Sécurité Financière [26] | Covers auditor independence, boardroom appointments, shareholders' rights, and disclosure guidelines | France |

*Source:* [7]

addressed financial risks, recent trends show governments are now including operational risk, board-level auditing, and risk governance. Table 7.2 shows two that cover companywide operational risk, one that covers risk governance, and three that focus on a particular component of enterprisewide operations: information security.

This chart shows that while information security regulations are recent examples of governments' reducing risks outside of companies (for the public), the other regulations are recent examples of governments' reducing risks within companies. As mentioned in Chapter 5 on process management, when companies are forced to comply with regulations that require operational risk management, the side effect is a tighter integration of three of the PePPR management activities: processes and projects are scrutinized even more for risk. The downside of early compliance panic, however, is the temporary marginalization of the fourth PePPR management activity: performance management. In the next sections, we will look at two of these regulations: SarbOx and Basel II, and at two risk management frameworks developed to help companies comply with these regulations: Committee of Sponsoring Organizations framework (COSO) and Turnbull. We will compare the two approaches to operational risk each regulation takes, then review the value-add of these regulations to integrated PePPR management.

## SarbOx

The Sarbanes-Oxley Act (SarbOx or SOX) was passed by the U.S. Congress in 2002 as a reaction to a string of highly visible corporate scandals. Then, to provide further guidance to accounting auditors, SarbOx created the Public Company Accounting Oversight Board (PCAOB) to act as a watchdog organization. Since the act so drastically affects the way companies are managed, it was decided to phase it in over several years. While the majority of the act focuses on improving financial statements, a small part of the act zeroes in on operational risk. For example, Section 404 states that each annual report is required

> to contain an internal control report, which shall
>
> 1. state the responsibility of management for establishing and maintaining an adequate internal control structure and procedures for financial reporting; and
>
> 2. contain an assessment, as of the end of the most recent fiscal year of the issuer, of the effectiveness of the internal control structure and procedures of the issuer for financial reporting. [21]

Though this was clarified slightly with the issuance of "Standard Number Two" by the PCAOB, SarbOx is a broadly written regulation. It applies to all U.S. public companies and can affect any international company that does business with public U.S. companies. While it doesn't provide for a way to implement operational risk management, it does require that it be done. In fact, executives are held accountable to the SEC on the accuracy of their companies' financial statements and adherence to operational risk controls.

## COSO

Back in the 1980s, the United States went through its savings-and-loan failures and experienced a series of corporate governance scandals. As a result, the government passed the FDICIA in 1991 to require the chief executive and financial officers of all SEC-registered banks to report on the quality of their internal controls. In enforcing this act, the SEC adopted a framework developed by a committee of the Treadway Commission called the Committee of Sponsoring Organizations (COSO). This framework outlined a set of best practices to follow for a company attempting to comply with this act.

Then, when SarbOx was passed in 2002, the newly created PCAOB decided to also adopt COSO as its recommended framework. But since SarbOx applied not just to banks but to any public company, COSO needed to be upgraded [10]. Fortunately, the Treadway Commission had this foresight and was already in the process of changing COSO; in 2004, the Committee of Sponsoring Organizations published the new COSO framework as "Enterprise Risk Management: Integrated Framework." Both the United States (with COSO) and the United Kingdom (with Turnbull) have realized that regulating corporate governance is a fluid process marked by evermore sophisticated regulatory acts. How governments evolve their enforcement of risk management in corporations tends to depend on extreme circumstances (e.g., reaction to several corporate blunders) and good planning (i.e., proaction to actual business needs). Figure 7.10 summarizes the core framework of COSO 2004. The three dimensions represent (1) the steps in risk management, (2) the applications of risk management, and (3) the participants in risk management.

- *Steps:* The COSO steps for enterprise risk align well with the basic model we reviewed. Figure 7.10 identifies those COSO steps that fit within each of the steps of our model.

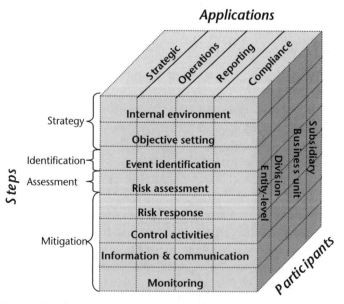

**Figure 7.10** The COSO cube.

- *Applications:* Here we see that COSO splits out risk applications into strategic risk management, operational risk management, the reporting of risk, and compliance. In this book, we argue that there is much overlap between these four applications of risk. For example, compliance with the regulations we cite requires the reporting of operational risk at the strategic (or summary) level to executives. This isn't much different from the approach COSO presents, except we promote integrated reporting of risks and performance metrics.

- *Participants:* Enterprisewide risk management is addressed at all levels of the organization. Top-down direction and framework promotion should come from the board and the executive office, respectively. Bottom-up risk identification should come from each staff member, to be filtered and prioritized by the various management layers.

## Basel II

In 1998, the Bank of International Settlement created a committee called the Basel Committee on Banking Supervision comprising bank supervisors from 13 leading economies. The resulting report, called the Basel II Accord, created "a three pillar regulatory structure of (1) capital charges against credit, market and operational risk, (2) supervisory review of bank risk management policies, and (3) greater information disclosure requirements" [22]. Contrary to SarbOx, which provides a vague pass-fail compliance dictate, Basel II provides for three different levels of qualification: (1) the basic indicator approach, (2) the standardized approach (e.g., by the board of directors), or (3) the advanced measurement approach (AMA). In other words, where SarbOx simply infers that a company is or is not complying, Basel provides a company with the option to meet different compliance levels. The higher the level of compliance, the more benefits the bank will receive. Banks that implement all AMAs by tracking key risk indicators (KRIs) are awarded better lending rates by government lending institutions. These lending rates can then be translated into improved revenues due to higher price margins.

Under AMAs, banks must be able to show the presence of six standards:

1. An *independent* operational risk management function;
2. *Integration* of the risk management system with day-to-day bank processes;
3. Regular *reporting* of risk exposure to management, senior management, and the board of directors;
4. A *well-documented* operational risk management system;
5. Regular *reviews* of operational risk management processes and measurement systems;
6. Verification that *internal validation processes* are operating in a satisfactory manner.

Basel II takes a more management-by-reward approach, as opposed to the management-by-fear approach of SarbOx. Instead of threats of prosecution and jail time for executives, Basel provides banks with the rewards of a smaller capital buffer to protect against investor flight. For example, under strict government regulations, if a bank loans out 100 euros, it needs to have 50 euros in its vaults; the rest is seen in the form of credit transfers. If the bank satisfies increasingly stricter Basel approaches, it can keep as little as 40 euros in its vaults and spend the resulting 10 euros on profitable investments.

### Basel versus SarbOx

While both Basel and SarbOx have as their primary goal the prevention of major risk control failures, Basel takes the perspective that a company must identify its risks before mitigating (or controlling) them. SarbOx, in contrast, looks primarily at how a company controls (or mitigates) risk. "PCAOB Standard 2 approaches the issue from a control versus a risk perspective" [27]. No mention is made of risk identification or assessment (two of the key steps of our earlier methodology). This leaves open the possibility that by focusing too heavily on control (or mitigation) mechanisms, a company may not be controlling the right risks. Banks that apply the Basel II AMA standards show risk alignment by categorizing the risks they've identified by business lines and by type of loss. Such a requirement to break down the corporate risk profile easily sets the company up to "support cause of failure and trend analysis" [27], two steps in the right direction. Unfortunately, neither SarbOx nor PCAOB provides guidelines on how to break down risks, let alone on how to report on them. In fact, according to Bruce McCuaig, author of "Can the Basel II Approach to Governance Work for SOX?" of those companies attempting to comply with SarbOx, 404 showed that they provided "vague, ambiguous reporting with insufficient detail to perform root cause or trend analysis" [27]. Fortunately, a new version of the COSO framework suggested by PCAOB will compliment SarbOx's pass-fail approach, providing a way to help companies categorize and align their risk profiles.

Basel's focus on risk management goes beyond just providing a complete picture of risk; it also provides a complete view of accountability. While SarbOx puts responsibility for risk control on the executives, Basel passes responsibility through all management layers. Alignment of the risk profile with the corporate strategy and integration of risk management throughout the company shows that Basel is first "designed as a management rather than an audit framework" [27]. Basel also goes to great length to describe the responsibility of the board of directors. While SarbOx does little more than explain that the audit committee should comprise independent directors who review major risk reports, Basel II goes much further. The Basel II accord explains that directors should not only understand the major risks but also set acceptable risk levels, monitor corporate risk management approaches (identification, measurement, and control), and review internal control mechanisms. While Basel II surpasses SarbOx in guiding companies to full compliance, Basel II lacks the rigorous timeline of SarbOx. From its inception in 1998 to its hopeful implementation in 2007, it will have taken nine years to realize. SarbOx, in comparison, took less than a year from the collapse of Enron in late 2001 to its implementation in 2002.

Turnbull

Where SarbOx applies to publicly traded companies in the United States and Basel II applies to banks in the European Community, Turnbull applies to companies listed with the London Stock Exchange (LSE). SarbOx and Basel II provide penalties for noncompliance and rewards for compliance. Turnbull is simply part of the listing rule disclosure requirements of the LSE and is the main document that provides guidance on corporate governance in the United Kingdom. Written by Nigel Turnbull and the Institute of Chartered Accountants in England and Wales, this report is based on earlier British government reports such as the Rutherman report (1994), the Hempel Combined Code (1998), and the Internal Control Guidance for Directors on the Combined Code (1999) [10, 16].

Turnbull has significance in risk management in that it addresses risk at the corporate governance level. At this level, such a regulation focuses on major corporate risks rather than on more detailed operational or project risks. Figure 7.11 shows how Turnbull combines governance (top-down risk management) with the two approaches to operational risk provided by SarbOx and Basel, namely ERM and internal control (bottom up). But one of the more interesting contributions of the Turnbull report is how it hints at "integrating the management of risk and organizational performance in general as part of a coherent approach to corporate governance" [5]. Here, we finally have an operational risk regulation that tries to guide companies into not ignoring performance management at the expense of risk man-

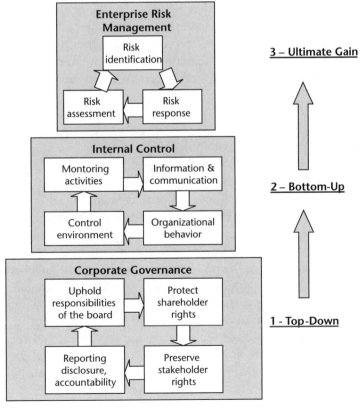

**Figure 7.11**   Turnbull framework.

agement compliance. Figure 7.11 shows how its internal control layer not only provides a foundation for risk management but also for strategic performance management. If we were to modify this diagram, we could easily, and logically, add a "Strategic Performance Management" block alongside the "Enterprise Risk Management" block. Turnbull goes beyond just providing a framework; it shows how to best incorporate risk management into the fabric of an enterprise. Some of these steps include:

1. Obtaining initial and ongoing buy-in of risk management at all levels of the organization through continual support and training efforts;
2. Focusing on improving business processes and culture;
3. Keeping it simple by rolling out risk management in phases and avoiding overloading the audit committee;
4. Integrating risk management into existing governance and management frameworks;
5. Strategizing, planning, and identifying objectives and prioritizing the tasks required to roll out risk management;
6. Monitoring output and tracking for trends in the key risk indicators [13].

In our PePPR model, compliance activities show themselves when reviewing projects for approval, monitoring processes for efficiency, and aligning performance metrics with corporate goals. If a company lacks control structures that address any of these three examples, then they risk not meeting operational compliance requirements. Establishing a formal enterprise risk management structure (either as an office or an accountable committee) sends a clear message to auditors on the importance of risk management. Integrating activity management components with the threads of risk management turns the message into execution.

## Value-add

Government regulations that control how businesses can operate have (1) been in place for centuries, (2) change annually, and (3) differ substantially between countries. At the turn of the millennium, however, some new regulations have focused particularly on how operational risk management is deployed in an organization. This has in turn heightened the need for risk-based processes in the core workings of companies. Nonetheless, as important as compliance is in the framework of enterprise risk management, it should be kept in perspective with all other risks companies face. For example, from 1999 to 2003, Booz Allen Hamilton conducted a survey of 1,200 companies with market capitalizations greater than $1 billion. A key finding of this survey was that more shareholder value was lost by these companies over 5 years from mismanagement and bad execution of strategy than was lost from all recent compliance scandals combined. To really bring this point home, Booz Allen Hamilton found that of the 360 worst financial performers from this survey, 87% of the lost value from the firms was due to strategic mistakes "and operational blunders, such as cost overruns and M&A integration problems. Only 13 percent of the value destruction suffered by these companies was caused by regulatory compliance failures or was a result of poor oversight of company operations by corporate boards" [15].

This shows that companies that implement risk management procedures for the sole purpose of regulatory compliance are only covering a small percentage of the reasons they could fail. Risk management should be about more than just compliance; it should be a process of assembling information to support leadership in making sound decisions about strategic direction [17]. While compliance activities should be a part of any risk management initiative, "confining risk management to compliance requirements is dangerous" [11]. According to John Oliveira, director of operations for Horizon Casualty Services, "People feel they don't have time to improve their business processes because they are so focused on addressing the compliance issues. But really, compliance is just the minimum quality standard" [28].

There are two basic categories of risk:

- *Defensive*: This category is usually associated with the internal or external compliance activities that strive to mitigate the abundance of small credit, market, and operational risks that constantly pop up daily.
- *Offensive*: This category includes risk management information that identifies strategic initiatives (or projects) and the criteria to evaluate them (project portfolio management) [11].

With either type of risk, the Turnbull report states that their management should be "incorporated within the company's normal management and governance processes, not treated as a separate exercise to meet regulatory requirements" (process management) [5]. So, instead of a narrow compliance vision to risk management, companies should embrace "an approach that contributes to sustainable organizational resilience" [7]. Offensive risk management from the top and defensive risk control from the bottom that is applied throughout the enterprise can lead to such organizationwide resilience.

### Business Continuity Risk

As has been shown, there can be many types of risk a company will need to address. Risks associated with personnel turnover, product delivery, environmental violations, weather, and the macroeconomy can all slow the forward progress of business. If not addressed and mitigated relentlessly, risks that seem minor at first can snowball into a set of catastrophes that can bring down the business. Many companies have layered how they address risks where the final layer, or last defensible position, is referred to as disaster recovery (DR). If a disaster occurs, crisis managers apply DR plans that describe the steps and the resources needed to get the company back to a recovered state. DR plans can be written for several scenarios and for different functional areas. Combined, they can fall under the umbrella of the company's business continuity (BC) plan.

David Brewer and William List, authors of "Measuring the Effectiveness of an Internal Control System," describe BC as a set of processes used to "(1) facilitate recovery from an event or to (2) minimize the impact of an event" [16]. But the ICM Computer Group claims that BC management has recently seen "a shift in focus to the *prevention* of such events, rather than the *cure* of DR. This has meant that DR has now become a subset of the whole process" [29]. Andrew McCrackan, author of "Is Business Continuity a Subset of Risk Management?" points out, "Business continuity should not be considered subordinate to risk management. There is a risk management function that sits within business continuity. There may also be a separate risk management function outside of this function, but not above, that deals with day-to-day risk of conducting business, depending on your organization" [30]. For example, retail stores invest in product-tracking systems to mitigate the risk of shoplifters. They also ensure leases are stable and long term to prevent business-busting rent increases. The former focuses more on day-to-day business risks, while the latter focuses on disaster prevention or business continuity.

Among BC and risk management (RM) experts, a classic chicken-or-egg discussion continues to brew. Is BC a part of RM, or is RM a part of BC? For a business to continue even under disastrous conditions, should compliance, security, and credit risk be part of the BC equation? Or should BC paper-based backup plans be in place as part of an enterprise risk management architecture that also includes compliance and credit risk? McCrackan claims that "business continuity management is the evolutionary result of developments in emergency planning, disaster recovery, security, health and safety, crisis management, and, dare I say it, risk management" [30]. By combining emergency management, IT disaster recovery, and operational risk management, DR plans were born. IT threat and risk assessments led to IT security management; process recovery needs led to business continuity plans (BCPs); identified event recovery (e.g., tornadoes, earthquakes) led to emergency management plans; and plan coordination led to crisis management plans. All of these fall under the umbrella of BCM, and only a subset of them addresses IT [29, 31, 32].

In this book, we'll consider BCM as a subset of the greater ERM architecture, but that is still an enterprisewide effort. For those who are considering such a large BC approach to mitigating unforeseen catastrophes [33], the ICM Computer Group claims there are three options: do nothing, buy insurance, or create a plan.

## Do Nothing

Doing nothing can be a very legitimate option. Such a decision to accept the probability of an event's occurring will usually be based on some sort of probability analysis. This could include something as simple as gut feel and experience or something as advanced as statistical and Monte Carlo analysis. The resulting choices made based upon these probabilities can be viewed as an organization's tolerance for risk. Brewer and List proposed an approach for assessing the tolerance of doing nothing versus doing something in their quantitative analysis of business continuity plans. Their model drew on the three core layers of security theory: prevention, detection, and eradication (or reaction). The model focuses on how detection time and eradication time ultimately affect the bottom line. If nothing is done to eradicate an identified threat, then one can assume that the cost to the business of the event's occurring is less than the value of the resources available to eradicate it. For example, if the local bully, in effect, demands $10 in protection money for me to operate my lemonade stand, I may feel it is more worthwhile to call his bluff and keep my $10. If sales are low, then the $10 is more valuable to me in my pocket than is the need for "security," or the prevention of a butt-kicking. But if the bully is intent on achieving dominance, then he or she might just get angrier the longer I delay payment. The result could be a more disastrous outcome, resulting in lost profits and more costs to rebuild the lemonade stand. By waiting to mitigate a risk until after it is preventable (building a stand in a different neighborhood), detected (receiving the threat), and fixable (paying the bully off), I put myself in a position to experience much graver outcomes if the risk is realized. Brewer and List's model (Table 7.3 and Figures 7.12 and 7.13) graphs money against time and tries to illustrate how the impact on profit ($l_f$) and the impact on costs ($c_f$) can be affected by delaying preparation for and responses to an adverse event.

Seven sublayers were created to represent different ratings of how any particular event is handled. If detection and then eradication times become too lengthy, then normal business operations can be affected. The graph in Figure 7.12 plots money versus time to show how the different time deltas can affect profits and costs to eradicate the problems caused by the event.

- Time of event: $T_e$;

**Table 7.3**  Brewer and List's Time Variables

| Class | Ability to Detect the Event and Take Recovery Action | Time Variables | Type |
|-------|------------------------------------------------------|----------------|------|
| 1 | Prevents the event or detects the event as it happens and prevents it from having any impact | Small $\Delta T_d$ and $\Delta T_f$ | Preventive |
| 2 | Detects the event and reacts quickly enough to fix it well within the time window | $\Delta T_d$ and $\Delta T_f \ll \Delta T_w$ | Detective |
| 3 | Detects the event and just reacts quickly enough to fix it within the time window | $\Delta T_d$ and $\Delta T_f < \Delta T_w$ | |
| 4 | Detects the event but cannot react quickly enough to fix it within the time window | $\Delta T_d < \Delta T_w$ $\Delta T_f > \Delta T_w$ | |
| 5 | Fails to detect the event but has a partially deployed BCP | $\Delta T_d$ and $\Delta T_f > \Delta T_w$ | Reactive |
| 6 | Fails to detect the event but does have a BCP | $\Delta T_d > \Delta T_w$ $\Delta T_f \gg \Delta T_w$ | |
| 7 | Fails to detect the event and does not have a BCP | $\Delta T_d > \Delta T_w$ $\Delta T_f \ggg \Delta T_w$ | |

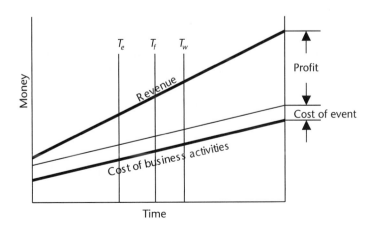

**Figure 7.12**  How adverse events can negatively affect profit over time.

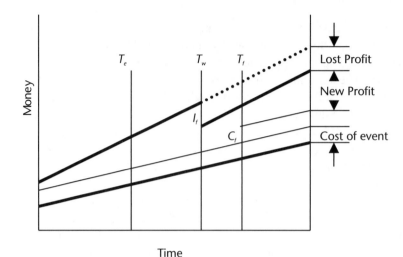

**Figure 7.13**  Reaction and proaction to events can minimize their effects on the bottom line. $I_f$ equals impact on profit of the business from late fix of problems associated with the event; $C_f$ equals cost to fix the problems associated with the event. Note that $T_w$ may never really be known until after the event is fixed. If timelines, deliverables, and costs of business for any activities (processes or projects) are not affected, then $T_f < T_w$. (*After* [16].)

- Time to detect the event: $\Delta T_d = T_e - T_d$;
- Time to fix the event: $\Delta T_f = T_e - T_f$;
- Time to fix the event before the event adversely affects the business: $\Delta T_w = T_e - T_w$.

This form of analysis helps rate how well the organization is losing by not managing its risks. If profits are being affected, then the cost of implementing risk management should be reviewed to determine if the lost profits are greater than the costs of risk management.

### Buy Insurance

For those who'd rather not invest in and maintain the resources to respond to a business-interrupting event, insurance can provide the capital to hire or buy such resources after an event occurs. Also, insurance can allow for compensation for lost business. Unfortunately, such business continuity insurance can be complex and lead to scenarios in which those who thought they would get compensated don't. Here are some examples of the types of insurance a business can invest in to cover disasters:

- *Denial of access (DOA):* This insurance covers losses when a facility other than your own prevents access to your facilities (e.g., a downed bridge or a flooded road.)
- *Increased cost of working cover (ICOW):* This covers payments to those who help bring the business back online (e.g., cleanup crews, public relations experts).

- *Business interruption:* This is a blanket policy that may fail to cover such specifics as DOA or ICOW.
- *Utilities extensions:* This provides for the interruption to essential services, such as gas and electricity.
- *Suppliers extensions:* This provides for the interruption to the supply of goods or services from external suppliers.
- *Contagious diseases extensions:* As an example, this would cover "you for the consequences of employing a chef with bubonic plague or some such ailment" [34].
- *Civil authorities extensions:* This covers "losses sustained as a result of government denial of access to your property, due to a covered loss at a location not owned by you" [34].

### Create a Plan

The lead-up activities to creating a plan should include some level of business analysis, risk assessment, and strategic review [28]. While going through these exercises, Brewer and List recommend you identify events, assets, impacts, and threats.

- *Events:* You should focus on identifying undesirable events that are very specific to your business. Failures such as loss of power, computer data, key personnel, or communication services are all examples.
- *Assets:* Identify the items that can be adversely affected by your list of events. Examples can include buildings, IT hardware and software, and any critical paper documents.
- *Impacts:* Marry the events and the assets by listing out not just the effect of the event on the assets but also the collateral damage to the company's ability to operate normally.
- *Threats:* List out the disasters that can occur, such as a snowstorm, earthquake, or epidemic, and then prioritize them to your particular business.

The result should be a list of low-probability, high-impact risks that started with the resulting failures (e.g., systems down, key personnel lost, transportation failure) rather than with the causes (e.g., tornado, strike, terrorist attack). With such failure scenarios, the business continuity group can then create what Brewer and List refer to as individual risk treatment plans. The consolidation of all such plans would result in the business continuity plan. Unfortunately, once a plan is completed, this is where most companies stumble. According to Barry Varley, author of "Creating Effective Business Continuity Plans," "Many businesses become complacent because they have a false sense of security built on the existence of their continuity plans. However when the plans are invoked, they fail unexpectedly" [33]. It all basically comes down to the risk profile of the company. If executives are risk averse, they should spend more money on business continuity plan tests, rehearsals, and scenario walk-throughs. If executives are comfortable with greater risk, funds can be diverted to other areas. Before a company can announce that it has addressed business continuity, however, it needs to train its staff and rehearse and test its plans [29, 34, 35].

## Risk and Performance Management

Whereas performance metrics look at recent events that have passed, risk metrics use past events to develop probabilities of future events' occurring. That is, performance and risk measurement draw their data from the same pool of metrics that all measure past activity. Along the bottom, Figure 7.14 illustrates these metrics, which typically have been associated with performance measurement but also feed risk measurement. When benchmarks and thresholds are added, the metrics can be tracked against set criteria. The benchmarks are actual metric results used to rate recent performance to historical activity. Thresholds are goals and desires for the future as set by management. Basing risk management on quantitative metrics and qualitative methods "is consistent with the approach adopted by modern corporate performance management" [5]: Both rely on historical quantitative data (benchmarks) and qualitative predictions about the future (thresholds) [5, 37]. However, such thresholds are only part of the visionary landscape. Risk analysis can provide metrics that monitor for hints or indications that a risk is more or less likely to happen. These monitoring points are referred to as key risk indicators, or KRIs. In contrast, by the time the key performance indicators have shown a significant deterioration, "it may be too late to prevent losses or other adverse effects" [13].

The probability analyses applied to corporate metrics to support enterprise risk management can be grouped in support of scenario analysis exercises. Then, once benchmarks and thresholds are established, clear options can be designed, and resources can be prepped. If enough of these scenarios or options are lined up and

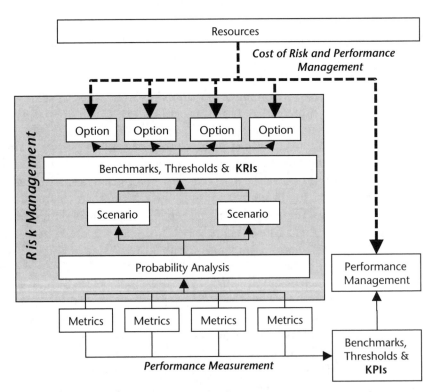

**Figure 7.14**   Risk versus performance management.

prepared for, a company is adopting more of an adaptive strategy. As was explained in Chapter 3, such an approach is good for companies with level 3 maturity or higher in today's dynamic markets. As events occur, the calculated probabilities that underlie these business-specific scenarios become less probable and more precise. That is, it can become clearer over time that certain previously predicted scenarios are coming to pass. This ultimately helps executives understand the impact of risk management on the bottom line (see Figure 7.14).

Some processes, such as security monitoring, asset management, and market tracking, are better analyzed with risk measures. The alternative would be performance measures that are of more value to operational measures than to executives. For example, surveys can be given after security training, trouble-ticket trends can be reviewed for particular assets, and best practice comparisons can be used to grade your marketing department. But such measures won't percolate well to an executive-level scorecard or dashboard. Risks of industrial espionage, collapsing bridges, and market blindsides, on the other hand, can carry some weight in the corner office. Integrating risk into the visualization of corporate activity rounds out the view executives need. Enterprise performance management initiatives can push too hard into the operational space and try to link metrics that don't make sense to executives. Therefore, it may be better in some cases to look more at risk than at performance.

## Summary

After reviewing operational risk and comparing it to other forms of risk, a consolidated, best practices methodology was presented. From here, we looked at such advanced risk management approaches as iterative risk mitigation to guard against risk "reflash"; risk benchmarking to prove the value of identification, assessment, and mitigation approaches; independent compliance-risk offices; and the pervasive subject of business continuity. By addressing all of these enterprisewide approaches to operational risk management, we were able to show that clear communication of the strategic risk profile, consistent assessment of risks, and aligned financing of risk mitigation projects are all activities supported by integrated PePPR management. For example, the Turnbull report encourages the creation of rollout processes that integrate performance with risk management. That is, when these two activity management silos are implemented in an organization, it is beneficial if they are done together. Furthermore, Sharon's hazard/probability/opportunity risk continuum laid the foundation for linking risk visibility to project execution, and Hewitt Roberts' risk identification model integrated project and process risk management across the enterprise. Sharon's continuum, Roberts' model, and Allan Holmes's consideration of risk when financing process improvement and systems implementation projects [19] are all examples of the integration of enterprise risk management with the other PePPR management silos. If you look closely at how operational risk is managed at the strategic level, you will invariably see opportunities for cross-communication and support with performance, process, and project portfolio management teams. Strong interaction at this level will help avoid the infighting that can occur when strategic priorities need to adapt on a dime.

# References

[1]   "Risk," *Merriam-Webster's Dictionary of Law*, Springfield, MA: Merriam-Webster, 1996.

[2]   "Risk," *The American Heritage Dictionary of the English Language*, 4th ed., Boston, MA: Houghton Mifflin Company, 2004, http://dictionary.reference.com/browse/risk (last accessed January 9, 2008).

[3]   Rosenzweig, Phil, "The Halo Effect, and Other Managerial Delusions," *McKinsey Quarterly*, No. 1, 2007.

[4]   Ward, Jeremy, "Operational Risk and Information Security Need to Co-Exist for Effective Risk Management," Continuity Central, March 23, 2005, www.continuitycentral.com/feature0189.htm (last accessed April 15, 2006).

[5]   Lawrie, G. J. G., D. C. Kaiff, and H. V. Andersen, "Integrating Risk Management with Existing Methods of Strategic Control: Avoiding Duplication within the Corporate Governance Agenda," 2GC Limited, August 1, 2003, www.2gc.co.uk/pdf/2GC-CP0803.pdf (last accessed on April 15, 2006).

[6]   Bailey, Michael A., and Edward T. Hida II, "2004 Global Risk Management Survey," Deloitte Development, LLC, 2004.

[7]   Crawford, Nicola, and Norman Hoppe, "Dragging Operational Risk Management into the 21st Century," Continuity Central, May 27, 2006, www.continuitycentral.com/feature0210.htm (last accessed on April 15, 2006).

[8]   "Integrated Risk Management Framework," Treasury Board of Canada Secretariat, April 1, 2001, www.tbs-sct.gc.ca/pubs_pol/dcgpubs/RiskManagement/rmf-cgr_e.asp (last accessed on April 15, 2006).

[9]   Sharon, Bill, "Emotion Rules: Ignoring It Won't Change Anything," Continuity Central, August 12, 2005, www.continuitycentral.com/feature0234.htm (last accessed on April 15, 2006).

[10]  Roberts, Hewitt, "Enterprise Risk Management: A Long-Term Solution for Compliance, Governance, and Sustained Growth in Shareholder Value," Continuity Central, May 5, 2005, www.continuitycentral.com/feature0202.htm (last accessed on April 15, 2006).

[11]  Sharon, Bill, "Risk Management: What Should Be, What Is and What Could Be," Continuity Central, July 29, 2005, www.continuitycentral.com/feature0231.htm (last accessed on April 15, 2006).

[12]  Sharon, Bill, "The Elusive 'Risk Culture'," Continuity Central, February 23, 2006, www.continuitycentral.com/feature0306.htm (last accessed on April 15, 2006).

[13]  Jones, Martyn E., and Gillian Sutherland, "Implementing Turnbull: A Boardroom Briefing," Centre for Business Performance, September 1, 1999, www.icaew.co.uk/index.cfm?route=120612 (last accessed on April 15, 2006).

[14]  Bies, Susan S., "Susan S. Bies: Managing Business Risks," *BIS Review*, June 16, 2003, www.bis.org/review/r030623c.pdf (last accessed on April 15, 2006).

[15]  Kocourek, Paul, Jim Newfrock, and Reggie VanLee, "It's Time to Take Your SOX Off," Strategy + Business, December 15, 2004, www.strategy-business.com/resiliencereport/resilience/rr00014?pg=all&tid=230 (last accessed on April 30, 2006).

[16]  Brewer, David, and William List, "Measuring the Effectiveness of an Internal Control System," Gamma Secure Systems, Ltd., William List and Company, 2004, www.gammassl.co.uk/topics/time/ (last accessed on April 15, 2006).

[17]  Sharon, B., "Operational Risk Management: The Difference Between Risk Management and Compliance," *Continuity Central*, September 16, 2005, http://www.continuitycentral.com/feature0243.htm (last accessed on April 15, 2006)

[18]  Berinato, Scott, "Playing with Fire," *CIO Magazine*, July 1, 2003, www.cio.com/archive/070103/fire.html (last accessed on April 30, 2006).

[19]   Lovallo, Dan P., "Distortions and Deceptions in Strategic Decisions," *McKinsey Quarterly*, www.bettermanagement.com/library/ library.aspx?pagetype=1&libraryid=13515 (last accessed on February 17, 2006).

[20]   Holmes, Allan, "Rx for Risk," *CIO Magazine*, March 15, 2006, pp. 56–62.

[21]   U.S. Congress, Sarbanes-Oxley Act, July 20, 2002, www.sec.gov/about/laws/soa2002.pdf (last accessed on September 13, 2007).

[22]   "Basel II: International Convergence of Capital Measurement and Capital Standards: A Revised Framework," Bank for International Settlements, June 2004, www.bis.org/publ/bcbs107.htm (last accessed on September 13, 2007).

[23]   U.S. Congress, "The Financial Modernization Act of 1999," Federal Trade Commission, 1999, www.ftc.gov/privacy/privacyinitiatives/glbact.html (last accessed on September 13, 2007).

[24]   "Data Protection Act 1998," UK Office of Public Sector Information, 1998, www.opsi.gov.uk/ACTS/acts1998/19980029.htm (last accessed on September 13, 2007).

[25]   U.S. Congress, "The HIPAA Statute," August 21, 1996, U.S. Department of Health and Human Services, http://aspe.hhs.gov/admnsimp/pl104191.htm (last accessed on September 13, 2007).

[26]   Kersnar, Janet, "Pay Now, Pay Later," *CFO Magazine*, November 2004, www.cfoeurope.com/displayStory.cfm/3350531 (last accessed on September 13, 2007).

[27]   McCuaig, Bruce, "Can the Basel II Approach to Governance Work for SOX?" Global Risk Regulator, October 1, 2004, www.globalriskregulator.com (last accessed on May 20, 2006).

[28]   Minsky, Steven, "Developing Risk Plans," EBizQ, June 24, 2005, www.ebizq.net/topics/bpm/features/6021.html?&pp=1 (last accessed on April 30, 2006).

[29]   "Beginners Guide to Business Continuity," ICM Computer Group, n.d., www.icm-computer.co.uk/newsroom/white_papers.asp?departmentID=6 (last accessed on April 15, 2006).

[30]   McCrackan, Andrew, "Is Business Continuity a Subset of Risk Management?" Continuity Central, February 25, 2005, www.continuitycentral.com/feature0178.htm (last accessed on April 15, 2006).

[31]   Thompson, Mike, "Business Continuity Management: The Nine Deadly Sins," Continuity Central, March 20, 2006, www.continuitycentral.com/feature0320.htm (last accessed on April 15, 2006).

[32]   McCrackan, Andrew, "Unraveling Business Continuity Terminology," Continuity Central, April 15, 2005, www.continuitycentral.com/feature0195.htm (last accessed on April 15, 2006).

[33]   "Beginner's Guide to Business Continuity," ICM COmputer Group, http://www.icmcomputergroup.c.uk/pdf/2GC-PMA02-2f.pdf (last accessed on April 15, 2006).

[34]   Miller, Ron, "Business Insurance—What You May Not Have Thought About . . .," Continuity Central, March 4, 2005, www.continuitycentral.com/ feature0181.htm (last accessed on April 15, 2006).

[35]   Varley, Barry, "Creating Effective Business Continuity Plans," Continuity Central, October 20, 2005, www.continuitycentral.com/feature0258.htm (last accessed on April 15, 2006).

[36]   Cornish, Malcolm, "The Highs and Lows of Continuity Software," Continuity Central, August 13, 2004, www.continuitycentral.com/feature0112.htm (last accessed on April 15, 2006).

[37]   Cobbold, Ian, and Gavin Lawrie, "The Development of the Balanced Scorecard as a Strategic Management Tool," 2GC Conference Paper, PMA 2002, Boston, MA.

## CHAPTER 8

# Integrated Execution

## Integrated Maturity

Any business with a desire to continue and grow implements some form of risk and performance management. At a minimum, such efforts are realized as summary reports (verbal or written) for the business owners. At best, such efforts are ingrained into the everyday processes of the organization's staff. As a company matures, it can maintain its risk- and performance-minded culture if it places trust in its staff through open-book management styles and provides clear direction through PePPR structures. This is especially important as executive time becomes consumed and priorities start to diverge from corporate goals. As a company matures, it also develops a growing need to efficiently manage its formal actions (i.e., its processes and projects). While all the organizations interviewed for this book were implementing all and integrating some of the four PePPR components, the more mature organizations tended to balance and control the integration of all four PePPR components with a small support staff. At nLight and Porter General Hospital, for example, a culture of process improvement, risk identification, and performance excellence was established among the entire staff. All of this was in turn supported through controlled but innovative growth provided by a project portfolio management (PPM) approach that satisfied the needs of investors, executives, and regulators at nLight and scrupulous doctors, needy patients, strict government auditors, and visionary administrators at Porter.

### The PePPR Components

With strategic performance, we showed how performance measurement frameworks (i.e., the Balanced Scorecard, the European Network for Advanced Performance Studies model [ENAPS], and the Performance Prism) helped us choose metrics that best fit the goals of the company. Automated enterprise performance management models and dashboards then provided the means to track and improve upon those metrics. With enterprise processes, we showed how process frameworks (e.g., Value Chain, Porter's Five Forces) helped us identify processes from a risk, performance, and project portfolio perspective. We then showed how these processes could be tracked and improved by implementing process improvement models, such as Kaizen and Six Sigma, and process-specific models, such as those supporting supply chain and information technology (IT). With project portfolios, we showed how portfolio management frameworks (e.g., the Project, Program, and Portfolio Management Maturity Model [P3M3] and the Organizational Project Management Maturity Model [OPM3]) helped construct project prioritization and auditing functions. Specifically, project tracking and improvement was realized through a combination of control and support of the project pipeline. Finally, with operational risks, we presented a framework (or methodology) that showed how to identify, track, mitigate, and improve operational risks at the enterprise level. In summary, we showed how the components of PePPR (metrics, processes, projects, and risks) are framed and managed using different industry models and international standards.

Performance management identifies, tracks, and aligns metrics; process management identifies, tracks, and improves processes; project portfolio management identifies, tracks, and supports projects; and risk management identifies, tracks, and mitigates risks. Each of these activity management silos has its own purpose and its own output. Historically, they have each operated independently, with their only opportunity for integration occurring at strategic reviews and, more visibly, during budget season. As each has evolved over the decades, the basic steps to accomplish their purpose have become remarkably similar. These basic steps are to find a framework that fits the company, identify the components to manage (metrics, processes, projects, and risks), prioritize the components according to the strategy, track and report on the output of the components (performance achievements, process improvements, project deliveries, and risk mitigations), and influence how each component can provide better support for management.

- *Frame:* Balanced Scorecard for performance management, Committee of Sponsoring Organizations standards (COSO) for risk management, the Organizational Project Management Maturity Model (OPM3) for project portfolio management, and the Information Technology Infrastructure Library for process management are all examples of frameworks that can be used for either an enterprise- or a department-level implementation. Before diving into implementing any PePPR component, lessons learned and best practices from others that have done it should be leveraged by using standard frameworks. Each of these frameworks has industry-specific options, and each recommends fitting the framework to the implementing organization.
- *Identify:* Once frameworks are chosen, metrics, processes, projects, and risks can more easily be identified. With the relentless support and guidance of executive management, those components can also be aligned with the stated requirements. Then, with the open participation of the entire organization, the PePPR components can be identified dependably.
- *Prioritize:* Before allocating resources to support a metric, improve a process, implement a project, or mitigate a risk, the company should prioritize the components. This allows management to better understand which components are most critical in improving the competitive advantage of the company. For example, with risk mitigation and process improvement, such prioritization efforts can be accomplished with the aid of an initiative submission and review process, typically associated with a project portfolio management office (PMO).
- *Track and report:* Performance management systems should be reviewed constantly to improve the quality of data and analytics given to executive management; processes should be benchmarked and tracked for quality improvement using such tools as Kaizen, Lean, and Six Sigma; project auditors should be

made available to validate project manager scoring; and risks should be monitored for mitigation. Tracking the elements of PePPR management is necessary before improvements or changes can be made. If a company has identified, prioritized, and tracked the state of all components of PePPR management, it can then report them. Two approaches to presenting PePPR component data include a central performance management dashboard or multiple departmental dashboards customized for focused needs (as seen at Verizon and Pinnacol Insurance in Chapter 4).

- *Provide Feedback and reframe:* Once the output of PePPR is distributed, constructive feedback can be used to improve the processes associated with performance, process, project portfolio, and risk management. This feedback loop is one of the most common elements of the highest level of maturity for most process maturity models.

Companies of different shapes and sizes will implement this model for each of their PePPR silos in different ways. Two basic ways they are implemented, however, are manually (i.e., the PePPR grind) or through some automation tool. I have seen very large companies with very mature PePPR cultures in place and that at the same time tracked and reported on their PePPR components in a rather manual fashion (e.g., Molson-Coors and Porter General). I also ran into companies that had prematurely implemented advanced automation systems for their PePPR components. As mentioned in Chapter 2, care should be taken first to implement a cultural foundation before rolling out an automation environment too soon. Either way, Table 8.1 shows how manual tasks in our least-common-denominator model can be implemented if an automated PePPR solution is installed.

Examples of events that could initiate research into a PePPR framework include a board request to start a risk analysis or a process improvement review to satisfy quality improvement needs. Only after a framework is adopted, risks are identified, or inefficient processes are found will the research team realize it doesn't have dependable methods for implementing mitigation or improvement projects. Worse

**Table 8.1**  Strategic Control Framework: Examples of Manual versus Automated Implementations

| Task | Manual | Automated |
|------|--------|-----------|
| Frame | Research and establish a framework | Framework is predefined by installed software |
| Identify | Iterate to determine components for each reporting level and then store them in a spreadsheet | Enter PePPR components into a database system |
| Prioritize | Score the components and then sort by score | Answer scoring questions in the software package, then leverage several best practices scoring models when generating prioritization reports |
| Track and report | Conduct field audits, implement e-mail updates, and write reports | Integrate systems with enterprise application integration packages, implement data warehouses and analytics engines, and autogenerate reports |
| Provide feedback and reframe | Alter PePPR statusing processes, reporting formats, and organizational responsibilities | Leverage automated feedback and trending mechanisms in the system; allow executives to manage their own ad hoc report formats |

yet, it may not realize this inadequacy until many projects have started and contributed to a cauldron of chaos. Before a company tries to lift a great weight, run a long distance, or leap across a wide crevice, it should be sure it is in good shape, or else serious injuries could result (e.g., disastrously failed projects). According to W. Chan Kim and Renee Mauborgne, authors of *Blue Ocean Strategy*, before launching into unexplored territory with new projects, a company should understand its execution risks, internal capabilities, and ability to perform [1]. Figure 8.1 then shows that if a company wants to implement the visibility components of PePPR (i.e., risk and performance management), it should first get its execution ducks (process and project portfolio management) in a row (Step 1, then Step 2).

Then, once frameworks are in place for all four PePPR components, processes, risks, and metric goals can be identified (3), prioritized (4), addressed (through projects, 5), and tracked (6). That is, by framing how risks will be identified, how processes will be reviewed, how projects will be controlled and supported, and how performance will be tracked, a company will be creating an ability to execute. Such a basic ability (1 and 2) should be a precursor to looking for reasons to start improvement or mitigation efforts (i.e., projects, 5). This allows the company to understand "the scope for the freedom within which people are allowed to act" [2]. This freedom is defined not just by identifying risks, metrics, and processes (3) but also by prioritizing them against the goals of the strategy and the execution capabilities of the organization (4). It is a "controlled" freedom that should be balanced between ensuring alignment with the corporate strategy and allowing opportunities for innovation, a balance that is more easily managed with PePPR controls in places. According to Peter M. Senge and Goran Carstedt, authors of "Innovating Our Way to the Next Industrial Revolution," and Phil Rosenzweig, author of "The Halo Effect, and Other Managerial Delusions," such activity is an essential part of the

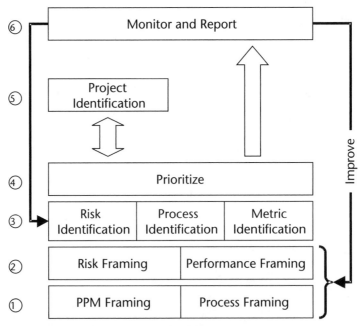

**Figure 8.1**  Siloed PePPR implementation methodology.

critical thinking required in today's dynamic environments before project-funding commitments are made [3, 4].

## An Integrated View

In Chapter 1, we showed how an organization can improve both its visibility and its execution through the implementation and integration of PePPR management components. Such integrated PePPR management was shown to be especially important for companies that hope to thrive in fast industries by executing efficiently on dynamic foundations. Smaller, prepublic companies would focus more on performance (or reactive visibility) than on risk (or proactive visibility). Then, with the swath of government and investor oversight that comes with a public offering, owners would shift to risk as being of higher priority than performance. That is, with newly public companies, key risk indicators (KRIs) carry more weight in decisions than key performance indicators.

Going public is just one of many scenarios that can cause the leadership of an organization to change its focus to a different PePPR silo. While the board may choose a pet project, focus on a process or quality improvement effort, or prefer risk analysis over performance results, the staff should be improving its ability to support any executive need. An efficient organization should be able to provide quick and accurate information on its inner workings. It should also be able to execute more quickly and effectively than its competition. Unfortunately, in today's tenuous executive suites, management vision and goals can change on a dime. So, to better weather the executive churn endemic in fast industries, organizations need to institutionalize (standardize and culturalize) the core business activities of PePPR management. The PePPR execution maturity model in Chapter 2 addressed this by integrating the output of nine PePPR-based maturity models. We ended up with four maturity stages:

1. *Ad hoc execution:* While leaders will reach for the "low hanging fruit" by supporting quick wins at the expense of long-term gain, staff will have started to show the beginnings of integrated PePPR management. For example, risks could be influencing project selection, performance metrics could be forcing process changes and vice versa, and project selection and process improvement processes could be repeating between project and process sets.

2. *Controlled execution:* When a company wants to select projects for its portfolio or to improve a process, it now does so by repeating a set of processes that worked for that company in the past. If executives want to better understand the future through risk-options analysis or performance trends, they are supported by a quick and capable staff. Also, executives are beginning to see the benefits of integrated PePPR management through strategic-level process monitoring metrics and a stream of risk mitigation and process improvement projects. Controls and the resulting efficiencies are well executed by an organization at this stage.

3. *Integrated execution:* Where control was the big gain in the previous stage, support is the big gain in this stage. All four PePPR management

components are well matured to the point of acting not only as control mechanisms for senior management but also as support tools to help corporate capabilities and project success rates improve in highly dynamic environments (as in Hiroyuki Itami's "dynamic resource fit" ). In Chapter 1 we referenced how C. A. Bartlett and S. Ghoshal highlighted the need for corporate support in order to infuse self-control into the organization. Such a focus on support lays the groundwork for the culturalized execution of the next stage.

4. *Culturalized execution:* When the components of PePPR no longer execute as silos, they execute like the crew of a racing sailboat or the team of a hospital emergency room. They each still excel in their specialty fields, but they also leverage their overlapping skills and common goals. Different project teams, divisions, and business units (BUs) are brought together by the champions of performance, process, project portfolio, and risk to cooperate in the development of a sound, yet adaptive, strategic plan (as in Kim and Mauborgne's "fair-process" approach to strategic development). These open and structured communications allow each part of the company to be aware of the actions of the others and to support and drive for mutual gain.

When we refer to ad hoc execution, we refer to piecemeal implementation of integrated PePPR. When we refer to controlled execution, we may refer to some of the more basic integration feeds (PePPR feeds 4, 7, and 8), but we claim that such feeds are well standardized and used within the organization. While these four stages represent the maturity of an organization when integrating PePPR management components, integration maturity is independent of an organization's maturity in each of the individual PePPR components. For example, an investment banking company could be at the highest maturity level for an organization that implements risk management principles, but does it consider risks associated with poor performance metrics or with poorly managed projects? Figure 8.2 overlays this integrated execution maturity model (from Chapter 2) with our siloed model defined in the last section and shown in Figure 8.1. Whereas Figure 8.1 simply illustrates an order in which each silo can be implemented relative to the others, Figure 8.2 shows how siloed PePPR maturity can evolve primarily within the control stage of our integrated maturity model. This figure also shows that since less mature companies will tend simply to identify and track metrics, processes, projects, and risks before adding any sort of structure or aligning frameworks, the initial framing efforts will require some realignment of previously identified PePPR components.

A mature, integrated PePPR organization can break down the communication walls created through decades of PePPR management silo implementations. Risk managers will no longer step on the feet of project portfolio directors, performance managers will work hand in hand with process improvement champions, and project portfolios will be well represented in any performance dashboards. Corporate flexibility and adaptability necessitate such open communications to reduce political roadblocks and "death by process." Model 2, organic, and open organizations allow for just the type of communications that support integrated PePPR management. According to the Deloitte/Utrecht survey referenced in Chapter 2, the more

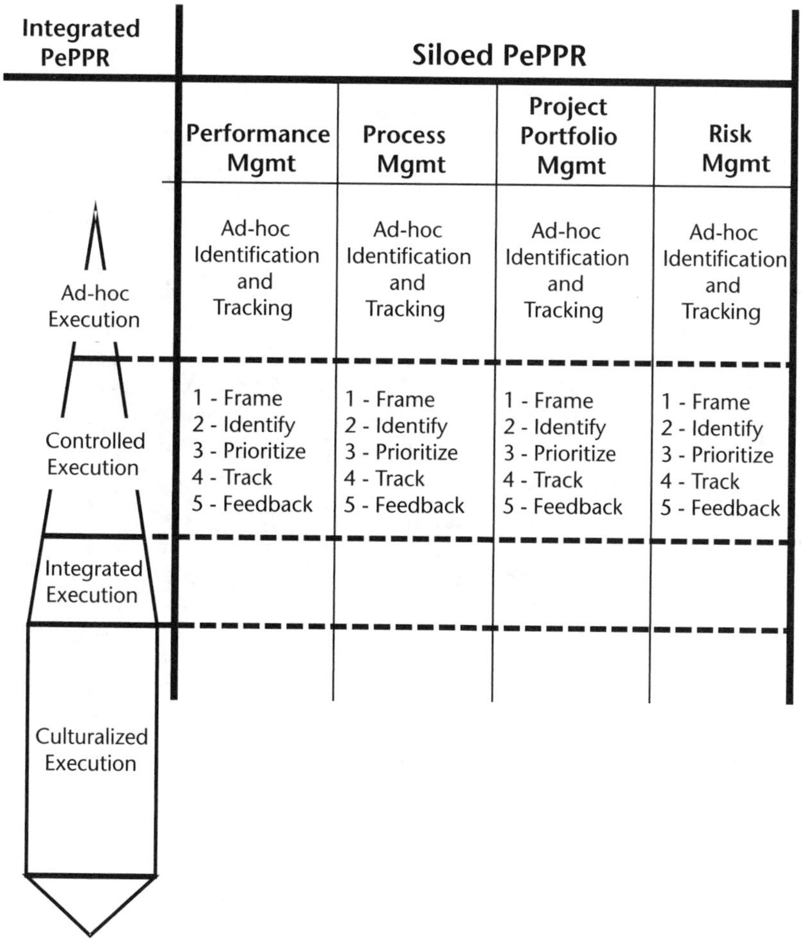

| Integrated PePPR | Siloed PePPR | | | |
|---|---|---|---|---|
| | **Performance Mgmt** | **Process Mgmt** | **Project Portfolio Mgmt** | **Risk Mgmt** |
| Ad-hoc Execution | Ad-hoc Identification and Tracking | Ad-hoc Identification and Tracking | Ad-hoc Identification and Tracking | Ad-hoc Identification and Tracking |
| Controlled Execution | 1 - Frame<br>2 - Identify<br>3 - Prioritize<br>4 - Track<br>5 - Feedback | 1 - Frame<br>2 - Identify<br>3 - Prioritize<br>4 - Track<br>5 - Feedback | 1 - Frame<br>2 - Identify<br>3 - Prioritize<br>4 - Track<br>5 - Feedback | 1 - Frame<br>2 - Identify<br>3 - Prioritize<br>4 - Track<br>5 - Feedback |
| Integrated Execution | | | | |
| Culturalized Execution | | | | |

**Figure 8.2**   Siloed PePPR control maturity.

mature and successful companies integrated the components of PePPR management. Yet, for a company to progress through the stages of PePPR execution maturity, it must first establish a culture of open communication.

Figure 8.3 shows how the four stages of PePPR execution maturity map to the seven Flamholtz and Randle (F&R) stages, the four STaRS stages, and the four business maturity model (BMM) stages presented in Chapter 2. Since establishing an open communication culture that is ripe for sound risk and performance management is easiest done from the beginning of a business, we have the first stage of PePPR execution occurring in F&R's expansion stage. For a company that is just trying to prove its viability in its earliest stage, the detail and added work involved with integrated PePPR management duties can distract the owners from the core tasks. Control needs to be introduced carefully; a balance should always be struck between controlled innovation and process overload. Controlled and integrated execution can slowly be introduced through expansion and professionalization of the company, out of the start-up stage and into the sustaining success and systems implementation stages of STaRS and BMM, respectively. Complete integrated PePPR value-add can even be realized before the company reaches F&R Stage 4

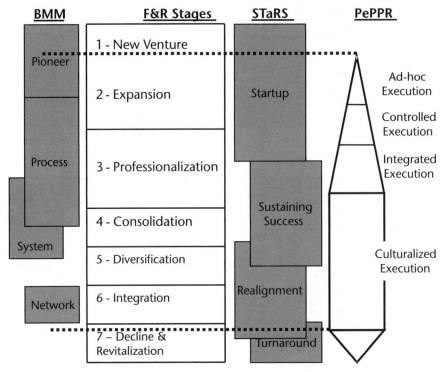

**Figure 8.3**  PePPR maturity mapped to business maturity.

(when a company realigns around a single strategic path). This mapping of PePPR to canned business maturity models should not be taken as gospel, however. It is just a balancing-act guide to illustrate that (1) you should take care when introducing processes before their time, and (2) it would be easier to introduce the organization-defining processes of PePPR earlier in a company's history. If the stages of PePPR execution are introduced later than shown, then organizational change efforts will be more dominant (see the "Organizational Considerations" section of this chapter).

We need to be careful not to claim a holy grail when referring to maturity models. According to David M. Fisher of Bearing Point, Inc., "Maturity models in and of themselves aren't valuable unless we can apply them and achieve benefits from them" [5]. In the case of siloed PePPR maturity models, each represents a sliced view of the organization and doesn't consider the maturity of other affecting activities. Integrated PePPR execution, on the other hand, refers to how the different activity dimensions support each other for more efficient execution and visibility. According to Andrew Spanyi, author of "Beyond Process Maturity to Process Competence," "After all, neither wisdom nor skill necessarily accompanies maturity. If it is performance that really counts, then we need to go beyond maturity to look at how an organization develops business process competence" [6]. In other words, when we refer to execution maturity, we need to consider the synergistic contribution of each of the players in the execution dance.

## PePPR Management Offices

Before the 1980s, the typical organizational chart was a hierarchy of branches, divisions, departments, offices, and groups. This structure continues to serve its purpose well in support of ongoing operations, but according to Bartlett and Ghoshal, authors of "Changing the Role of Top Management: Beyond Structure to Process," it has "little built-in capability for renewal—for discarding old ideas and assumptions as they [become] obsolete" [7]. That is, as large companies grew through the 1980s and 1990s, they "were becoming increasingly inflexible, slow to innovate, and resistant to change" [7]. In order to bypass barriers to innovation, competence building, and renewal, executives would launch pet projects, build alliances, and acquire other companies. However, these efforts didn't remove the organizational barriers; "they only sidestepped them" [7]. As a result, in today's dynamic marketplace, companies executives are viewing their companies less as a hierarchy of static positions and more as a "portfolio of dynamic processes" [7].

When executives grow tired of throwing money over a one-year wall for large capital expenditures, they start looking for better ways to track and control such costly initiatives. Even innovative companies willing to accept a certain number of dead-end approaches, bad ideas, and project failures would still like to keep a finger on such developments as they occur rather than after the fact. Such controls are more often being implemented by what Marius Leibold, Gilbert Probst, and Michael Gibbert refer to as "shadow organizations," what Robert Grant refers to as "parallel structures," and what Robert S. Kaplan and David P. Norton refer to as "shared services groups." Figure 8.4(a) shows how such a matrixed "shadow" structure can coexist with the functional structure in one company. Figure 8.4(b) shows that while measures for process risks and performance percolate up the functional structure, measures for project risks and performance percolate up the matrixed structure. The performance levels of both ultimately feed some performance monitoring interface for executives.

The parallel structures that are being built to support rapid internal dynamics borrow from the matrixed structures so common to project teams. With matrixed organizations, staff would have two bosses who would influence their performance evaluations: the functional boss and the project manager. That is, authority (e.g., compensation, time off) over the matrixed resource would be split between two or more supervisors. The drawback to such split authority is visible when each manager wants 100% of the resource's time. A similar drawback is evident when PePPR management offices (MOs) are created to transfer responsibility for strategic-level performance, risk, process, or project portfolio from the functional leaders. The resulting strain isn't over use of a resource but over the loss of turf and the gain in new auditors. Where matrixed organizations distribute authority over resource activity between managers, mature PePPR management organizations distribute authority over strategic activity between divisions and strategic activity management offices. Regardless of the turf battles, Lee G. Bolman and Terrence E. Deal, authors of *Reframing Organizations: Artistry, Choice, and Leadership* (see Chapter 2), still feel that matrixed structures provide the best "communications necessary to handle rapid change" [8].

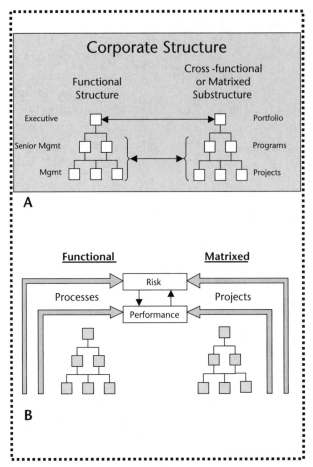

**Figure 8.4**  PePPR management in corporate structures. The structures are shown in (a) and the paths of communications are shown in (b).

On the good side, interfunction communication and support can lead to companies that execute systemically. On the bad side, "matrixed structures create means of lateral linkage and integration but are notorious for creating conflict and confusion" [8]. So, to help understand whether enterprise-level matrices are appropriate for your company, Bolman and Deal have come up with six dimensions that should be considered when deciding how expansive your matrixed PePPR organization should become (see Table 8.2 for a summary).

- *Size and age:* "As a company gets larger and older, the complexity and formalization can increase" [8]. This in turn necessitates the checks-and-balances found in a matrixed structure.
- *Core process:* More project-centric organizations should adopt more controlling structures (e.g., matrix) due to the subjective nature of projects. More process-centric organizations can lean more toward a functional structure.
- *Environment:* A simpler (e.g., functional) structure works better in a stable environment. More complex (e.g., matrixed) structures are favored for more uncertain, turbulent environments.

**Table 8.2** Criteria for Functional versus Matrixed Structures

| | Functional (Vertical) | Matrixed (Horizontal) |
|---|---|---|
| Size and age | Simple and informal (small) | Complex and formal (large) |
| Environment | Stable, simple | Turbulent |
| Strategy and goals | Less clear → more centralized | Clearer → more decentralized |
| IT | Poorly implemented, siloed | Advanced, well implemented, cross-functional |
| Workforce | Less educated; wants controlling leadership | More educated; wants autonomy |
| Core processes | Processcentric, individualistic | Projectcentric, team oriented |

- *Strategy and goals:* "Variation in clarity and consistency of goals requires appropriate structural adaptations"[8]. The clearer the goals, the more decentralized you can be. As decentralization occurs and an independent culture propagates, other distributed controls, such as with a matrixed auditor, are needed to keep the kids in line. The less clear the goals and the less these goals are enforced, the more chaotic a decentralized organization will become.

- *Information technology:* "Information technology permits flatter, more flexible, and more decentralized structure" [8]. That is, due to the increased visibility (i.e., speed and accuracy) provided by well-implemented IT systems, fewer human (or organizational) controls, such as a matrixed auditor, may be necessary.

- *Nature of the workforce:* "More educated and professional workers need and want greater autonomy and discretion" [8]. This is where functional, or vertical, direction gets replaced by a matrixed structure that provides more support than control. Coincidentally, such support inevitably leads to a culture of self-control. According to Bartlett and Ghoshal, "Only when a company has developed a strong sense of self-discipline and control can its top management undertake the kind of radical decentralization" proposed by a matrixed PePPR architecture [7]. Unfortunately, many PePPR management offices are implemented with a mission to be controlling auditors rather than supporting agents. Such an improper implementation can counter the benefits offered to an advanced workforce by a matrixed structure.

## Siloed PePPR Management Offices

Performance, process, project portfolio, and risk management offices (RMOs) are very common in private, public, and nonprofit organizations around the world. Figure 8.5 shows how these four management offices can exist in an organization. Each of them has its own special tasks to complete (only a small subset is listed here), but each also has redundant tasks. We will briefly review how some organizations have implemented these and then consider the value-add of consolidating the offices into a single entity. Figure 8.5 also shows two key elements to keep in mind as we review each of these offices: (1) each office may require its own executive sponsorship, and (2) during strategic design sessions, each office may have differing

**Figure 8.5**  Siloed PePPR management offices with multiple strategic views, multiple executive sponsors, and redundant activities.

strategic visions. Ultimately, we hope to show that a consolidated strategic activity management office will reduce costs, improve PePPR management success, improve corporate adaptability, reduce executive workload, and quicken strategic development efforts.

### Virtualizing Process and Performance MOs

As the need for business process realignment and reengineering continues and grows with faster industries, process management offices have continued to become part of the structure of organizations. For example, the Federal Bureau of Investigation [9], Genentech [10], Sun Microsystems [11], and Emerson [12] have all created such an office to help implement process improvement, process change, IT systems efforts, or some combination thereof. These offices can be used to coordinate Six Sigma black belts, train staff in statistical process control, conduct organizational change assessments for project proposals, or help write project requirements. The business analysts managed and trained by the process management office will more than likely be the same analysts who recommend and manage the strategic performance metrics that link to operational process metrics.

Even though process and performance management offices can overlap in their use of business analysts, performance management offices are unique in their technical application. As we outlined in Chapter 4 and Chapter 5, the adoption of strategic performance management by your company requires a broad analytical approach to doing business. Not only do systems have to be in place to support such automated processes as business intelligence, data warehousing, and business activity management, but "changes in culture, process, behavior and skills for multiple employees" will have to be made [13].

The way many companies address the organizational upheavals from implementing a strategic process or performance management architecture is the same way they address similar upheavals from implementing operational risk management and project portfolio management architectures: they create a matrixed organization to distribute ownership for PePPR management between central offices and the different functional units. Examples of this would include the business advisors and the analytic specialists at Quaker Chemical [13] and the analysts at Harrah's casinos. Depending on the culture of the company, these process and performance management specialists can report to different business unit leaders or to a central body (e.g., a functional group or a performance management office). Quaker Chemical has these analysts reporting to each of the BU heads and Harrah's, because of its strong focus on customer-loyalty programs, has them reporting to the marketing department [13].

Toyota Motor Corporation took a similar approach to Harrah's, except it has such business analysts reporting to the chief information officer (CIO) due to its push for business IT alignment [14]. Whichever reporting structure is chosen, it is usually done to enhance the communication between the various BUs (those that have a profit-and-loss responsibility) and some business support units (BSUs), such as marketing or IT. Whether they report to business units [Figure 8.6(a)] or to business support units [Figure 8.6(b)] can depend on a myriad of factors, including culture, strategy, executive whim, and internal "politics."

The BSU in Figure 8.6(a) shows what can also be called a virtual PePPR MO (Harrah's and Toyota). Its actual footprint in the organization is small, but its breadth of coverage is large. This is achieved by having the small staff of the PePPR MO act to coordinate the various business analysts, technical architects, executives, and auditors. These specialists continue to report to their functional managers, but they are also committed to supporting the needs of the virtual PePPR MO. In contrast to this approach, we have the illustration in Figure 8.6(b), where the specialists report to the PePPR MO (Quaker). If usage of process analysts is required by executives for projects or for periodic process reviews, then bottlenecks can occur if the PePPR MO isn't staffed to the business needs. On the other hand, if demand for such talent is low, unused resources could be sitting on the "beach." Therefore, care must be taken to align staffing levels with the current and pending directions of the company. One way to do this is by keeping an ear to the proposed project pipeline, as can be done in an integrated PePPR MO.

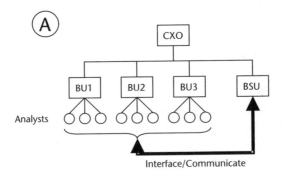

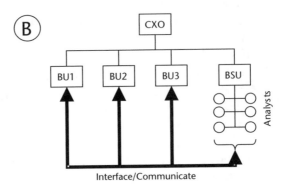

**Figure 8.6** In a business support unit (BSU) such as a central PePPR management office, analysts can report to their business units and be matrixed to the BSU (a) or report to the BSU and be matrixed back to their business units (b).

### Operational Risk MOs

*Executive Autonomy*    In a virtual risk management office (VRMO), staff should be responsible for ensuring organizational participation rather than "defining the meaning of risk and demanding that the organization respond" [15]; that's the job of the sponsoring executive committee. The company should also focus on avoiding "putting in place unnecessary bureaucracy" and especially avoiding "usurping the role of the executive committee" that reviews risks [2]. This allows the RMO staff to maintain a level of objectivity while coordinating enterprisewide operational risk. It also adds credibility to the RMO when it helps define KRIs and then report on KRI status to executives and the rest of the organization. Steven Minsky [16] expands on this concept by splitting out the three players in corporate risk management:

1. *Auditors are the police:* They find the problems.
2. *Compliance groups are the lawyers:* They interpret the regulations and state the framework.
3. *Risk managers are the mediators:* They evaluate the risk and liability data based upon business metrics and help establish a framework.

*Leveraging Operations*    None of these three roles includes the authority to take action on risks. For one thing, they don't normally have the resources to mitigate risk. But if relationships exist with performance, project portfolio, and process management, synergies can result in more efficient risk identification, assessment, and mitigation. This works primarily because these other three PePPR components have relationships with operational staff (i.e., the executors of change) that risk managers may not have. Bill Sharon, author of "Emotion Rules: Ignoring It Won't Change Anything," believes that risks should first evolve from the self-interests of operational staff to provide the technical details and then be aligned with the business strategy to get the best of both worlds [17]. That is, rather than trying to create a "risk culture" from scratch, efforts should be applied to add risk management to the existing culture [15].

The two extremes of implementing an RMO would be either (1) to establish an RMO managed by a senior risk manager (sometimes referred to as the chief risk officer [CRO]), or (2) to create risk architectures run by multiple business unit leaders [18]. A VRMO would combine these two approaches, which is similar to the approach taken by process and performance MOs. Specifically, when rolling out a VRMO, Martyn E. Jones and Gillian Sutherland, authors of "Implementing Turnbull: A Boardroom Briefing," suggest the following steps:

- Distribute a "kick-off" memo from the executive sponsor of the RMO to all members of management and staff.
- Conduct risk management roundtables and workshops at different levels of the company.
- Allocate some training budget for business risk training.
- Communicate
  - The general risk management policy;
  - The key business goals and the associated risks;
  - Policies on how significant risks are to be mitigated or managed.
- Involve staff in identifying (early warnings) and responding (nonproject mitigations) to problems.
- Establish channels of communication to report suspected problems.
- Create an environment in which people are not willing to sit on problems.
- Introduce a common risk management vocabulary [2].

*Horizontal Committees*   By parsing out responsibility for risk management to specialists and business unit leaders, a wide range of risk management approaches can develop. In the biotech industry, G. J. G. Lawrie, D. C. Kaiff, and H. V. Andersen, authors of "Integrating Risk Management with Existing Methods of Strategic Control: Avoiding Duplication within the Corporate Governance Agenda," identify five possible committees: audit, finance and planning, human resources, information communication and technology, and gene technology. In this case the committees were "composed of relevant subject matter experts from within the appropriate functional areas of the organization, assisted by the Strategy & Risk department" [19]. Real operational risk management requires "a robust matrix structure that reaches to everyone in the organization" [20]. Then, to adequately develop a companywide operational risk management approach, the decentralized risk managers need to coordinate with each other. Not only does this avoid redundant work, but it allows for a uniform presentation of the company's risk management message. Unfortunately, the various units or groups that make up the risk environment tend to compete rather than collaborate with each other, "particularly when budgets are at stake" [20]. Without a central authority that can aid communication and collaboration between these disparate risk managers, increased costs can result from:

- Duplication of work/loss of productivity;
- Confusion of work priorities;
- Restriction or loss of knowledge;
- Variance in quality [20].

*Organizational Maturity*    How risk governance is implemented was one of the subjects of a biannual survey conducted by Deloitte and Touche. This 2004 survey focused on an industry well known for its highly structured approach to risk management: the financial services industry. It found that the number of companies that created a chief risk officer (CRO) post (81% of financial institutions) varied mostly by the size of the company. For example, smaller companies tend to adopt more of a centralized CRO who reports to either the chief executive officer (CEO) or to the board of directors. Larger companies, on the other hand, generally apply a combination of centralized and decentralized approaches to risk management. That is, a company will have a central CRO and several business-unit-specific or risk-type-specific (i.e., credit versus market versus operational) risk managers throughout the company. Such a hybrid approach then combines an integrated view of the company's risks "across the enterprise with the flexibility required by the business units to respond quickly to changing market conditions" [21].

> Some companies that have tried to put all of their risk management silos under a single "czar" have failed because they attempted either to homogenize the silos or to assume central control of a process that more properly should have been managed by the specialists. While there should be a central point of coordination (such as a chief risk officer), this role should not be one of overarching control. The business units should always remain responsible for taking and managing risk and maintaining ownership for the risks they assume [22].

With a centralized office that facilitates communication among the different risk managers, consolidated risk prioritization and centralized "bucketing" can occur. If a particular risk affects the entire company, an RMO can bucket it with other strategic-level risks. If other risks affect small projects or business processes, then managers can bucket them with other nonstrategic risks and delegate them to risk specialists. The larger the company or more risk averse the industry, the more structure will be applied to strategic risk mitigation. The smaller the company or more risk-free the industry the more likely risks will be considered nonstrategic and be mitigated on the fly. Nonetheless, setting some structure early in the lifetime of a company "could reduce the costs of transition once they have grown or been hit by an unforeseen event" [2].

## Architecting Project Portfolio MOs

Many names have been given to this office. I have heard enterprise project management office, strategic program office, enterprise portfolio office, and project portfolio management office. Therefore, whenever a company talks with another company, consultant, or trade organization, it is worthwhile to align the syntax used by each for this office. In this book, we have referred to the strategic-level office that supports, monitors, and approves all projects and programs as the project portfolio management office, or PMO).

A PMO can start from the top down or from the bottom up. If it is initiated from the executive suite, it is usually done as a quick-fix solution using some fancy software package. As illustrated in Chapter 1, this can end up creating more headaches (i.e., time and money costs) than value-add. A more successful approach has been to first create a culture of project management in an organization from the bottom up. This is similar to the approaches taken in successfully rolling out strategic performance and operational risk management cultures. Such bottom-up PMO efforts many times start in a single department that is able to prove measurable and sustainable successes; in the late 1990s, this was more times than naught the IT department. From these successes, other departments may take notice and try to implement its own permutation of a PMO. Product managers, marketers, and plant managers are some of the business unit leaders that can see the value in applying project portfolio management principles.

Once multiple departments have established their own PMOs, executives can provide a layered PMO approach, or an operational portfolio architecture. This is a structured way for a company to spread the successes of a departmental PMO across the organization. According to a 1999 survey of over 250 companies by Robert G. Cooper, Scott J. Edgett, and Elko J. Kleinschmidt, "A significant number of businesses . . . operate portfolio management within the business unit, and they also have a centralized or corporate portfolio management method (44.7 percent of respondents)" [23]. This is similar to the mature RMO structures implemented by companies in the Deloitte survey.

Molson-Coors is an example of an organization that successfully implemented a "vertical" operational portfolio architecture. In this case, the company placed portfolio management offices at various vertical levels in the organization (see Figure 8.7). The topmost level (actually shown as the bottommost position in Figure 8.7) was named the global PMO and addressed more of the strategic duties of a typical PMO. At the lower levels (shown as the next level from the bottom), strategic business units (SBUs) had their own PMOs that oversaw departmental PMOs (e.g., IT, product development, and large capital expenditure projects). These lower-level PMOs focused less on strategy development and propagation and more on portfolio-level project support duties, such as interproject architecture, asset, resource, knowledge, and vendor management [24]. Figure 8.7 illustrates how the CEO received information on project health from the accountable parties (SBU CEOs), as well as from an objective or neutral party (the global PMO). Besides a cleaner, more dependable vision of the corporate dynamics, such an architecture also allowed for cascading rewards for those sub-PMOs that demonstrated higher maturity (similar to the approach taken by the state of California referenced in Chapter 6).

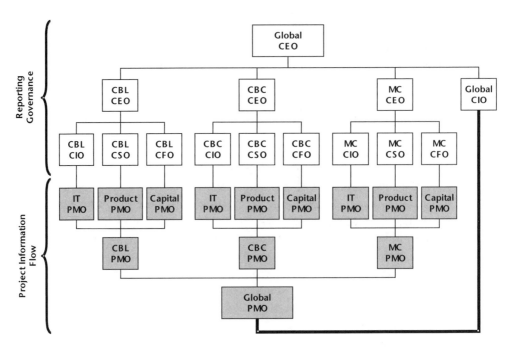

**Figure 8.7** Vertical portfolio architecture (CBL = Coors Brewers Limited, CBC = Coors Brewing Company, MC = Molson Canada). (*After* [23].)

Besides a vertical architecture, there can also be a horizontal project portfolio architecture, similar to the horizontal risk committees implemented by the biotech industry. Bryan Maizlish and Robert Handler, in their book *IT Portfolio Management*, refer to some of the boxes on the left and right side in Figure 8.8 as subportfolios within a PMO. The cylinder in the middle of the figure represents the project pipeline we referenced in Chapter 6. This form of PMO architecture helps develop what the Molson-Coors team referred to as "communities of practice" across the organization, which in turn allowed for more efficient inter-PMO communications and support [24].

### Roller Coaster MOs

I've talked with several PMO directors who ran a PePPR management office of one employee but had at one time managed much larger organizations. Whether their MOs had been downsized due to corporate budget woes, turf fighting, poor MO execution, or lack of executive focus is hard to determine, though the most popular excuse was the latter. In the case of project portfolio management offices, executives would launch a PMO initiative to counter a problem with poor project success rates. Unfortunately, once a hearty PMO was able to prove that projects were doing much better, it would have its funding cut off in favor of some other executive need. The organization would continue for a period, and then renewed project failure rates would lead to executive support for a rejuvenated PMO. This same problem can occur with process quality audits. For example, one of the major strategic mistakes made by McDonald's, the global restaurant corporation, was to bend to the pres-

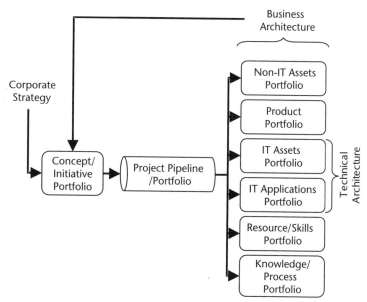

**Figure 8.8**  Horizontal (or functional) portfolio architecture. (*After* [23].)

sures of franchisees and eliminated corporate inspection of many restaurants. This resulted in such a degradation of quality that the restaurant chain's image was adversely affected. Many years later, a new CEO reintroduced corporate auditing of all restaurants [8].

Market winds, capability obsolescence, or executive churn are all reasons why an organization may lose enthusiasm over any particular PePPR component. The drawback of an office's experiencing such a roller coaster of executive support is that it takes time to relaunch an effort that has had time to collect dust (and lose expertise). Sure, some companies build themselves on a cultural foundation of one or maybe two PePPR activities. But the majority will experience waves of enthusiasm for the remaining activities. Once ISO9000 certification is achieved, are the same number of resources made available to maintain and improve on this status? Once project success rates and visibility surpass the competition, do project portfolio management offices maintain their level of executive commitment? What if 20% of the performance management metrics are proven erroneous? Are projects financed to repair them, or do executives return to deriving enterprise performance from manual status reports and chief financial officer (CFO) risk assessments? As mentioned earlier, a company should guard these activity management family jewels by standardizing and culturalizing the PePPR processes. This allows a company to maintain what martial artists refer to as "form" in the long term, regardless of whatever skunk work "techniques" may sprout up in the near term.

## A PePPR Architecture

In the mid-1990s, Bartlett and Ghoshal [7, 25] reviewed several large companies, including 3M, Corning, and Komatsu, and found that certain management processes could be integrated at the highest levels to promote corporate flexibility. But seeing that corporate head offices were becoming smaller across industries, they recommended that the processes associated with these offices be propagated through the layers of the company, just as would be done with a PePPR architecture. The three core (horizontal) processes they focused on were the entrepreneurial process, the competence-building process (improving and deploying organizational capabilities), and the renewal process (molding organizational vision and executing change). They then looked at three core (vertical) layers of a company that these processes could be delegated to: the corporate-level (executive management), the cross-business-unit coordinators (middle management), and the business unit leaders (frontline management). In other words, Bartlett and Ghoshal were promoting the virtualization of the strategic management office into an architecture similar to how RMOs and PMOs have evolved recently.

Combined, PePPR MOs provide a balanced view of the organization and a balanced ability to execute. Some common threads between the different siloed PePPR MOs are that as companies grow, MOs go from being single offices to architectures of offices, both vertically and horizontally. Such expansion of these parallel organizational structures can help avoid the problems found with roller coaster commitment by the executive suite. As PePPR management becomes more pervasive in a culture, however, it is important to avoid PePPR empire building, but not at the expense of unbiased objectivity, open communications, and executive autonomy. This leads us to the recommended structure of having the global integrated PePPR MO report directly to the CEO and having the subordinate MOs report to the PePPR MO. This global office could be a division of the enterprise strategy office, or it could be its own entity. Either way, it should be kept small and be supported diligently by executives from the top, by an architecture from below, and by the organization as a whole.

To set the organizationwide support needed, we return to the entrepreneurial environment that breeds in an open culture. While PePPR control will provide executives with the visibility needed to make quick decisions, PePPR support will lead to an organization able to react quickly on executive decisions. Such support can come in the form of improved bottom-up visibility through empowerment, inclusion, and open-book cultures and through improved top-down execution through project support. If such an environment exists, then companies are in a better position to grow from the ground up through entrepreneurship. 3M provides an example of a company that had established just such a culture. "Generations of top management at 3M have viewed their organization as growing from the bottom—the project team—up. Under a principle the company calls 'grow and divide'" [7, 25].

### The Integrated PePPR MO

Figure 8.9 shows how an integrated PePPR management office (IPMO) can look. While the PePPR components still require special skills, certifications, software, and personalities to be effective, they also leverage common activities. This was evident with processes and projects when, in Chapter 3, we showed how Hoshin Kanri integrated these activity management silos under one framework, yet also highlighted the need to keep some supporting activities separate. The true value-add for integrated PePPR occurs when the leaders of each silo agree on a common direction

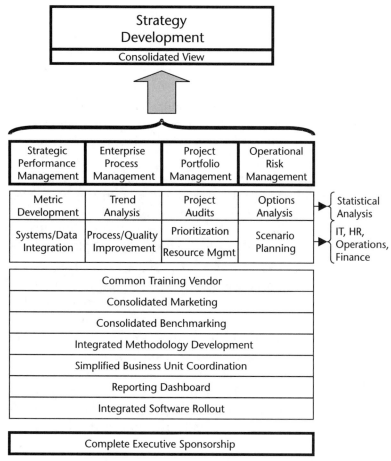

**Figure 8.9** Centralized strategic management office with a single strategic view, consolidated executive sponsorship, and integrated support activities.

for the company during strategic design. However, other cost savings can result. Starting from the top, we can see that IPMO staff can be trained on statistical analysis and then apply this knowledge across all four silos. Also, the IPMO staff size can shrink due to leveraging resources available in other departments (i.e., reduce work). IT can help with systems and data integration for performance management, human resources can support resource management for project portfolio management, operations can support process improvement efforts, and finance can help with project prioritization and scenario planning. IPMO staff can be further reduced, and siloed PePPR management successes can be increased if common activities are leveraged.

- *Strategic design:* With regard to structure, businesses tend to organize themselves around core specialties or functions (e.g., human resources, finance, marketing, manufacturing, IT, and research and development). While these functions act as the operational core of an organization, integrated PePPR management crosses and consolidates the functions and helps steer the company toward its vision or strategy through controlled execution. That is, while siloed performance, process, project portfolio, and risk management may bridge the gap between operational and strategic management, integrated PePPR management provides a more efficient development of the strategic design. Such efficiency can in turn lead to a more adaptive corporation, government, or nonprofit.

- *Common training vendor:* Training vendors today are offering courses that cover all the areas of PePPR management. Costs can be saved by contracting with a single vendor rather than allowing siloed PePPR managers to choose their own.

- *Consolidated marketing:* Staff frustration can be reduced if a single, consolidated PePPR strategy is communicated. Oftentimes, one PePPR component may be championed at the expense of another: should we focus on metric development, risk identification, or new project ideas? This can be avoided if the same team represents the IPMO during PePPR "road trips."

- *Consolidated benchmarking:* As with marketing, IPMO staff can reduce staff frustrations by conducting benchmark interviews in parallel. When operational staff members are interviewed to identify potential metrics, they can also be interviewed to identify potential risks, projects, or process improvements. Why make several trips and consume valuable staff time?

- *Integrated methodology development:* The risk management component of a project management methodology should integrate with the operational risk management efforts. The approval process for performance metrics should consider the checks-and-balances provided by key risk indicators and project statuses. In other words, standards and methodologies developed for the PePPR components should no longer be developed in a vacuum if an IPMO exists.

- *Simplified business unit coordination:* When projects are prioritized, this should be done with an architecture review committee and an organizational assessment committee. When performance metrics are chosen, this should be done with representatives from operations and finance. When risks are prioritized, this should be done with representatives from different business units. Coordinating these business unit committees can be simplified if done through a single IPMO entity rather than through four separate PePPR management offices.

- *Reporting dashboard:* Physically grouping the PePPR organizations into one will help ensure the goals referenced in Chapter 4. Namely, performance dashboards that consolidated project statuses with process metrics and key risk indicators can provide a more balanced view of the activities of the organization. The design of such a consolidated dashboard can be iterated to meet changing markets and executive needs more quickly if the different PePPR teams work closer together, as in an IPMO.

- *Integrated software rollout:* Software packages can be purchased to support any one of the four PePPR components; however, more advanced software is available that integrates these components. The stronger inter-PePPR team communications that can be found in an IPMO will help ensure that software is purchased that can satisfy the needs of more than one PePPR silo.

• *Complete executive sponsorship:* Rather than spread executive involvement across each of the four PePPR initiatives, executives can now choose a customized PePPR strategy and present a consolidated and persistent message to the organization, thus reducing strategic activity management workload. "This company will focus on achieving world-class performance by meeting our project goals and squashing risks," or "Company ABC will become the icon of product quality in our industry through strict adherence to Six Sigma process improvement." Whatever mix of PePPR is chosen, the IPMO will have the tools, experience, relationships, and respect in the organization to execute the strategy. Destructive in-fighting will be reduced, results will be achieved sooner, and confusing, nonstandard reports will be eliminated.

## Organizational Considerations

It can be a difficult task to establish a culture of risk identification, process improvement, project management, and performance measurement that provides value to both operational staff and executives. As we mentioned in Chapter 1, it can take those companies that hope to instill such a culture where there wasn't already one (the most common scenario) many years to do so. If the added efforts required of staff to support such activity management aren't instilled early in the culture of an organization, it can take some effort to convince staff members that new efforts won't adversely affect their ability to get their jobs done. According to Russ Banham, author of "Seeing the Big Picture: New Data Tools Are Enabling CEOs to Get a Better Handle on Performance Across Their Organizations—Technology—Business Performance Management," such changes in the organization no doubt bring with them the risks of cultural upheaval from management reorganizations and resistance to process changes [26]. More specifically, establishing an office to manage new processes (thus an updated culture) will be resisted as power and authority are transferred from the individual functions and passed to an organization that is focused on the entire enterprise. Some lessons we can draw from how siloed PePPR MOs have been successful with other organizations include:

1. Keep a small MO footprint.
2. Reduce perceptions of bias through independent governance.
3. Combine or piggyback PePPR MO rollout.
4. Understand your tenuous position and build relationships.
5. Hold managers accountable.
6. Be fast.
7. Benchmark and prove constant "wins."
8. Nurture and advertise your executive sponsorship.

*Small Footprint*    One lesson we can draw from the VRMO is that a key to its success is its small footprint in the organization. The bigger it is, the harder it will fall. If an organization were created to handle all risk-related activities in an organization, backlash would turn to rejection and ultimate closure of the new activity management office. Roller-coasting of your integrated PePPR MO can also be avoided if it doesn't appear to be another bureaucratic cost center. By adopting a virtual PePPR MO approach, the organization will be spreading responsibility for success throughout the company. While the smaller PePPR MO will primarily act as a guide to various support committees, it is understood that such committees will be apt to provide the hard work required to develop methodologies, roll out PePPR management software, prioritize and audit projects, manage performance management systems and metrics, conduct risk scenario analysis, or champion process improvement frameworks. Temporary, dedicated resources, whether internal or outsourced, may be needed to establish processes or automation support in early stages.

*Independent Governance*   Another lesson we can pull from VRMOs is the importance of independence and objectivity. If such an office is under the control of an organization that gets rated for process and project performance, then a perception of bias can exist when departmental health reports are released. As was shown in Chapter 6, the optimal scenario would be for a consolidated PePPR MO to report directly to the CEO. According to Bartlett and Ghoshal, such "a well-established sense of fairness serves as an organizational safety net for risk takers" [7].

*Piggybacked Rollout*   Some feel that since performance management shouldn't be rolled out without the checks-and-balances of a risk management approach, opportunities exist to minimize organizational backlash issues while rolling out both. In fact, Jones and Sutherland feel that a good risk management rollout "has the potential to re-orient the whole organization around performance management" [2]. Since performance and risk management share the same goal of achieving the organization's strategic objectives, they should be marketed as such. Besides, according to Lawrie, Kaiff, and Andersen, the main difference is only that performance management focuses on achieving good results while risk management focuses on avoiding bad results [19]. Since new risk or performance management initiatives may cause great organizational change, it can be beneficial to "piggyback" such efforts [2]. Many times executives will launch such efforts only to see them wither due to a lack of organizational commitment. If one such effort has failed in the past, any new effort will be met with heightened skepticism. If there is a long-term executive commitment to risk and performance management, then such initiatives should be pushed equally through the ranks to reduce organizational rejection and increase synergy.

Moreover, the Treasury Board of Canada's Secretariat feels that to get a company to focus specifically on risk management, for example, this PePPR component should be integrated not just with the rollout of another PePPR component but also with the responsibilities of an existing unit [27]. For that matter, piggybacking any of the PePPR components on the other PePPR components will allow for easier updates to the PePPR culture of the day. For example, if executives have burned out from trying to push an enterprise process improvement effort (e.g., Six Sigma) and want to refocus resources on project portfolio management, then they can do so by marketing PPM as an evolution of process management. The same resources can be used, the same training slots can be leveraged, and the same business unit representatives can stay involved. At Lowe's, the CIO took advantage of his IT PMO and integrated process management tasks to create the company's Business Solutions Group. Since this organization was tasked with business value reviews, architecture reviews, and project reviews, it ended up growing to a larger size. It consisted of 85 staff members who held such titles as business analyst, project manager, and technical architect [28].

*Relationship Building*    Where matrixed supervisors derive authority from having input into performance evaluations, PePPR managers only have authority as long as executives hold the rest of the organization to the recommendations of the PePPR management office. Since executive marketing of PePPR isn't a standard process like performance evaluations, it can be difficult to get the necessary consistent support from the executives. Bolman and Deal use product managers as an example of those who must work with a range of groups outside their authority to achieve success [8]. But with thin authority, getting business units to buy in to PePPR concepts tends to be accomplished more with a carrot than with a stick. "To augment efforts of formal groups, coordinating roles or units spring up, using persuasion and negotiation to help others integrate their efforts" [8].

*Manager Accountability*    According to Kim and Mauborgne, tipping-point leadership is a technique to help expedite the type of organizational change we can find with PePPR MO rollouts [1]. With this technique, PePPR MO champions and executive sponsors understand that middle management can be the greatest impediment to change. To resolve this organizational change hurdle, tipping-point leaders "focus on three factors of disproportionate influence in motivating employees": (1) put most of your effort into getting supervisors and managers on board (referred to as kingpins), (2) place a spotlight on these managers and hold them accountable to the entire company (referred to as fishbowl management), and then (3) break the tasks down into clearly achievable elements (referred to as atomization) [1]. Since traditional top-down organizational change looks first for executive support, followed by early-adopting managers, then by organizationwide grass roots, and finally by rogue managers, tipping-point leaders will be better prepared to overcome problems with this last group before they reach it.

*Speed*    As discussed in Chapter 3, we don't want to be a slave to our competitors' tactics or to the results of an uncontrolled project. "If we have the initiative, our tactics are generally slave to our strategy" [29]. When rolling out an integrated PePPR MO, organizationwide scrutiny will be sufficient to warrant a focus on some quick wins that are aligned with the long-term PePPR goals.

*Benchmark*    In Chapters 3 and 6, we referenced the need to benchmark the failure rates of projects before implementing a PMO. This will allow a PMO to then prove value-add as project failure rates are reduced. This is an absolutely critical step for the survival of a PMO. But what about the identification of risks, the improvement of processes, or the creation of well-regarded metrics? For executives to best understand how their risk, performance, and process improvement cultures are improving, they need a way to compare status to some earlier state. The best way to do this is to apply the benchmarking that is necessary for PMO success to the remaining PePPR components.

*Executive Sponsorship*    We save the best for last. All is lost without executive support in the strategic activity management world. So much organizational commitment, enthusiasm, and change is required that different management styles must be made available. Management by reward and management by fear can only be used if a PePPR management team is not just accountable for success but also has the authority to get staff on board. There is no better way to achieve this than to link PePPR participation and success to performance. This performance can be in the form of metrics that track risk identification, project successes, and process improvement initiatives. Or it can be in the form of links to personnel performance reviews. In the first case, departmental budget allocations can be influenced by performance metrics. In the latter, promotions and compensation can be influenced by personnel reviews. With executives providing such authority to PePPR champions and then relentlessly advertising the importance of PePPR management, the need for management by fear will be eclipsed by organizational passion.

## Summary

If you were to introduce performance, process, project portfolio, or risk management to your organization, you would most likely follow some framework that had proven successful with other organizations. After choosing such a framework, industry standard maturity models referenced in Chapter 2 generally promote four other stages: identify, prioritize, track and report, and provide feedback and reframe. When implementing any one of the four PePPR silos, such approaches to improving the maturity of the organization are well proven. But how should these silos be rolled out so that they feed on each other to produce the optimal consolidated benefits for the company? After first presenting an order that the components of the different PePPR management silos could be rolled out, we then looked at how this approach fit into both the PePPR execution maturity model and the business maturity models we reviewed in Chapter 2. While we addressed organizational maturity in the first section, in the second section, we addressed organizational structure. Several keys to success in this area were presented, with two being fairly strong: (1) keep the organizational structure small, and (2) distribute ownership, accountability, and support throughout the organization. Such virtual strategic management offices (VSMOs) have met with success in the risk management and project portfolio management world. But to reduce the effects of a roller coaster of executive commitment, an advanced form of VSMOs, which we call PePPR management architectures, can bring activity management closer to the grass roots while still being very visible to the executives. By looking first at siloed management offices, we were able to come up with an approach to creating a virtual integrated PePPR management office (IPMO).

The benefits of a virtual IPMO are to break down interdepartmental communication barriers while also avoiding the perception of bureaucratic growth. Each of these activity management silos is meant to increase efficiency of visibility and execution in its own right. However, when efficiencies are lost due to redundant workloads, confused staff (through multiple strategic messages), frustrated executives (through multiple reports and commitments), and complex strategic design sessions, siloed implementation of performance, process, project portfolio, or risk management may be introducing more pain than value. An early organizational change effort can minimize middle-manager resistance and waning passions before they snowball and cause a classic roller coaster PePPR implementation. Stage 2 companies of the integrated PePPR maturity model will have figured out the need for organizational change management while rolling out any of the individual activity management silos. By the time they reach Stages 3 and 4, the organization will already be prepped for the internal tacks needed to accommodate the external winds.

## References

[1] Kim, W. Chan, and Renee Mauborgne, *Blue Ocean Strategy*, Cambridge, MA: Harvard Business School Press, 2005.

[2] Jones, Martyn E., and Gillian Sutherland, "Implementing Turnbull: A Boardroom Briefing," Center for Business Performance, September 1, 1999, www.icaew.co.uk/ index.cfm? route=120612 (last accessed on April 15, 2006).

[3] Senge, Peter M., and Goran Carstedt, "Innovating Our Way to the Next Industrial Revolution," Harvard Business Online, December 1, 2001.

[4] Rosenzweig, Phil, "The Halo Effect, and Other Managerial Delusions," *McKinsey Quarterly*, No. 1, 2007.

[5] Fisher, David M., "The Business Process Maturity Model—A Practical Approach for Identifying Opportunities for Optimization," Bearing Point, Inc., September 1, 2004.

[6] Spanyi, Andrew, "Beyond Process Maturity to Process Competence," BPTrends, June 1, 2004, www.bptrends.com.

[7] Bartlett, C. A., and S. Ghoshal, "Changing the Role of Top Management: Beyond Structure to Process," *Harvard Business Review*, January–February 1995, pp. 87–96.

[8] Bolman, Lee G., and Terrence E. Deal, *Reframing Organizations: Artistry, Choice, and Leadership*, 3rd ed., San Francisco, CA: Jossey-Bass, 2003.

[9] Boyd, K., "Business Process Reengineering at the FBI," presented at the Brainstorm BPM conference, Washington, D.C., September 20, 2006.

[10] Vellequette, Mary Baumgartner, "Case Study: Aligning BPM to Business Stakeholder Value," BPM Institute, www.bpminstitute.org/presentations/all-presentations/article/case-study-aligning-bpm-to-business-stakeholder-value/news-browse/2.html (last accessed on December 27, 2007).

[11] Lauchlan, Stuart, "Picking Your Standard," MIS Asia, February 1, 2005, www.misweb.com/magarticle.asp?doc_id=24256&rgid=2&listed_months=0 (last accessed on December 27, 2007).

[12] "Control Performance Improvement," Fisher-Rosemount Systems, Inc., March 2007, www.sureservice.com/pd/SDS_CntlPerfImprv.pdf (last accessed on December 27, 2007).

[13] Davenport, Thomas, "Competing on Analytics," *Optimize*, February 1, 2006, pp. 41–46.

[14] Wailgum, Thomas, "Toyota's Big Fix: An IS Department Turnaround," *CIO Magazine*, April 15, 2005, www.cio.com/article/print/110851 (last accessed on January 27, 2007).

[15] Sharon, Bill, "The Elusive 'Risk Culture'," Continuity Central, February 23, 2006, www.continuitycentral.com/feature0306.htm (last accessed on April 15, 2006).

[16] Minsky, Steven, "Developing Risk Plans," EBizQ, June 24, 2005, www.ebizq.net/topics/bpm/features/6021.html?&pp=1 (last accessed on April 30, 2006).

[17] Sharon, Bill, "Emotion Rules: Ignoring It Won't Change Anything," Continuity Central, August 12, 2005, www.continuitycentral.com/feature0234.htm (last accessed on April 15, 2006).

[18] Kocourek, Paul, Jim Newfrock, and Reggie VanLee, "It's Time to Take Your SOX Off," Strategy + Business, December 15, 2004, www.strategy-business.com/resiliencereport/resilience/rr00014?pg=all&tid=230 (last accessed on April 30, 2006).

[19] Lawrie, G. J. G., D. C. Kaiff, and H. V. Andersen, "Integrating Risk Management with Existing Methods of Strategic Control: Avoiding Duplication within the Corporate Governance Agenda," 2GC Limited, August 1, 2003, www.2gc.co.uk/pdf/2GC-CP0803.pdf (last accessed on April 15, 2006).

[20] Crawford, Nicola, and Norman Hoppe, "Dragging Operational Risk Management into the 21st Century," Continuity Central, May 27, 2006, www.continuitycentral.com/feature0210.htm (last accessed on April 15, 2006).

[21] Bailey, Michael A., and Edward T. Hida II, "2004 Global Risk Management Survey," Deloitte Development, LLC, 2004.

[22] Layton, Mark, and Rick Funston, "The Risk Intelligent Enterprise," Deloitte Development, LLC, 2006.

[23] Cooper R. G., Edgett, S. J., and Kleinschmidt, E. J., "Best Practices for Managing R&D Portfolios," Project Portfolio Management, Lowell D. Dye and James S. Pennypacker, (eds.), West-Chester, PA: Center for Business Practices, 1999, pp. 309–328.

[24] Bonham, Stephen, et al., "The Molson-Coors Operational Portfolio Architecture," CAIS, December 2006.

[25] Bartlett, C. A., and S. Ghoshal, "The Myth of the General Manager: New Personal Competencies for New Management Roles," *California Management Review*, Vol. 40, Fall 1997, pp. 92–116.

[26] Banham, Russ, "Seeing the Big Picture: New Data Tools Are Enabling CEOs to Get a Better Handle on Performance Across Their Organizations—Technology—Business Performance Management," *Chief Executive*, November 1, 2003, www.findarticles.com/p/articles/mi_m4070/is_193/ai_110811916/print (last accessed on February 17, 2006).

[27] "Integrated Risk Management Framework," Treasury Board of Canada Secretariat, April 1, 2001, www.tbs-sct.gc.ca/pubs_pol/dcgpubs/RiskManagement/rmf-cgr_e.asp (last accessed on April 15, 2006).

[28] Waxer, Cindy, "Portfolio Management: How Lowe's Grows," *CIO Magazine*, December 1, 2005.

[29] Huffman, Brian, "What Makes a Strategy Brilliant?" in *Strategic Management in the Knowledge Economy*, by M. Leibold, G. J. B. Probst, and M. Gibbert, (eds.), New York, NY: Wiley, 2002, pp. 106–117.

# List of Acronyms

| | |
|---|---|
| **AARK** | Architecture, Asset, Resource, and Knowledge |
| **AARKV** | Architecture, Asset, Resource, Knowledge, and Vendor |
| **ABPMP** | Association of Business Process Management Professionals |
| **AMA** | Advanced Measurement Approach |
| **BAM** | Business Activity Monitoring |
| **BC** | Business Continuity |
| **BCP** | Business Continuity Plan |
| **BI** | Business Intelligence |
| **BMM** | Business Maturity Model |
| **BPA** | Business Process Automation |
| **BPM** | Business Performance Management |
| **BPR** | Business Process Reengineering |
| **BSU** | Business Support Unit |
| **BU** | Business Unit |
| **CAD** | Computer Aided Design |
| **CEO** | Chief Executive Officer |
| **CFO** | Chief Financial Officer |
| **CIMRU** | Computer Integrated Manufacturing Research Unit |
| **CIO** | Chief Information Officer |
| **CIS** | Computerized Information System |
| **CMM** | Capability Maturity Model |
| **CMMI** | Capability Maturity Model Integrated |
| **CMP** | Crisis Management Plan |
| **CMS** | Colorado Medical Society |
| **COBIT** | Control Objectives for Information and Related Technology |
| **COSO** | Committee Of Sponsoring Organizations |
| **COTS** | Commercial Off the Shelf |
| **CPM** | Corporate Performance Management |
| **CPM** | Critical Path Management |
| **CRM** | Customer Relationship Management |
| **CSF** | Critical Success Factor |
| **DMAIC** | Define, Measure, Analyze, Improve, Control |
| **DOA** | Denial of Access |
| **DPMO** | Defects Per Million Opportunities |

| | |
|---|---|
| **DR** | Disaster Recovery |
| **DW** | Data Warehouse |
| **EAI** | Enterprise Application Integration |
| **EBIT** | Earnings Before Interest and Taxes |
| **EBITDA** | Earnings Before Interest, Taxes, Depreciation, and Amortization |
| **EIS** | Executive Information System |
| **EMP** | Emergency Management Plan |
| **ENAPS** | European Network for Advanced Performance Studies |
| **EPM** | Enterprise Performance Management |
| **EPM** | Enterprise Portfolio Management |
| **EPS** | Earnings Per Share |
| **ERM** | Enterprise Risk Management |
| **ERP** | Enterprise Resource Planning |
| **EVA** | Earned Value Analysis |
| **FBI** | Federal Bureau of Investigation |
| **FDA** | Food and Drug Administration |
| **FDICIA** | Federal Deposit Insurance Corporation Improvement Act |
| **FMEA** | Failure Mode and Effect Analysis |
| **GE** | General Electric |
| **GIS** | Geographical Information System |
| **GLB** | Gramm-Leach-Bliley Act |
| **GNP** | Grupo Nacional Provincial |
| **GPS** | Geographic Positioning Satellite |
| **GSCF** | Global Supply Chain Forum |
| **GUI** | Graphical User Interface |
| **HIPAA** | Health Insurance Portability and Accountability Act |
| **HR** | Human Resources |
| **ICAEW** | Institute of Chartered Accountants in England and Wales |
| **ICOW** | Increased Cost of Working Cover |
| **IPMO** | Integrated PePPR Management Office |
| **IPOC** | Independent Process Oversight Consultant |
| **ISACA** | Information Systems Audit and Control Association |
| **ISO 9000** | International Standards Organization 9000 |
| **IT** | Information Technology |
| **ITIL** | Information Technology Infrastructure Library |
| **IV&V** | Independent Validation and Verification |
| **JCAHO** | Joint Commission on the Accreditation of Healthcare Organizations |
| **KB** | Knowledge Base |
| **KM** | Knowledge Management |

| | |
|---|---|
| KPI | Key Performance Indicator |
| KRI | Key Risk Indicator |
| LSE | London Stock Exchange |
| M&A | Mergers and Acquisitions |
| MO | Management Office |
| MPT | Modern Portfolio Theory |
| NFP | Not For Profit |
| NPD | New Product Development |
| NPP | New Product and Packages |
| NPV | Net Present Value |
| OGC | Organization of Government Commerce |
| OPM3 | Organizational Project Management Maturity Model |
| ORM | Operational Risk Management |
| OSHA | Organizational Safety and Health Act |
| OSM | Office of Strategy Management |
| OTROS | Office of Technology Review, Oversight, and Security |
| P&L | Profit and Loss |
| P3M3 | Project, Program, Portfolio Management Maturity Model |
| PCAOB | Public Company Accounting Oversight Board |
| PDCA | Plan, Do, Change, Act |
| PePPR | Performance, Process, Project Portfolio, and Risk |
| PERT | Program Evaluation and Review Technique |
| PEST | Political, Economic, Social, and Technological |
| PIMS | Profit Impact of Market Strategy |
| PM | Project Manager |
| PMBOK | Project Management Body of Knowledge |
| PMI | Project Management Institute |
| PMO | Portfolio Management Office - usually prepended with an S (Strategic) or an E (Enterprise) to differentiate from a Program or Project Management Office |
| PPM | Project Portfolio Management or Process Performance Management, depending on context |
| PRINCE2 | Projects In Controlled Environments 2 |
| R&D | Research and Development |
| RBV | Resource Based View |
| RFID | Radio Frequency Identification |
| RFP | Request For Proposal |
| RMO | Risk Management Office |
| RMO | Risk Management |
| ROCE | Return on Capital Employed |
| ROI | Return On Investment |

| | |
|---|---|
| **SAC** | Strategic Action Committee |
| **SarbOx/SOX** | Sarbanes-Oxley Act |
| **SBN** | Strategic Business Network |
| **SBS** | Strategic Business Systems |
| **SBU** | Strategic Business Unit |
| **SCM** | Supply Chain Management |
| **SCOR** | Supply Chain Operations References |
| **SEC** | Securities and Exchange Commission |
| **SEI** | Software Engineering Institute |
| **SFA** | Sales Force Automation |
| **SLA** | Service Level Agreement |
| **SMO** | Strategic Management Office |
| **SNMP** | Simple Network Management Protocol |
| **SOA** | Service Oriented Architecture |
| **SOP** | Standard Operating Procedure |
| **SPC** | Statistical Process Control |
| **SQC** | Statistical Quality Control |
| **STaRS** | Start-up, Turn-around, Realignment, and Sustaining Success |
| **SWOT** | Strengths, Weaknesses, Opportunities, and Threats |
| **TLA** | Three Letter Acronym |
| **TQC** | Total Quality Control |
| **TQM** | Total Quality Management |
| **TRB** | Technology Review Board |
| **TWI** | Training Within Industry |
| **VID** | Vehicle Identification |
| **VP** | Vice President |
| **VSMO** | Virtual Strategy Management Office |

# About the Author

**Stephen S. Bonham** is the president of TrueCourse Solutions, Inc. in Denver, Colorado. Author of the best-selling IT Project Portfolio Management, he has over 18 years of experience working for several small technology companies, and consulting for many Fortune 500 companies, international governments, and nonprofit agencies. He has held positions in most areas of information technology, software product development, and program management. In recent years, he has been supporting organizations in their quest for actionable strategies. Mr. Bonham holds an M.E. in Computer Science from the University of Colorado, and an M.B.A. from the University of Denver.

# Index

## Recent Titles in the Artech House
## Technology Management and
## Professional Development Library

Bruce Elbert, Series Editor

*A Practical Guide to Managing Information Security,* Steve Purser

*Preparing and Delivering Effective Technical Presentations,* Second Edition, David Adamy

*Reengineering Yourself and Your Company: From Engineer to Manager to Leader,* Howard Eisner

*The Requirements Engineering Handbook,* Ralph R. Young

*Running the Successful Hi-Tech Project Office,* Eduardo Miranda

*Successful Marketing Strategy for High-Tech Firms, Second Edition,* Eric Viardot

*Successful Proposal Strategies for Small Businesses: Using Knowledge Management to Win Government, Private Sector, and International Contracts, Fourth Edition,* Robert S. Frey

*Systems Approach to Engineering Design,* Peter H. Sydenham

*Systems Engineering Principles and Practice,* H. Robert Westerman

*Systems Reliability and Failure Prevention,* Herbert Hecht

*Team Development for High-Tech Project Managers,* James Williams

For further information on these and other Artech House titles, including previously considered out-of-print books now available through our In-Print-Forever® (IPF®) program, contact:

Artech House
685 Canton Street
Norwood, MA 02062
Phone: 781-769-9750
Fax: 781-769-6334
e-mail: artech@artechhouse.com

Artech House
46 Gillingham Street
London SW1V 1AH UK
Phone: +44 (0)20 7596-8750
Fax: +44 (0)20 7630-0166
e-mail: artech-uk@artechhouse.com

Find us on the World Wide Web at:
www.artechhouse.com